Cataloging in Publication Data—DK
Courtesy: D.K. Agencies (P) Ltd. <docinfo@dkagencies.com>

Workshop on Perspective of Security and Development in North East India (2002 : Shillong, India)
Perspective of security and development in North East India / edited by S.K. Agnihotri, B. Datta Ray.
p. cm.
Papers presented at the Workshop on Perspective of Security and Development in North East India, held at Shillong on 9th December 2002.
Includes bibliographical references.
Includes index.
ISBN 8180691659

1. Internal security—India, Northeastern—Congresses. 2. Insurgency—India, Northeastern—Congresses. 3. India, Northeastern—Economic conditions—Congresses. 4. National security—India, Northeastern—Congresses. I. Agnihotri, S. K. (Shailendra Kumar), 1942- II. Datta Ray, B. (Basudeb), 1925- III. Title.

DDC 355.021 805 41 21

ISBN 81-8069-165-9

First Published 2005

Published and Printed by
Ashok Kumar Mittal
Concept Publishing Company
A/15-16, Commercial Block, Mohan Garden
NEW DELHI-110059 (India)

Phones : 25351460, 25351794
Fax : +91-11-25357103
Email : publishing@conceptpub.com

PERSPECTIVE OF SECURITY AND DEVELOPMENT IN NORTH EAST INDIA

Edited by

S.K. AGNIHOTRI

B. DATTA RAY

CONCEPT PUBLISHING COMPANY, NEW DELHI-110059

Books Published for NEICSSR, Shillong

- Reorganisation of North East India since 1947, **B. Datta Ray**
- Sociological Constraints to Industrial Development in North East India, **B.K. Datta Ray, *et al.***
- Population, Poverty and Environment in North East India, **B. Datta Ray, *et al.***
- Agenda for North East India, **B. Datta Ray** (Ed.)
- Development Priorities in North East India, **Bimal J. Deb** (Ed.)
- Linguistic Situation in North East India, **Mrinal Miri** (Ed.)

Releasing Shortly

- Ethnic Issues, Secularism and Conflict Resolution in North East India

---

About the Editors

S.K. Agnihotri is currently Secretary, National Foundation for Communal Harmony, New Delhi. Formerly, he was Chief Secretary of Arunachal Pradesh. He has rich security, strategic and administrative experience at higher level. He had authored many publications on small tribes of North East India.

B. Datta Ray is a fighter for freedom and social science research. He is Founder Secretary of North East India Council for Social Science Research. He has to his credit two books, namely, *Administrative History of North East India and Tribal Identity* and *Tensions in North East India*. Also, he has edited 16 books on North East India.

PERSPECTIVE OF SECURITY AND DEVELOPMENT
IN
NORTH EAST INDIA

PREFACE

North East India Council for Social Science Research, the premier social science research body in North East India, held on 9 December, 2002 a workshop on 'Perspective of Security and Development in North East India'.

The basic objective of this workshop was to start an intensive dialogue among scholars and policy-makers on the subjects dealing with: (a) The security scenario, internal security issues with reference to North East India, (b) External security threat, relating to arm supply, human, wildlife and drug trafficking, (c) Militancy and its adverse impact on the economic and industrial development of North East India, major targets of attack being on oil, coal, tea and power infrastructure, (d) Conflict resolution measures sub-regional co-operation on manage-ment of militancy through sharing of water, trade and transit facilities, management of migration, trafficking, narcotic problems, etc.

The workshop analysed the reasons behind the deteriorating situation in North East India. It came to the conclusion that the issue of security and development must be considered together. The lack of good Governance at all levels is one of the major causes of deteriorated situation over time.

We take this opportunity to thank National Foundation for Communal Harmony and North Eastern Regional Centre of ICSSR for their generous support to hold the workshop. Mr. Ashok Kumar Mittal and Concept Publishing Company, New Delhi deserve special thanks for undertaking expeditious publication of this volume.

Editors

CONTENTS

LIST OF TABLES

LIST OF FIGURES

LIST OF CONTRIBUTORS

Bandyopadhyay, P.K.
Scholar currently with Ministry of Defence, New Delhi

Bandyopadhyay, Sabari
Department of Economics, Vidyasagar University, Kharagpur, West Bengal

Bhattacharjee, R.P.
NE Regional Institute of Science and Technology Nirjuli, Itanagar, Arunachal Pradesh

Borkakoti, Sanjib Kumar
Department of Economics, ADP College, Nagaon, Assam

Chakrabarti, Subhendu
Economic Research Unit, Indian Statistical Institute, Kolkata

Chakraborty, Gorky
Department of Economics, Doom Dooma College, Doom Dooma, Assam

Deka, Meeta
Department of History, Gauhati University, Guwahati

Datta, B.B.
Former Member, Rajya Sabha

Dutta, P.C.
Department of Statistics, S.S. College, Hailakandi, Assam

Ganguly, J.B.
Formerly Vice-Chancellor, Tripura University, Agartala

Goswami, Pranay Jyoti
Department of Economics, G.C. College, Silchar, Assam

Kar, M.
Scholar, Shillong

Kumar, B.B.
Editor, *Dialogue*, New Delhi

Lahiri, Tarun Bikas
Formerly of North-Eastern Hill University and Visva Bharati

Maiti, Asok
Formerly of Sociological Research Unit, Indian Statistical Institute, Kolkata

Mao, Xavier P.
Department of Philosophy, North-Eastern Hill University, Shillong

Mazumdar, Sukhendu
Scholar, C/o 99 APO

Purkayastha, R.K.
Department of Political Science, St. Anthony's College, Shillong

Ray, Asok Kumar
Scholar, New Delhi

Sen, Gautam
Formerly Financial Adviser, North-Eastern Council and of Assam Rifles, Currently Financial Adviser, Defence, New Delhi

Singh, Konsam Ibo
Department of Political Science, Manipur University, Imphal, Manipur

Sinha, A.C.
Department of Sociology, North-Eastern Hill University, Shillong

Sudhir, H.
Department of History, Manipur University, Imphal

INTRODUCTION

North East India is a strategic area of significance with 5,500 km. length of international boundary. It is connected with the rest of India by a narrow strip of land, known as chicken's neck. It has assumed considerable importance during the last fifty years more so since 1962.

No other region of India has international borders as extensive as that of North East India. It shares about one-third of India's international border. North East India shares about 1,643 km. border with Myanmar, about 1,000 km. with China, about 1,956 km. with Bangladesh and about 650 km. with Bhutan. It is a land locked mass of land. It has no coast line or exclusive maritime economic zone. As a result North East India's relations with the neighbouring countries have far reaching implications, strategic and developmental. North East India's security and development issues are linked directly with its neighbouring countries with which it has borders.

Security of country, external or internal, has a great bearing on its social, human and economic development. In fact, security and development, in its multidimension aspects reinforce each other. A secure environment encourages the entrepreneurs to undertake higher level of investment in production activities by minimising the uncertainties and risk factors and thereby strengthening the process of development, the latter in term enables the state to further improve its security environment through higher level of investment in strategic and critical inputs. Thus security and development go hand in hand. The more secure a region or a country is, it is more likely to attract global investment in productive activities and in human development. The more developed a country is, it is more capable to support an elaborate security arrangements.

The development implications of vulnerable security perceptions of a state are felt more in bordering areas than in the hinterland. It is because of this, traditional security perception tends to consider its bordering region like North East India more vulnerable to external threats. This perception in turn tends to affect development activities in the bordering areas. India-China relation in the eastern sector is a glaring instance.

Any strategic change in the neighbouring countries has serious security and development implications for India. A good neighbourly relation, no doubt, improves the security environment, a hostile relation negatively affect development activities by way of diversion of scarce resources from development to security needs, external as well as internal. The current stand off with Pakistan is a pointer. The uneasy relations between India and Pakistan and India and China severely impeded the social and economic development of South Asia. Therefore it is of utmost importance to study how our relation with immediate neighbours and security concerns arising out of that have affected our pace of development particularly of North East India during the last five decades. Our relations with neighbouring countries have serious long-term development and security implication for North East India.

There are more than 100 major ethnic groups in North East India. The motivation of different ethnic groups for preserving their identities has been a dynamic phenomenon in reorganising of North East India on broad ethnic boundaries. The Constitution of India adopted a federal approach to accommodate ethnic aspiration and creating a security environment by the mechanism of Fifth and Sixth Schedules to the Constitution and also by re-organisation of State boundaries. The process started in 1954 with the creation of North East Frontier Agency. The dream of composite Assam ended in 1972. Reorganisation is a continuous process to accommodate ethnic aspirations and for creating development and security environment.

The break-up of composite Assam by 1972 necessitated the birth of North Eastern Council for co-ordinated planned development of social and economic infrastructure in North East India. The need for regional security was expected also to be looked into by an independent body under North Eastern Council which is a recognition of the interdependence of economic development and security environment in North East India.

Since 1990, neighbouring Bangladesh has harboured North East India insurgent groups and allowed them to import arms to their bases in India through Cox Bazar and Chittagong Hill Tracts. Some top insurgent leaders continue to live in Bangladesh. Extra religious groups are trying to gain a foothold in the border states of North East India. The adverse security implication of this development acquires a sinister overtone when we realise that Bangladesh is a small country. It needs space. The rise of far right religious groups to state-power has sharpened the unresolved identity crisis and has a serious challenge to internal security of Bangladesh and to the peace, security and development of North East India. The insurgent camps of Bhutan forests and the five decade old of insurgency in Upper Myanmar bordering North East India have security and development implication for North East India. North East India cannot continue to remain a soft underbelly. As a core power, India can ill-afford to ignore or minimise the gravity of the situation. The crying need is an effective security, and economic development strategy package.

S.K. AGNIHOTRI
B. DATTA RAY

1

SECURITY FOR WHOM? HUMAN OR THE NATIONAL? A Plea for Comprehensive Security in India

A.C. SINHA

Security has been of paramount concern of the human beings from the very beginning of the human history. To begin with, it raises the issue of individual *vis-a-vis* collective security. Should an individual be considered as an atom or a faceless common man or a citizen of a civil State? At what level, should one identify the collectivity? Community, tribe/cast, 'State', world-wide civilized humanity, or United Nations Organisation (UNO)? Is it not a fact that current security obsession has something to do with colonial heritage? The former British colonizers' concern for the security of their Indian empire and consequent 'Forward Policy to the Himalayas' as a part of 'the Great Game' in the Central Asia is too familiar. The two Great World Wards further developed the obsession of their national securities to the extent that the rivalry between the world powers turned into 'cold war' between the world power blocks. So much so that even when one of them, the USSR collapsed, the only super power in the world, USA, is so much concerned with its national security, that she has identified her counterpoise in the form of a world-wide Islamic terrorist movement.

It is nobody's surprise that today every member of the civilized world is terror-stricken because of the deteriorating security environment all over the world. In this brief paper, our effort is to examine the security concern from Indian point of view. There are a number of aspects in this presentation. Firstly, we propose to provide a brief historical background of the security concern. Secondly, we seek to identify the various security concerns in India. Thirdly, we intend to survey the security scenario from vantage point of North Eastern Frontiers of the Indian State. And lastly, we end our presentation with a plea that the one-sided concern for either the individual or the 'State' security is logically misplaced. We should endeavour for a comprehensive human security world over. And only then, every individual, community, or the 'State' will have a sense of security. Till then, we keep on trying to acquire it.

The Background of the Security

The prehistoric man terribly insecure in the face of the daunting natural objects. He was awfully afraid of the natural forces: fire, water, wild creatures, flood, earthquack, sun. He was invariably awe-struck because of the fact of human technological and mental infancy. In course of time, the rational man, who lived in woods along with wild creatures, developed a moral and spiritual approach to the physical and natural forces. Man as well realised the strength of the collectivity when he formed the tribal bands. And thus, he had the first experience of communal living. Chieftainship, principalities, kingdoms, states and empires did emerge in course of time in different parts of the world in different forms. However, valours in the wars against the adversaries got engrained in, the psyche of the various communities and nationalities. Thus, one finds folk heroes and folk warriors all over the world as the centres of the legends and myths. The classical literature abounds in the songs, ballads and exploits of these folk heroes. Needless to add that one of the most potent principles of the state formation has been the principle of conquest, with its validity till date.

In course of time, individual valour came to be replaced with excellence of armaments, because of increasing scientific inventions and improved technology. This process gave birth to arms race among the nations to collect/develop more and more of articles and weapons of mass destruction. Connivance of the callous men and materials of mass destruction during the two World Wars further increased the appetite to search for more potent weapons of mass destruction: nuclear, hydrogen and chemical. These means of mass destruction were used sparingly, but when they were used against all forms of live force: human, animal, bird, insect and vegetation. This has been the phase of human experience, when the 'State' appears to be all powerful entity, unchallenged and drunk with its own might against the individual dissent.

Refusal to accommodate some of dissent gave birth to individual or ideological desperation. There have been occasions, when 'States' appear to be helpless against well-armed and desperate extremists, who manage to create a psychosis of insecurity and destruction. There are occasions, when the all powerful states appear increasingly helpless and insecure against such fanatic adversaries and they even are unable to provide basic security to life to the common citizenry. As the 'State', whether the welfare one or the totalitarian one, appear to be unable to facilitate the basic security to the citizen—one of the rationale for its existence—man is left at loose, as a helpless and mindless entity. In such a situation, a common man's physical, mental and moral strength is no match to this new form of challenge to its existence.

In such a situation, what does one expect from the state apparatus? What should be the security scenario today? Whose security are we referring to? Granted that the 'State' has turned out to be ineffective, how does an individual, an ordinary citizen, ensure his security on the teeth of desperate havoc of a terrorist? Is there any mechanism available to an average human being against this menace? In case there is no tangible remedy to this menace, then in the absence of the state structure, who will ensure even the very physical continuation of the individual against such an adversary? Thus, in the ultimate analysis, human rights and human security, which are certainly distinct from state security, have to be accommodated within the ambit of the state security. This is because of the fact that once the institution of 'State' goes, the very existence of humanity is at stake, a risk, which cannot be and must not be taken knowingly.

Dimension of Security

The classical definition of security is that "a nation is secured to the extent to which it is not in danger of having sacrifice core values, if it wishes to avoid, and it is able, if challenged, to maintain them by such victory, in such a war" (Raghavan, V.R.: 2001). Hence, war is accorded primacy to preserve a country's national security leading to defence preparedness. Such a perception in one country may cause apprehensions, and thus, insecurity in another, possibly a neighbouring country, leading to an armed race between two or more neighbouring powers. However, security in its widest and true sense of the term should result in the well-being of the people at large. After all, there can be little security in a state of endemic poverty, illiteracy, and absence of health care. That's the reason why some of the scholars talk about security. By human security, they imply that "ultimately state is for individual security. In the end, the State is the provider of security for the citizenry; it is a means to security (of its inhabitants) and its security cannot be end of security" (Bajpai, K.: 2002).

To begin with, at the conceptual level, security does encompass a series of aspects. Some of them may be arranged in the following order:

(i) *Economic Security*

(a) Free movement of work force across the national boundaries can be an area of co-operation between nations; and

(b) Tariff and trade barriers, if reduced, will enhance the economic security among the nations.

(ii) *Environmental Security*

(a) Depletion of prime resources such as water, clean air will affect the security of both—the state and its population even across the national boundaries; and

(b) Energy security and its impact on the people is a matter of concern among the nations.

(iii) *Political Security*

The challenge of harmonising plural societies *versus* a distinct national identity as a determinant of security needs in a state is fraught with serious consequences and thus, such efforts need to be studied in greater details.

(iv) *Societal Security*

(a) Migration of population segments across the national boundaries may pose security risk;

(b) Influx of refugees from one to another country after a possible persecution may endanger the security environment among the nations; and

(c) Lack of participation in the State sponsored development plans by the civil society may lead to a totalitarian regime.

Security Concerns from the Indian Regions

Delhi Policy Group has been organising a series of seminars on security related aspects. Its first such seminar was called in January 2001 on 'Comprehensive Security for South Asia', scholars and policy planners from SAARC countries participated and the proceedings of the seminar were made public within few months. The second seminar in the series was organised in August 2001 and it was on 'Comprehensive Security: Perspectives from India's Regions'. After a three-day long deliberations on the presentations from the various regions of the country, certain common concerns were identified as the summery on the issue (Raghavan, V.R.: 2002). They may be enumerated in the following:

1. Issue of poverty, economic backwardness and economic growth;

2. Problems of governance, dissonance between resolutions and implementations; and
3. Problems of identity, migration and social fragmentation.

North Eastern Concern for its Security

The above security concerns from the Indian regions were equally applicable to this region. However, certain points needed to be emphasised and some unique ones to the region are to be added to. Among them mention may be made of the following:

Identity

We held a seminar in 1978 on the problems of youth as a part of an all India exercise in North-Eastern Hill University. Unlike other regions of the country, the issue of ethnic identity, and not poverty and unemployment, were the key concerns within the region. The problem of identity continues to be of cardinal significance even today. There are communities, which have been rightly as the 'bridge communities', while there are others, which have been functioning as the 'buffer' ones. The relatively smaller ethnic groups in the region have seen both the processes of fragmentation and consolidation of the smaller entities into larger ones *vis-a-vis* larger socio-cultural units. These are the reasons for being apprehensive of their submergence in the ethnic melting pot of the Indian Union.

Migration

The local ethnic groups rarely resort to a sizeable out-migration; but thinly populated region is subject to in-migration from Bangladesh, Myanmar, Nepal, Tibet and other states of the Indian Union. In such a situation, the small ethnic groups naturally feel encapsulated and drowned. They apprehend that their forested hill tracts may be turned into an alien land to them within no time. The Assamese are yet to get over Sir Sahdulla's encouragement to settle the British Assam with immigrant Bengal Muslims in second quarter of 20th century.

Social Fragmentation

The North Eastern Frontier region of India is naturally identified with reference to the Indian Union. The region, which was known as British Assam during the colonial period of its history, has not been able to evolve a regional identity. It has a tenuous link in terms of racial, ethnic, linguistic, religious and even historical context with rest of India. Even historical linkages are problematic, formal and legal one and there is a limited emotional involvement in Indian things. Within the region, again the 'seven sisters' have a plethora of social, religious, ethnic and other types of combinations. There are really very limited fora actively engaged in the region for social integration of the region with the Indian cultural commonwealth.

Lack of Effective Governance

Fragmentation of composite state of Assam led to emergence of small states with limited revenue and considerable expenditure. The Indian Union treats them as a special category states because of their limited revenue base, on-going insurgency, location on the backward frontier region and predominance of the scheduled tribes. These states suffer from lack of fore-sighted, committed, and effective leadership. The state level decision-making process is far from satisfactory to deliver the welfare programmes to the grassroots level. In such a situation, the common man of the region is lost, insecure and always apprehensive.

The North Eastern region of India as a whole is subjected to an intense insecurity at all the levels. The Indian States, the federal and the provinces, and its denizens, indigenous and migrants, all are insecure in the region, because of the contested legitimacy. Insurgency and counter-insurgency operations cost a considerable amount of investment in terms of men and material. On the other hand, human dignity to the citizens cannot be ensured because limited economic resources are thinly distributed even among the aliens. Poor quality of life and high level of political consciousness breed an atmosphere of insecurity in which political unrest ensures a chain of violence, suppression and reprisal.

One may pose an obvious question: what type of security scenario for the 'State' and human dignity for the individual emerge from the above survey? Add to this is the security scenario from the neighbouring countries. Sri Lanka and Pakistan had their internal problems, which invariably spilled over to India. Similarly, Myanmar and Tibet have been in turmoil for decades now. Of late, even Nepal, Bhutan and Bangladesh have turned out to be locales of pronounced anti-state uprisings. There have been persistent reports that the agent-provocators of Inter Service Intelligence of Pakistan have established a network of spionage in India in general and North Eastern region in particular. It is invariably reported that the chain of Islamic theological schools (*Madarsas*) are extensively used for anti-Indian activities. We have noted elsewhere how even the legendary loyal members of the Gorkha background have been recruited for creating unrest and causing harm to men and materials (Sinha, A.C.: 2002).

The picture presented above indicates enough dark spots on the security map of India. There are aspects of security, which go beyond our national boundary; in which co-operation from the neighbouring countries is urgently needed. Needless to add that our security policy continues to be state centric, which is possibly a colonial inheritance. It has to be broadened and human dimension has to be added to it. Defence related strategy is a must, which has to be persued by qualified policy-makers. However, no defence policy will succeed unless common interests are identified with countries, which have common borders with us. We continue to be captive of the past colonial heritage in the matters of defence. For example, we have open borders with Nepal and Bhutan, but we raising electric wire fencing on our Bangladesh borders. We know that the history of both the situations is different; still we should review the strategic concerns together with the neighbouring countries. Can we not help to chalk out "a security charter of the SAARC countries" minus the stumbling block of Pakistan? One imagines that the time has come to think aloud and take unconventional and bold steps in this direction. And only then the above dark picture of national and human security will be different and pleasant one.

REFERENCES

Bajpai, K. (2002), "Beyond Comprehensive Security: Human Security" in *Comparative Security: Perspectives from India's Regions*, (ed.) by V.R. Raghavan, Delhi Policy Group, New Delhi.

Raghavan, V.R. (2001). *Comprehensive Security for South Asia*, Delhi Policy Group, New Delhi.

Sinha, A.C. (2002). "The Indians of Nepalese Origin and Security of North East Region" in *Comprehensive Security: Perspectives from India's Regions*, (ed.) by V.R. Raghavan, Delhi Policy Group, New Delhi.

2

CONTOURS OF NATIONAL SECURITY THREATS AND THREAT PERCEPTIONS IN INDIA

B.B. DATTA

The Concept of National Security

In the pre-capitalist era with no nation state in sight, there was hardly any sanctity of what we call an "international boundary". Boundaries of kingdoms were violated with impunity. Invasion and plunder was the rule of the game. In fact, in those days, this was the way "power projection" was done by kings, monarchs and emperors.

With the emergence of modern nation states, protecting the sanctity of national boundaries became one of the top priority functions of a state. The attributes of such a nation state include a demarcated geographic territory, a population living within its boundaries with a common cultural heritage and a shared history with a common ideal for the future and the sovereignty of the people as vested in the state.

The classical definition of security throws a good deal of light on the main concern of security. It says, "a nation is secured to the extent to which it is not in danger of having to sacrifice core-values, if it wishes to avoid war, and is able, if challenged, to maintain them by such victory in such a war". If we add to "core-values", whatever other concerns are integral to the existence of a modern nation state, the definition is a perfect one.

Threat Perception

Threats to national security have to be understood and analysed with reference to two basic points. Firstly, what lies within the capacity and competence of a state to deal with by way of providing good governance, must not be brought under the cover of security threats. Dissent, agitations, peaceful or violent, challenge to authority arising out of deprivations of perceived justice—economic, political, social or cultural—may originate from faulty policies in governance. To the extent it is so, they are not matters of concern for national security. But when such a situation is sought to be exploited by external powers in connivance with elements within, it poses a national security concern. The line is thin. Still it is a line of demarcation indicating where the solution lies and what specific measures are called for involving the need to restore good governance and taking appropriate security measures.

Second, threat to security is a matter of perception. There may be threats to the state from a neighbouring or distant power and it may or may not be perceived by the targeted nation. Perceived threats activate nations towards defence preparedness. Unperceived threats remain dormant till the time it makes a surprise appearance on the unprepared victim at a time of the enemy's choosing. The degree to which a nation is capable of reading the whole range of threats to its security now or in near future, is determined by the degree to which a nation is awake and alert with a sense of history and armed with the necessary economic, political and defence intelligence of those nations who are or likely to be hostile and compare them with its own strengths in respective spheres.

The extent to which a nation perceives its vulnerability is a matter of its own judgement about threats. Threat perceptions are time and space specific. A nation is unprepared without a vulnerability analysis of its own on a continuous basis.

Security Management

Historically speaking, war has been the main instrument of dealing with security threats. The war, as an instrument to secure peace, whatever be its nature—localised, conventional, limited or nuclear calls for defence preparedness and is still today the most important instrument of security management with the primacy of its own.

Two strategies are very important for adequate defence preparedness: (i) to ensure that it has state of the art defence mechanism comparable to those of other countries that are considered "potential security threats"; (ii) to keep on fighting a diplomatic war to maintain certain equilibrium in international relations to make sure that it is not disadvantageous to itself.

It is interesting to note that there is an unchanging paradigm in the twin strategy in defence preparedness. The salient principles of diplomacy have remained more or less the same throughout. Regarding the other part, while the war has become high precision, high tech, with immense capacity for mass destruction, and threatening to transform warfare into a process of annihilation through biological or ecological warfare, the basics remain the same. To quote Satpal, "In canto III (*Yuddha Kanda*) of *Valmiki Ramayana*, Hanuman explains to Lord Rama that Lanka was absolutely invincible because it had well in place all the four elements which make a country inaccessible even to gods. It had a deep moat; it had high mountains; a dense forest; and impregnable fortress. The mountain and moat paradigm of defence have not changed with the changing times of technologies. All that is happening is a slight redefining of the mountain and the moat, and the forest and the fort.

In the present context, for India, electronic warfare (EW) in the air, and anti-missile batteries throughout the landmass of the country can make it very difficult for the enemy men or machines to approach the targets and hence can be viewed as mountain and forest respectively. Similarly, the Indian Ocean can act as partial moat with nuclear submarines growling like alligators. The choice of site for engaging the enemy will have to be flexible. This will necessarily make the "Portable Fort" a military reality in any future warfare but it will be a fort anyway".[1]

However it is true that the concept of national security has undergone a sea change in twentieth century world particularly to its later decades and, beginning of the twenty-first. The concept has become so comprehensive in its meaning and scope that it encompasses all issues extending far beyond external military threats in the traditional sense as well as non-military, non-traditional security threats emanating from "Drugs", "Aids", "migration of population", proxy wars and the like which affect the concerns and sensitivities, cultural identity and value system of a nation.

The concept of national security can best be grasped with reference to the state structure of a modern nation state with its well-defined functions indicating the province of government. A state by definition has to have all the necessary instruments in place to protect its territory, the life and property of the people living within its jurisdiction and ensure justice, fair play and well being of its people through spontaneous and effective functioning of its various organs for the fulfilment of those very purposes for which the state has emerged as the highest form of social organisation at the apex of the "social pyramid".

Threats to national security have to be perceived in this light. Whenever the effective and spontaneous functioning of the state is affected because of factors operating either from outside or from within or both challenging the State's capacity to discharge its responsibilities, a security threat has emerged. Threats therefore maybe either external or internal. By internal threat we refer to any threat, maybe political, social, economic or cultural, which has arisen due to either internal political conflict, or through abetment by the foreign agencies having a direct bearing on the law and order situation of the country. By external threat we refer primarily to that kind of threat, which is by and large anticipated in view of the troubled international relations or one country having any direct vested interest within another country.

To provide an effective security cover to the country the state has to ensure two things: (i) physical security in terms of defending the territorial integrity safeguarding the border with patrolling, fencing, canalising, border demarcation when and wherever necessary; and (ii) ongoing counter intelligence operations covering (a) espionage, (b) sabotage, and (c) subversion.

National security is very much concerned with economic, technological capabilities of a nation and its diplomatic efficiency as reflected in the global and regional power equations. It also concerns the characteristic traits of a nation as reflected in its responses to political, psychological and diplomatic pressures mounted upon it by another nation or a group of nations.

However, all said and done, "power" remains at the heart of international relations and one cannot think of security management without referring to power. The concept of power is also changing in its scope. Phrases like economic power, military power or moral power are indicative of this. But on the question of security it is the military capability of a nation that matters most though even a military power needs steady economic and moral support to provide itself an invincible bulwark of defence against any attack. This is security as a derivative of power.

National security is also being seen as a derivative of "peace". Here the indications are that cooperative security or harmonious coexistence would alone ensure the lasting peace and tranquillity that nations desire. According to this school of thought national security is nothing but "human security" or the "defence of a healthy and happy population". If this is not what we are defending then it may be that one day we are left with nothing to defend, they argue.

In an increasingly globalised and multipolar world with many non-governmental actors active new ideas of security as well as of threats keep on evolving and the concept of security has a tendency to go beyond territory and embrace economy, education, environment, inequalities and imbalances. In such a context security implies not merely "absence of war" but "the rule of law", transparency and accountability.

While many healthy ideas can be connected with a nation's security concerns or even those of the international bodies, the precursors of a global state and coining phrases like "food security", "educational security", "health security", the fact is that the world of today does not yet permit a sovereign nation to de-link itself from the concept of security as a derivative of power. In India the Nehruvian period between 1947 and 1962 was marked by a bold experiment to shape the country as a moral power, the defence bulwark being moral excellence and cultural politics with diplomatic peace offensive rather than a state of the art military preparedness. But that collapsed in 1962 when the Chinese army entered the North East Frontier areas of India. India was forced to seek American help with a policy shift. She awoke to her needs of defence and with Soviet help forthcoming defence preparedness was on way.

Earlier in 1947-48 when the Pakistani sponsored tribal militia attacked Kashmir on the heel of Maharaja Hari Singh's declaration that as per options given under the terms of British withdrawal, Kashmir had joined India, Indian Army had to intervene to repulse the attack. And then at a point when the Indian Army was well poised to drive out the attackers, Nehru took the matter to the United Nations. A partisan UN rewarded India with a Lein of Control with the armies of Pakistan and India pitted against each other. The military dictatorship in Pakistan inspired by the success it had, in partnership with the US, in Afghanistan, sought to apply the strategy of state sponsored terrorism into Jammu & Kashmir. It worked well in internationalising the issue with mounting pressure on India to solve the Kashmir problem with Pakistan. The September 11th attack on the US knocked out the very basis of the strategy. Had India solved the problem militarily, of which it was fully capable, Hindus, Muslims, Buddhists and others of Kashmir would not have been the worst victims of a continuing tragedy. The cacophony about South Asia being in the danger of nuclear holocaust would not have been heard. India sought peace, acted morally, with full trust in the Charter of the UN and got in return a never-ending hydra-headed war.

These frustrating experiences in India's foreign policy were not enough to force Indian rulers to undertake a pragmatic assessment of policy objectives to prioritise the nation's interest from the security perspective. A humiliated India kept on committing the blunders of not projecting herself as a power. Power projection is at the heart of security management involving both defence and foreign policies. A nation's prestige is a derivative of the reputation of being a power among the fellow states, a reputation that inspires awe and respect. To quote John Spanier, "Prestige, like love, is in the eye of the beholder. It is to be sure, acquired as a result of past action. In short, a state's power has credibility."[2]

India did the nuclear implosion in 1974. It was her ideal opportunity to enter into the nuclear club. She did not do so for reasons best known to the rulers of the time. Had India availed herself of the good work done by her scientists and technologists, she would have assumed the status of a regional power, which she is by her sheer size, long history and culture spreading beyond her boundaries. It would have a very salubrious effect on both North Western and North Eastern regions of India where external and internal threats, inextricably mixed up, were assuming an alarming proportion. Her tenacious advocacy for total disarmament, seeking to demonstrate her moral superiority as a non-nuclear power did not cut any ice. Had she become a nuclear power by then, her opinion would have received more respectful attention. The emergence of China as a nuclear power testifies to the farsighted policies of the Chinese rulers, who decided as early as 1963 to go nuclear so that China would not be bullied by the big powers. By 1998 when India at long last went for a nuclear explosion, Pakistan, which had followed closely on the trail of India, did the same and derived legitimacy from Indian actions. And what is more important, established a nuclear parity with India which otherwise she could never have dreamt of. This achievement of Pakistan is in spite of so many inherent lacunae behind the façade of their nuclear posture. India's delayed decision had cost her the legitimate membership of the nuclear club and economic sanctions. Yet India, having gone nuclear has got the power projection it badly needed. The immediate benefit was a radical shift in the US foreign policy objectives from China to India.

There is a second kind of threat. The threat to social and cultural cohesiveness of the nation. Here the attacks, covert or overt, are on one or more points of the social pyramid at the apex of which sits the state. These attacks have started from within and joined by forces from outside. India today has the spectacle of facing an inextricable mix-up with increasing external and internal threats with inter-community, inter-tribe and inter-clan conflicts. In such a scenario anti-Indian foreign powers, particularly the religious fundamentalists who have set a goal to conquer India, are busy helping mutually antagonistic interests with money, weapons and training, setting community against community, tribe against tribe, clan against clan, to keep India's North Eastern as well as North Western regions destabilised, with the specific objective of weakening her militarily and economically. To deal with this kind of threat India certainly needs a well-equipped defence force with high expertise on counter insurgency operations. But this has to be accompanied by radical reforms in the institutional framework provided by the Constitution and in Indianising education rooting youths to their own rich heritage retaining full emphasis on science, technology and spirituality. In the area of ethnic chaos and conflicts the challenge has to be met by, to quote His Holiness Sri Sri Ravishankar, "the deepening of roots and broadening of vision."

Lack of good governance and efficient administration has developed internal strife, consisting of threats from regionalism, widening economic disparities, steady migration from rural to urban areas, social imbalances creating unrest, unemployment, degradation of environment and basic amenities. With the pressure of population on the increase, mounting demands are met with disillusionment and frustrations. In the heartland of India the emerging picture, though somewhat different from the North East and North West, is equally disturbing. The presence and the operation of the Maoist Communist Centre and People's War Group or even the presence of brigands like Veerapan complement the picture of insurgencies in the North East and terrorism in Jammu and Kashmir. When one considers that about 115 insurgent groups are operating in the North East and about 35 are active in J&K and Punjab areas and the major groups with a full coordination amongst themselves running parallel governments in certain areas, collecting taxes every month from villagers, businessmen and civil servants alike, the intensity of threats to our internal security can be gauged. The political class which is increasingly becoming dependent on money and mafia to retain power is unable to run the civil administration without more and more help from police, paramilitary and sometimes even on military forces. Today the spectacle before an Indian citizen is: the protectors need protection more than the vulnerable citizens. The military suffers a loss of character by being involved in quelling internal revolt. Corruption and criminality have corroded every rung of the social order. These are, strictly speaking not matters of national security concern but of badly needed reforms in administrative and electoral systems to safeguard the fundamental rights of a citizen in a free, open, pluralistic society and ensure that the fruits of development reach in a fair measure to all sections of the people. There must not be any confusion between the demands of national security management with those of good governance and efficient administration.

There is a third kind of a threat—civilisational threat. Each nation does belong to a civilisation. And a civilisation has certain core values which inform the society and politics of the country. The ethos of a civilisation continues to influence the working of a nation through many channels including the cherished customs and traditions. When a nation finds that by certain developments in the society and politics, these core values are being attacked and mauled, a real civilisational threat emerges. It may potentially be present at the periphery and grow in intensity silently over time, unnoticed for long. The core values of Indian civilisation may be found in the abiding spirit of secularism, democracy, separation of religion and politics, tolerance and appreciation for other's religion, non-conversion, emphasising the fact that each religion is essentially true. The core values are to be found in the spiritual traditions, which have nurtured through centuries the flowering of the Indian genius. To such a society, any aggressive religion or ideology with a blind faith that it alone is true and others are false, with a spirit of conquering others by coercive means such as threat or temptations is an aggressor on its core values. India's secular democratic polity gives them all opportunities to enjoy their rights, in some cases special rights and hence the security threat emanating from them runs through a maze of immense complexity. The emergence of two Islamic states in India's North West and in the North East with a character that relegates non-Muslims to a status of second class citizens subject to discriminatory treatment. This has created a situation leading to gradual expulsion of minorities into neighbouring countries, particularly to India. Viewed from India's security standpoint these two countries appear to be two bridgeheads of pan-Islamism. Never in the history of India even in the heydays of the Mughal period such a thing happened. Hindus and Muslims lived together sharing the same political destiny, the same economy and the environment of toleration and love.

In post-Independent India the vast demographic change with the consequences of partition ceaselessly at work, a grave security challenge to the civilisation is fast developing. In the areas covered by North Eastern and Eastern region states, the threat is much more acute with the growing immigrant population. It has created social unrest and political turmoil.

In the North East there is a compact geographic area sharing a highly sensitive international border which is home to three Christian majority states, Nagaland, Mizoram and Meghalaya, having English as the state language. As tribals they are in minority in the region though having more land under their possession. The Coupland Plan or the Reid Plan for separation of these tribal areas, constituting them into a "Crown Colony" could have posed a security threat to India. But the Christians and the tribal people have rejected the idea themselves with their instinctive wisdom. Only conversion and that too not by the large Christian group but by zealots belonging to smaller denominations create problems. In Tripura the insurgents tried to adopt conversion as a weapon by issuing threats along with instruction of dos and don'ts. This has somewhat abated but it is still there.

Vigorous conversion drive in Arunachal carries with it a political motive. It looks like there is an effort in some quarters to give both geographical and religious depth to Christian tribals so as to ensure the emergence of a Christian political force in India's North East, in a very strategic location. The canvas calls for a critical security assessment and an appropriate policy application. The threat from the Islamic fundamentalists, who are busy in implanting a picture of a very rich Islamic dreamland in the minds of the Muslim youth comprising Bangladesh, North Eastern region states, and parts of Bihar and Orissa, is too dangerous to be ignored. In the area described above, the Muslims are already in a majority. Ten to fifteen kilometres inside India along the Indo-Bangla border Muslims over the years have acquired a majority status capturing in many places village leaderships from non-Muslims as the non-Muslims have kept on migrating to the towns or deep inside the interiors for safety reasons. This presents us with a picture of Muslim majority on both sides of Indo-Bangla border. Indeed a hard time for not only for those who watch and protect the borders but also for loyal Indian Muslims. The Inter-Services Intelligence (ISI) of Pakistan is very active with funds coming from Islamic countries to implement programmes of sabotage and subversion.

The threat is very complex in nature as it calls for segregating the loyal from the disloyal, genuine Indian citizens from the infiltrators, criminals from the law abiding etc. To meet this threat a strategy has to be evolved combining defence policy, foreign policy and population policy completely sealing off migration. Pre-emptive actions have to be taken to ensure protection of minorities in Bangladesh and dismantling of clandestine training camps for insurgents operating in India. The civilisational threat cannot be tackled only by military action. The role of culture, ecology and democracy are equally important.

For India the security spectrum is indeed very complex. Bleeding through the evil consequences of fissures created by an ill conceived partition, India's national objectives are to assure herself of physical survival, territorial integrity and political independence. These objectives are not attainable by themselves. The achievements require the following:

(i) That India projects herself as a "power" among the fellow states.

(ii) That she acquires economic strength adequate enough to give economic security to her national goal.

(iii) That she meets the objective of national welfare which has acquired tremendous importance due to the twin facts of mass mobilisation being an indispensable part of governance and providing the masses an ever increasing share of material comforts made available by mass industrial production.

(iv) That she plays her role to secure the protection of her environment and ecology in concert with other nations as a responsible member of global community.

The growth of United Nations after the demise of the League of Nations with it numerous World Bodies active in all spheres of political, social and cultural lives of the human family has caused, slowly and imperceptibly, erosion in the sovereignty of states. Given the pace of globalisation, mainly powered by economic factors, it is not unlikely that a day may come when the world will become one country with one government. Whatever be the scenario of the future, the concept of security and its management shall remain an abiding responsibility of the states even in a new World Order and the phase preceding it. With nationalism loosing its teeth, the nation state may find a serious challenge from the big powers. Defence preparedness, diplomatic initiatives and economic bargaining power have to be mixed in varying proportions as dictated by situation to evolve appropriate defence mechanism. It is worth quoting Dr. A.P.J. Abdul Kalam, the President of India, who told the nation in his inaugural address on 25th July 2002: "National security is a national priority . . . indeed, making India strong and self-reliant economically, socially and militarily is our foremost duty to our Motherland, to ourselves and to our future generations. . . . 'Thinking' is the key to progress and 'non-thinking' is distraction from vision. When a nation does not think, smaller minds overpower it." It is time the political tribe pay heed to what he had said.

NOTES

1. Satpal, "New Security Paradigm", *Pioneer*, March 1st, 1990.
2. John Spanier, *Games Nations Play*, New Delhi, McMillan (Seventh Edition), pp. 77-78.

3

SECURITY AND DEVELOPMENT
A Conceptual Frame

ASOK KUMAR RAY

The question of "Security and Development" has been a challenging one in the post-reform development literature. Recent World Bank literature of post-reform era on this issue is burgeoning. The term'security' has been viewed from a special angle and in cases, it has been strategically conditioned with 'Governance' and 'Social Capital'. The context in which these jargons have become the commonplace ones is that of globalisation under the New Economic Policy. The political economy of Globalisation made a major shift in the classical synergy of State, Capital and Market. In the post-reform era, the stake of development has been shifted from government to the non-government organisations and to the private sector. The New Economic Policy pleaded for minimal role of the government in development. Decentralisation, promotion of private sector, organisational pluralism and institutional reforms became the prime agenda in current development administration.[1] The state, far from being a direct stakeholder of development, has rather become a facilitator, enabler and a guide to it. De-institutionalisation of public sector has logically come to be linked with promotion and rationalisation of private sector. It is in this context that "Security and Development" can be viewed in this article.

The very fundamental academic question is: "Security for what"? In the context of Globalisation and New Economic Policy, this security is by and large that of 'finance capital'. The operation of finance capital under the New Economic Policy demands proper defence strategy. This is because of the inherent contradiction within the philosophy of private-owned finance capital *vis-a-vis* mass exclusion and alienation with the potentials for opposition. For the purpose of creating an enabling environment in which finance capital may safely operate, two major and related strategic measures are thought of:

Governance and Institutions

In the political front the concept of governance appeared in the backdrop of downsizing of the state power and growing need for decentralisation of power. In the economic front institutions were regarded important for growth, especially important were protection of property rights, capable bureaucracy and political stability as the initial conditions for growth. The hypothesis was: good institutions facilitate growth and weak institutions negatively affect growth. The policy implications of institutional reforms lie in linking it up with the conditionalities of foreign aid, below market-rate loan, and technical assistance provided by the World Bank to the poor countries. Further policy implications of institutional reforms are: efficiency of investment, enforcement of property rights both for their direct effects on growth (more efficient investment) and for their indirect effects in terms of larger investments. In the quest for determining socio-political determinants of growth, Alesina identified some of the variables of weak institutions that affect growth. These are: ethno-linguistic fractionalisation, rule of law, quality of bureaucracy, corruption, democracy, political assassination, government crisis revolutions and coups, government change, strikes, black market premium and human capital. Alesina has drawn a Correlation Matrix for selected political variables, growth and human capital and has shown how these variables affect growth.[2]

Social Capital

It has been recognised that a market system cannot operate solely on the basis of narrow self-interest. The informational problems in market interactions offer many chances of opportunistic behaviour. Without some minimal amount of social trust and civil norms, social interactions would be reduced to a minimum of tentative and distrustful commodity trades. The success of a market economy cannot be understood in terms of narrow economic incentives. Norms, social institutions, social capital and trust play critical roles in economic growth. It is this *social contract* implicit in social capital that is necessary to successful operation of market society. This cannot be simply legalised, decreed or installed by a reform government. Behind these social norms stands the machinery of the law which itself stands apart from the market.[3]

Thus according to the proponents of social capital theory, "it is not by destroying the old norms and constraints in order to clean the slate without allowing for the time consuming process of consuming new norms, the new legalised institutions may well not take hold." This points to a marked departure from the classical capitalist view that traditional relationships and ways of life impede the process of development and reiterate the view that social relations among corporate and political elites were a primary mechanism of capitalist exploitation.[4]

THE CRITICAL ISSUES

Viewed from the angle of correlating growth theory with political economy, governance and institutional reform stand as an agenda of economic reforms under globalisation. The intellectual root of the term 'Governance' is political economy. Under the umbrella of globalisation, the NEP agenda is to globalise privatisation of capital and allow MNCs to go for FDI in the under-developed countries. Dominance of finance capital has been the instrument of post-War neo-colonialism. This has eventually let loose a few risks:

- The contradiction between economic globalisation *vis-à-vis* economic nationalism[5] and the resultant political reaction.

- Denial of social value of labour in the production process of globalisation.
- Insulate the poor and the marginal section of the society from the production and consumption processes of globalisation.
- Labour alienation of the unskilled workers and the eventual crises.
- Doubtful promises for social development.[6]
- Likelihood of political reaction, violence and conflict.

Governance is a brief formula of mitigating all these risks and ensuring fuller security of FDI, capital investment by the MNCs and ensuring smooth flow of international debt and profit.[7] The expectation from governance norms and strong institutions is that the latter must be in a position to resist violence and instability of any kind that might affect the volume and efficiency of foreign direct investment. The term 'security risk' has a still greater connotation. The World Bank intends to insulate itself from the society in which its finance capital operates. This may be termed as 'secessionism of the rich'.[8] Keeping the administrative question of foreign debt in view, governance norms have been directed towards establishing administrative efficiency, personal security of the administrators, creation of enabling social and political environment for running the foreign aided industries and projects and towards maintenance of law and order and surveillance. For reducing security risk and conflict resolution, the World Bank promoted another concept, namely, participatory development. Participation has been regarded as a norm of good governance. The anticipation is that participation reduces the risks of security and promotes peoples involvement. The accountability of development is bounced back to the people as if the people are the stakeholders of development. Within the institutional matrix of globalisation and privatisation of capital, peoples' participation cannot lead to a 'fit' and eventually it calls for a hiatus between behvioural and structural approaches to conflict resolution and security risk mitigation.[9]

The formula of Governance is expected to create 'capital trenching'. In rationalising this formula, the political economists of globalisation (Alberto Alesina, Robert Perotti) have discovered SPI indicators. (Socio-political Instability Indicators).[10] Through the application of SPI indicator, there has been an attempt to show a negative impact of these indicators on 'Growth' through probate regression analysis. It has been shown that,

- Political instability causes inflation
- Hinders the process of growth
- Increases the volume of debt
- Discourages FDI
- Reduces GDP
- Causes lack of far-sightedness in formulating economic policy.

The role of governance has been highlighted in order to contain politico-economic unrest and this role has been felt more significant in the under-developed countries. The institutional question is related to that of governance. The institutional conditionality is equivalent to governance conditionality and this equation has become *sine qua non* for the recipient countries to receive foreign debt.

These conditionalities have provoked the World Bank to decline support to those countries, which have weak institutions.[11] Commitments to governance and maintenance of institutional standard need among others, a few things:

- The under-developed countries should have surveillance and knowledge about the hindrances of good governance
- Creation of appropriate social and political environment
- Ensure administrative transparency and accountability
- Adequate reforms at policy level
- Change weak structure and systems
- Adequate law and constitutional reforms
- Create an environment receptive to NEP
- Define role of government in the light of globalisation and NEP reforms
- Ensure efficiency and eligibility in the process of administration

- Institutional reforms and decentralisation
- Develop the people based organisations
- Decentralisation in decision-making and policy formulation.

Thus, parallel to the SPI indicators, the institutional indicators have also been developed. These include:

- Security of bilateral and multilateral economic agreements and property right indicator
- Corruption indicator
- Judicial system and delay in justice indicator
- Political stability indicator
- Political efficiency indicator
- Market efficiency indicator
- Social and political rights indicator
- Institutional achievement indicator
- Social capital indicator

In the neo model of institutionalisation many more points are there like, efficiency of goods and services and flexibility of government institutions in marketing these, service-oriented and desired institutionalisation, collective efforts of private bodies, CSOs and the media, to include a few.[12]

The core question of governance and institutional reforms evolves round that of downsizing the state power in the under-developed countries so that the latter could never become a powerful contestant to the western states nor they could take concrete and sovereign decisions on socio-economic and political development. The institutional question is raised by the western power not only for the sake of political-economic exchange but also for the sake of keeping police surveillance over rights including the intellectual property rights created through this exchange, being transferred to the MNCs and for keeping the bilateral and multilateral agreements activated. The attenuating circumstances arose out of the need of institutionalisation has hard pressed the law and order infrastructure of the under-developed states and has impelled the latter to introduce coercive legislation. There has also been growing deficit budget to meet such expenditure.[13]

Despite all rhetoric on governance and institutional reforms, in the pursuit of global market, the role of institutional force has not been ignored. In the peace mission of global marketisation, the "*peace building rules and triggers*"[14] have got a place and accordingly, use of institutionalised force has been prescribed to subdue any kind of democratic movement in the under-developed countries.

In the globalisation context, the concept of social capital is caught in its own dilemma. Social capital formation among the poor and the disadvantaged so far could not lead to any kind of social contract that is necessary for a market society. Given the inherent contradiction between productive forces (highly privatised) and the production relation (characterised by poverty, lack of gainful employment, lower purchasing power of the common people and so on) the social contract proves to be highly utopian. Though theoretically social capital offers a way to bridge sociological and economic perspectives and provide potentially richer and better explanation of economic development, social interactions between community and institutions may not necessarily shape economic performance. In fact Woolcock and Narayan themselves have admitted that "having high level of social solidarity of informal groups does not necessarily lead to economic prosperity.[16] Rather social solidarity even in our country has resisted the process of private capital investment. (The case of Du Pont in Goa).

But the more serious issue is poverty *vis-à-vis* social capital. Far from gaining from the concept, the contradiction between private capital and the disadvantaged is logically to take a deep root in the society.

NOTES

1. *Quarterly Journal of Public Administration*, XLIV, No. 4, 1998.
2. Alberto Alesina (2000), *The Political Economy of High and Low Growth*, Annual World Bank Conference on Development Economics, 1997. Also see Jannie Aron, *Research Observer* 15(1), IBRD-World Bank.

3. J.E. Stigliz (1999), *Whither Reform? Ten Years of the Transition*, Annual World Bank Conference on Development Economics, The World Bank, Washington DC.
4. Michael Woolcock, Deepa Narayan (2000), "Social Capital—Implications for Development Theory", *Research Observer* 15(2), IBRD-World Bank.
5. Baldevraj Nayar (1997), "Globalisation, Nationalism and Economic Policy Reform", *Economic and Political Weekly*, July 7.
6. Social Summit—Copenhagen, The Draft Plan 1994.
7. Dr. Asok Kumar Ray (2000), *Sushashan, Pratisthanic Prashna avam Visyayan*, International Conference, Department of International Relations, Jadavpur University.
8. Prabhat Patnaik (1995). "Nation State in the Era of Globalisation", *Economic and Political Weekly*, August 19.
9. Dr. Asok Kumar Ray, *Civil Society Under Globalisation—A Case Study of Assam Rural Infrastructure and Agricultural Services Project*, Seminar paper in NEICSSR, Shillong.
10. Alberto Alesina and Robert Perotti, (1994), "The Political Economy of Growth", *The World Bank Economic Review*, Washington DC.
11. Alberto Alesina (1997), *The Political Economy of High and Low Growth*, Annual World Bank Conference on Development Economics. Also see Jannie Aron (2000), *Research Observer*, 15(1), IBRD-World Bank.
12. The World Bank, *Research Observer*, Vol. 15, Washington DC.
13. Erole D'Souza (1996), "How did the Reforms get Acceptability", *Economic and Political Weekly*, July.
14. "The State of World Hunger", 10th Annual Report, *BFW*, US.
15. Planning Commission, Government of India, 2002.
16. Michael Woolcock, Deepa Narayan (2000), "Social Capital—Implications for Development Theory", *Research Observer*, 15(2), IBRD-World Bank.

4

DEVELOPMENT AND DEFENCE
Some Conceptual Questions

ASOK MAITI and SUBHENDU CHAKRABARTI

Development and defence are understood by most of the nation states today (especially after Second World War) as contradictory phenomena. The reason behind such understanding is that, if you spend more on food, health, education or welfare, you would have less for your armaments. Defence of one's geographical territory is so fundamental for the nation remaining sovereign that no discourse regarding 'Defence' is permitted even in the highest forum like the Parliament. Whatever the Government or for that matter the ruling parties say about defence is final and questioning the argument of government in this matter is looked down upon as unpatriotic. The members we send to the parliament consider it as a solemn duty not to question the authenticity or reliability of the claims regarding requirement, performance or efficiency of the government in the matter of defence. Any and every issue of the defence is treated as sacrosanct. Even scams regarding purchase of Bofors guns or Coffins are dismissed by Prime Ministers as minor things which should not be deliberated upon. They treat 'defence' as 'secret' never to be shared with the people whose 'will' we all know as sovereign. Again, mingling of military secrets (which are very necessary for the success of any operation) with 'defence' gives the government as ploy to hide the facts from the people and protect the persons responsible for non-performance, dishonesty and inefficiency.

In a democracy, the questions and issues related to defence is matter of public interests and the peoples have right to know about the aims, objectives and retionale about our preparedness. At the same time it is also very important to understand that the army administration is entrusted to maintain military matters as closely guarded secret. Public access to such secrets is untenable because all security measures consist of different activities—espionage, counter-espionage, camouflage etc. to which public access is rightly denied. But the policies of defence for democratic states cannot be secret. The people have right to know what government thinks, whether it intends to defend its own people from foreign invasion or subjugate other nations by force of arms, whether the government honour peaceful co-existence or aspire to be a super power. The Government should be quite straightforward in the matter of defence and take the entire population into confidence regarding the formulation of our defence policies, security issues and the like. Peoples' awareness about the defence needs, their participation in the matter of defence preparedness, their alertness and vigilance can protect a nation against foreign invasion. Otherwise there can be alienation of the people from the government as well as from the army. There cannot be proper self-defence without fullest cooperation and direct involvement of the population in the matter of defence.

Let us now consider the question of 'development' in relation to the country's security or defence. There is a saying that "the army marches on its belly". If there is no food for the army supplied by the nation, the army is bound to fail. In the medieval as well as in colonial times many armies were extinct as there was no food for soldiers as well as for general public. So it is imperative that, the people of the country concerned should at least be free from hunger, should have fulfilment of basic minimum needs and sufficient infrastructural facilities for their armies to march. During the colonial days the army of a colonial power would be sustained by plunder of the people. These mercenary soldiers were not accountable to the people and they would be guided by their generals not for defence of any country but for subjugating other countries. The value system in colonial armies are therefore irrelevant and dangerous in case of armies nurtured in democracies. In a Democracy, the army should be trained in a value system which build their allegiance to the people. They know that they are children of the nation and they are entrusted to defend their own people even at the cost of their own lives. They should know that their countrymen caters to basic needs of army men first as patriotic duty and are ready for greater sacrifices if the situation so demands. That is how they should be and are duty bound to the people and to their country.

Understanding 'defence' and 'development' from this paradigm helps us in eliminating the so-called competitiveness of the economic ends with respect to resource allocation. It is true that with the scarce resources at hand, there would be certain problems of making judicious allocation for development and defence needs. But innovations in these fields can be of much help and efforts should be made for the same.

Let us take an example from the erstwhile Soviet Union where machine tractor stations were converted to tank-building establishments during Second World War. This shows how development goals and defence objectives have some common points. Reverting an industry meant for agricultural production into armament-industry was possible and desirable at that point of time. Moscow's Metro was not only meant for commuters, but also was used as Air-raid shelters. In present day technology, fertilizer factories can easily be converted to explosives factory and the like.

The point which we want to make is that *Defence and Development have many complimentarities* and not mere competitiveness alone. Can we not make the complimentaries predominant? Constructing roads and railways along and across the country would not only strengthen our defence preparedness, the efficiency of the supply lines and such other things but also open up avenues of various economic activities especially trade and commerce.

If the peoples are not made aware about the maintenance of territorial integrity, no amount of military preparations can prevent cross-border infiltration and crimes. The people should feel that they are to defend their territory in their own interest and defence is only a part of development. They should also feel that their own children are guarding the borders in order that there can be no aggression on their territory and they can pursue their economic, social and cultural activities remaining free from fear of external aggression.

Understanding development and defence as complimentary is a quest for the quality of life. Fascism or imperialism never ever appreciate the quality of life peoples all over the world want and aspire for. They can have no respect for the peoples and sovereignty of other countries. On the contrary, Democratic Republics having no design to colonise other countries or destroy peoples of other countries should unite in order that Defence and Development become complimentary in all such countries. To begin with, we can attempt this in SAARC countries. This regional alliance among different states would mutually guarantee each others' sovereignty and user in brilliant economic co-operation to the benefit of our peoples. If the government of our country and those of our neighbours are wise enough they should see that our economics (weak compared to countries in the north) can thrive well if we respect each others sovereignty and work for the welfare of the peoples of our own countries. Most of the expenses of Arms-Race can then be useless and the resources so saved can be spent for the greatest good of the greatest number of peoples.

Another point, which needs be understood carefully, is that *security is a function of utmost vigilance of the peoples.* Infiltration, cross-border terrorism and other such undesirable activities can be meaningfully and successfully dealt only with the fullest cooperation and utmost vigilance of the peoples. What is normal-trade in border-areas can be 'smuggling' in the eye of law in respective countries. There should therefore be a clear delineation between normal trade and illegal activities. Unless the peoples in the border areas are not enough educated and alert, the entire matter is left at the hands of armies of either side and the images of armies are also tarnished in the eyes of the people.

The people living in international border area are distinctly different from those in other parts of the country. The border region peoples have no access to centres of growth (cities, state capitals, industrial estates etc.). They are in difficult terrain and there was very little development of infrastructure by the state powers on either side of the border. In most of the settlements of the border areas the governments are not at all known to the people and if known, they understood Government as trigger-happy army-men. So they generally try to avoid those people armed to teeth and consider them as alien or outsiders. Since these people have a long tradition of friendship and mutual interdependence with people on the other side of the border, they cannot remain dissociated from them. They have been exchanging their necessary goods on barter system. Since most of the economies were pre-monetised there was no question of money as a medium. Even when the government came and the economy was gradually monetised both the currencies were accepted in localised border trade on either side of the border.

The story does not end with the mutual dependence of the people of either side of the border in respect of only commodities. There are social exchange as well as cultural affinity of the people living in either side of the border. For example, Nagaland and Manipur have similar cultural traits with those of the people of Myanmar living in border areas. Again the people of Arunachal Pradesh have religious affinity towards people living in Tibet region of China. In other words, peoples in the border region have different kinds of ties, namely, economic, cultural and religious, with their counterparts of the other side of the border. Can defence policy be realistic without considering these common heritages of the people having their nationality differences. We would argue that these aspects of the relationships should be addressed in formulating a dynamic and progressive policy.

In this context, let us look into the situation of North East Indian states in our country. These states are said to be strategically vulnerable border states as they are.

North East India (previously Assam and NEFA) had no defined boundary even in 1960. This was due to the legacy of the British rule in India. Being expansionist the British Imperialists kept this border undefined. Later the borders were demarcated and a kind of actual line of control appeared in the Indian map. One-third of the India's international border occurs in north east. That is how north east India is recognised as a strategic area of significance with around 5500 km length of international border. Being a very difficult terrain it is not always possible to maintain constant vigilance on the entire length of the border. In this part of the country we have 1643 km of border with Myanmar, about 1000 km with China, 1956 km with Bangladesh and 650 km with Bhutan. While Bhutan is a protectorate of India, the others are not. There had been problems in finally demarcating the border between China and India. The border between Myanmar and India and between Bangladesh and India are allegedly porous. The Government of India may be due to its foreign policy compulsions maintained different degrees of vigilance in borders covering different countries. Even though the Government of India expresses its concern about the areas and people living in those areas having international border, it seemed to have no comprehensive policy of border area development.

What we would like to argue is that there should be a comprehensive policy of defence and development for border states. Such policies would not only be meant for physical protection of our geographical territories but also for development of our people in all fronts. Improvement in their livelihood situation and their entitlement to health and education would generate a sense of belonging among these peoples who would zealously guard the country's international border remaining friendly with peoples living on other sides of the borders. A kind of good neighbourliness will no longer remain a distant cry if the governments of the countries treat defence and development in a positive way.

5

INSURGENCY, MILITANCY AND INSECURITY
Roots and Its Ramifications

TARUN BIKAS LAHIRI

The Region and Its Unique Distinctiveness

With rugged terrain and torrents, the mighty Brahmaputra Valley, with dense forests, people having diverse ethnic-socio-cultural characteristics, with international frontiers all-around except the narrow isthmus in North West, the connecting corridor with mainland of India; N.E. India is a remarkably distinctive region of the Indian Union.

The region referred to as seven sisters covering the states of Arunachal Pradesh, Assam, Manipur, Meghalaya, Mizoram, Nagaland and Tripura has an area of 2.5 lakh sq.m., habitat of 38.5 million persons (2001). Thanks to dominantly rugged physiography, N.E. region has an apparently favourable land-man ratio. The region covers about 7.8 per cent of geographical area of the country but holds about 3.7 per cent of India's population (2001).

However, in spite of its valuable natural resources, scenic grandeur, substantial advance in literacy levels, cultural wealth of some communities, the region has remained backward, a formidable retarding factor being the internal strife between the communities, at times eroding as under-current at times highly destructive through violent eruptions.

Human behavioural characteristics may not be viewed in

isolation. It has roots in family lineage as well as larger societal mind-set. Disquiet in the North East too has also manifold linkages.

Historical Retrospection

Though in epic like *Mahabharata*, the region found a noteworthy place and there is also mention of Kamrupa on the Allahabad Pillar inscription made at the time of most powerful emperor of the Gupta Dynasty, i.e., Samudra Gupta but N.E. Region by and large was never under the hegemony of the central rulers of India in ancient or medieval eras. Only once Mira Jumla, the General of the Mughal Emperor Aurangzeb defeated the Ahom King in the Brahmaputra Valley. But the success was short-lived, Ahom Kings recaptured their kingdom soon.

However, Ahom Kings did not enjoy supreme power over the entire region. Power of governance was shared by the dynastic kingdoms of Manipur, Khasi and Jaintia Kingdoms, Manikya Rulers of Tripura. Bodos at one time occupied a large part of the Brahmaputra Valley though they had not been able to set up a dynastic rule. In Nagaland, Mizoram and Arunachal Pradesh various ethno-cultural-religious principalities ruled in their respective segments. Though, Ahoms at times extended their influence over marginal area of others' territories in the hills of the N.E.

Thus, the North Eastern region was never under a unified command either centrally or regionally.

Desperate Ethno-Cultural-Linguistic Affiliations

Widely desperate ethno-cultural composition of the population of N.E. Region was the dominant factor for simultaneous existence of virtually independent principalities having suzerainty in their respective habitats.

N.E. Region has absorbed waves of migrations from Myanmar, Tibet and Thailand. Considerable admixture took place between two major ethnic groups, viz. the caucasoid and mongoloid. Most mignants brought various Tibeto-Burman languages. Mention may also be made of Austric language represented by the people of the Khasi and Jaintia hills of Meghalaya. However, the dominant population group constituted by Ahoms—a mixture of caucasoid Aryans and mongoloid migrants from Myanmar—in course of time was Hinduised and adopted Assamese language derived mainly from Sanskrit. As a matter of fact, 'Asom' is a Sanskrit word which means peerless or unparallel, socio-cultural influence of the Ahoms was paramount in the Brahmaputra Valley where they ruled from 1228 to 1826. Grahgaon, the Capital of the Ahom Kingdom was the important power centre of N.E. Region in pre-colonial era.

Colonial Era: Radical Change of Guard

The British took over control of Assam from the Ahom King Purandar Singh in 1838 with tacit support of Myanmar. Under the British rule in India, for the first time, almost the entire North Eastern Region was brought under the umbrella of the Central Command located at Delhi. In the sensitive frontier region South of Macmohan Line (Arunachal Pradesh), for effective control, the British organised Frontier Administrative Service. The officers under this service, played the role of soldier-administrators. They also performed a kind of paternal role model particularly along the Macmohan Line, boundary line with Tibet (China).

But unlike the Ahom Kings, the British adopted a very successful strategy of consolidation of their influence by promoting large-scale baptisation of the tribals. They termed the process of conversion of tribals into Christianity as 'humanising' initiated by David Scot, the first Commissioner of Assam appointed in 1836. Christian converts developed a negative perception of Indians from other parts of the country which gave rise to separatist tendencies. Christianisation of the tribal population vastly changed their native socio-cultural characteristics. By and large, they adopted English as the medium of instruction.

Loyalty to the British, was amply demonstrated by the Nagas, almost wholly converted to Christianity. During World War-II, they actively supported the British and offered stiff resistance to the Japanese-INA force during seize of Kohima in 1944. Divisive policy of the British gradually eroded whatever friendly relations existed between hills and plains people. Previously Daylas, Mismis etc. of Arunachal had trade with plains people and they could speak in Assamese.

Unrest on the Eve of Independence

However apparent peace and unification of the North East under colonial rule started witnessing early tremors by disintegrating forces as stranglehold of the British showed signals of retreat in near future.

In connection with visit of the Simon Commission, Khasi National Durbar pressed for Khasi State. In 1945-46, Khasi States, People's Union also demanded Khasi State. Naga Hill Council led by Mr. Phizo, demanded even a sovereign Naga State at the time of Indian Independence in 1947. Mizos too wanted recognition of their separate identity. On the whole, separatist tendencies kept under the carpet during colonial rule surfaced again on the eve of and after independence. Only the Brahmaputra Valley leaders who participated at the freedom struggle and Maharaja Virchandra Manikya Bahadur, the enlightened tribal King of Tripura willingly joined independent Indian Union. Rest of the tribal ethno-cultural affiliations had no positive attitude towards new-born Indian Union.

Constitutional Provisions Made

Certain constitutional provisions were made to satisfy urge of the tribal principalities for autonomy. The VIth Schedule of the Constitution granted regional autonomy for hills people. It was followed by the N.E. Act of 1971 which in course of time saw the birth of tiny states—Nagaland, Meghalaya and Mizoram. Arunachal Pradesh, previously designated as North East Frontier Agency (NEFA) was also granted statehood. Tripura and Manipur too were recognised as autonomous states. Size of erstwhile Assam Province (later on state) was very substantially reduced. The geographical area of the North Eastern Region is now divided into seven autonomous states, referred to as seven sisters though love relations between the sisters, if exists at all, are often under clouds.

Reorganisation of States could not bring Peace

North Eastern Region is still an active area of insurgents and militants. Separatist strifes here are xenophobic manifestations of deep-rooted ethno-cultural and emotional differences.

Facets of ravaging hostilities in the North East may broadly be grouped as below:

> All the tribal groups are united in their feeling against non-tribal people and resentment against Central Government. However, negative attitude of the tribals towards non-tribals is not confined to North East States only. Perhaps out of the feeling of mistrust and sense of insecurity, all India presents a polarised dwelling pattern of tribals. Generally speaking, about three-fifth of tribal population in India live in districts where they are either in majority or from very substantial minority. But, outside North East, mutual distrust between the tribals and non-tribals has not yet led to conflagration.

Apart from tribals *versus* non-tribals, there are hostilities between tribal factions, clashes for territorial expansions and in economic interests. Rivalry between tribals and plains people is also related to these factors.

Insurgent Groups and their Goals

The National Socialist Council of Nagalim (NSCN-IM) is the largest, best equipped and most dominant insurgent group in the entire region. It is regarded as the mother insurgent group feeding other militant outfits in the region like United Liberation Front of Assam (ULFA), the two Bodo Groups in Assam, People's Liberation Army (PLA) in Manipur. The Smaller Naga faction followed Khaplang, a Hemi from Myanmar. This factor is referred to as NSCN(K). NSCN's activities are spread over Nagaland, Manipur, Assam and Tirap-Changland region of Arunachal

Pradesh. The objective of the insurgency is to create a sovereign independent Greater Nagaland called 'Nagalim' covering all the areas where Nagas live.

Currently conflict between Meiti plainsman and Tangkhul Naga hill tribes in Manipur has assumed serious proportion. Meitis with Vaishnavite culture is very different from Tangkhul Nagas who are devout Christians. There is a clash of economic interests also. Meities cannot acquire land in hill areas where Nagas live. But Nagas are acquiring properties in Meiti areas in and around Imphal Valley of Manipur. Nagas demand that parts of Manipur where Nagas live should be included in Nagalim.

Tribes fighting against tribes is yet another aspect of unrest in the North East. Kuki Naga clashed are at times quite violent. Paradox is that both Kukis and Nagas are Christians and tribes. Kuki National Army (KNA) and Kuki Liberation Organisation (KLO) were organised to protect Kuki villages from the onslaught of Nagas. Both the tribes are fighting each other to monopolise control of the narcotics trade along Indo-Myanmar border with centres at Morch (in India) and Tamu (in Myanmar).

The root of Kuki-Naga problem was rooted in the shrewd British policy of governance. They baptised and patronised Nagas. But to check ascendancy of Nagas, promoted migration of Kukis living in Chin Hills of Myanmar into India in the 19th Century.

Assam is the theatre of operations of three militant organisations, ULFA wanted a sovereign Assam. Bodo Land Tiger Force (BLTF) and National Democratic Front of Bodoland (NDFB) want a separate state out of Assam along the north bank of the Brahmaputra river. Skirmishes between Nagas and Assamese along Assam-Nagaland border contributes to restlessness in the region.

After independence, liberal tribal king of Tripura allowed entry of waves of refugees from erstwhile East Pakistan (now Bangladesh). That changed the demographic and habitat structure of tribal population of Tripura. Plain lands were mostly occupied by Bengali refugees and tribal dwellings were polarised in hilly areas. Conflict of interests made Bengalis and tribals antagonistic to each other. Confrontation between Bengalis living in plains and Chakma, Reang and Jamatiya tribal groups living mainly in rugged terrain often take the form of violent clashes.

Mizos are also not easy with Chakmas or Hmars in Mizoram. Rivalry between tribal groups disturb peace in the State.

Taking advantage of relative calm in Arunachal Pradesh, militant outfits NSCN(K), ULFA and Bodos have set up their training camps and operating bases in Tirap-Changlong Region of Arunachal Pradesh.

So, no state in the North Eastern Region is free from clashes between warring groups. Internal strife is being actively abetted by motivated help extended from neighbouring foreign countries.

Foreign Factor

Disquiet in North Eastern Region provided opportunities to Pakistan for opening a subsidiary theatre for its proxy war with India. It has been reliably learnt that Pakistan has set up a network of espionage bases and insurgent training camps in Bangladesh. These camps are mainly located in Chittagong Hill Tracts in South East and Sylhet-Karimganj Region in North East of Bangladesh. Illegal arms are mainly acquired from arms bazar near Bangkok and transported by sea to coastal area around Cox's Bazar in Bangladesh. Supply of arms are passed on to insurgents of N.E. India through infiltrators *via* Indo-Bangladesh-Myanmar borders. Such foreign help is escalating hostilities in North East Region and destabilising India.

ISI of Pakistan is also active inside North East States. Illicit immigrants from Bangladesh provide ISI launching pads. It has also created fundamentalist Islamic Groups with the help of a small local community of Manipuri Muslims (Pangals).

LTTE connection with expatriate Tamil community from Myanmar and its resultant contribution in helping militant activities should also not be excluded from the vista.

Developmental efforts are suffering due to prolonged restlessness prevailing in one or other part of the region. In spite of substantial central assistance and its natural resources, the region has remained backward, its relative development index is nearly half of national average. Politicians-militant nexus is a constraint for eradication of hostilities.

Outlook: Reconciliation and Development

Recently in January 2003, a memorandum of understanding (MOU) has been signed between the Government of India and the premier and most resourceful insurgent organisation of the North East Region, viz. NSCN(IM) who pledged no more fighting against Indian Security forces, Mr. Isaac Chisi Swu and Mr. Thuingalang Muivah, two top leaders of NSCN(IM) even visited Rajghat, samadhi of Mahatma Gandhi at Delhi and paid homage to the father of the nation. These developments may be the harbinger of long awaited peace in the North East. Though neither NSCN(IM) nor NSCN(K) has deviated from their demand for Nagalim. But NSCN(IM) has agreed to negotiate for it peacefully.

However, Ms. Addino Phizo, President of the Naga National Council, has challenged the authority of Swu and Muivah to sign the MOU on behalf of the Nagas. Ms. Phizo, daughter of late Mr. Phizo who first demanded independent Nagaland in 1947, claimed that the mantle of leadership of the Nagas lie with her organisation only. NSCN(K) has also denounced the agreement reached between NSCN(IM) and Government of India. Notwithstanding these noises, which may not be wholly hollow, the process of reconciliation started should be welcomed as the right step and expression of faith in democracy by both sides. Dialogue and understanding with other warring groups could bring stable peace in the region. But terrorist and espionage activities emanating from foreign lands are to be dealt decisively where military may have to play the major role—in the context of the present geo-political scenario of the subcontinent. Otherwise, outside agents will continue to fuel latent terrorist tendencies.

Side by side of political processes, all possible avenues need to be followed to step up development efforts and its true percolation at the grassroots level. In this connection, performance of Army Development Groups (ADGs) first created after 1962 and revived in 1990s at the initiative of General Shankar

Roychowdhury is noteworthy. ADGs carried out basic civic developments in the frontier locations of the North East Region. The group teams were composed of construction engineers, medical and vaterinary officers, electrical and mechanical engineers and educational corps. They built foot tracks on the hills, arranged water supply, health care, primary education and other community facilities, all in very remote and difficult areas. The soft face of the army has earned appreciation of population vitally important for the army. ADGs, operating in limited areas for short periods were successful as they were corruption-free. However, Army Welfare Missions cannot cover entire population, neither it is the primary role of the army. It is the job of elected civilian leaders who may take some guidance from the approach of ADGs which rested on twin pillars, viz. right choice of programmes and no corruption.

REFERENCES

Deb, Bimal J. (ed.) (2002), *Development Priorities in North East India*, Concept Publishing Company, New Delhi.

Hazarika, Sanjoy (2003), "A major step forward," *The Statesman*, Kolkata Edition, February 1.

Roy Burman, B.K. (1971), "Distribution of Scheduled Tribes in India," Paper included in *An Indo-USSR Collaborative Study*, Census of India.

Roychowdhury, Sankar (2002), *Officially at Peace*, Viking Penguin India.

Vidyarthi, L.P. (1993), *Art And Culture of North East India*, Publications Division, Government of India.

6

THE STILWELL ROAD AND THE CHINA SYNDROME

MEETA DEKA

A consideration of the revival and development of the Stilwell Road, originally the Ledo Road, in North East India is to be studied from a geo-political perspective; primarily because its (embarkment point is) in a region of great strategic importance and second, because the 'potential' Chinese threat, or the so-called 'China Syndrome' may give vent to its inclination of assuming greater control of South Asian politics, where India's interest may be sidetracked. The China Syndrome, then, poses a serious security threat perception. The concept of national security is perceived as consisting of several interrelated elements or as an interplay of national interests, as well as of political aims, studied as a cohesive whole, which in turn converts a geographical entity into a geo-political one.

Defence analysts point out that the safeguarding the national interests would explain the country's national security concept. The foremost national interests of any sovereign country are "the safeguarding of the national frontiers, freedom of action in the international fora," so that their freedom or existence cannot be curbed by others although there may be norms imposed by the UN, "economic independence, despite rules and regulations of the WTO, and most important of all, security of the people," of the common man, be it from political harassment, by protecting national frontiers, or from elements within, or to ensure his economic welfare. Strategic analysts, therefore, maintain that the present geo-political circumstances have interlinked external and internal threats to the security of India[1] and the present scenario of this region is a manifestation of this. The paper focuses on the strategic importance of the Stilwell Road, then and now, *vis-a-vis* the security environment of the region and related problems like insurgency for instance, on the question of its reopening.

Upon its construction, "Stilwell justified the strategic importance of the road by stating that it would be the most potent winning factor," in the war against Japan. Field Marshal William Slim wrote that many people, Americans as well as British, questioned whether the Ledo Road could be built, whether the Chinese would ever be able to drive back the Japanese and clear the route, whether the Ledo railway would carry and maintain the troops, labour, equipment and material required, whether any road builders could overcome the monsoon climate combined with the extreme difficulty of the terrain. Many, 'even of those who believed it possible', did not think that the road would ever repay the expenditure in men and resources that would be required. He wrote: "Indeed at this time, Stilwell was almost alone in his faith. . . ."

Slim was in agreement with Stilwell in so far as the feasibility was concerned that properly equipped and efficiently led Chinese troops could defeat the Japanese if, as would be the case with his Ledo force, they were numerically stronger, and that so far as the engineering skill is concerned, British engineers had experiences of building roads on as difficult terrain with less technical equipment. However, "Slim doubted 'the overwhelming war-winning value of this road', and believed that it was starting from the wrong place." He stated that the 'American amphibious strategy' in the Pacific, of hopping from island to island would be more effective than an overland advance across Asia with a Chinese army yet to be formed. In any case, if the road was to be really effective, its feeder railway should start from Rangoon, not from Calcutta. "On military grounds", he asserted, "I would have used the immense resources required for this road, not to build a new highway to China, but to bring forward the largest possible combat forces to destroy the Japanese army in Burma." Once this was accomplished, the old route to China would be open and over it would flow a much greater tonnage than could ever come *via* Ledo, and the Allied Forces in Burma would be available for use elsewhere.

"This became the fundamental difference between the American and the British outlook in Burma." To the Americans, the reconquest of Burma was merely incidental to the reopening of land communications with China, and needed to be pursued only to the limited extent necessary for that purpose. To the British, the reoccupation of Burma was not only an end in itself, the liberation of British territory, but, by the capture of Rangoon, the best means of opening up a really effective link with China.[2] Thus, it was the debate on the merits and demerits of the Stilwell Road that provoked opposition and rivalry within the American group and this had its bearing on the future war strategy of the Allied Forces.

In a discussion of the strategic importance of the area and the road, it is important to note that approximately 57 km of the road lies in India, 23 km and more in Assam jurisdiction and around 36 km in Arunachal Pradesh, 1040 km in Myanmar and about 639 km in China, approximately. The total stretch of the road is 1736 km, of which the Burma road comprises only 911 km approx.[3] The Ledo road was finally linked to the Burma road in May 1945. Only two major convoys travelled over the road to Yunan before the end of the war made it redundant and very soon fell into disuse and disrepair. The pontoon bridge across the Irrawady was dismantled in 1947 to allow river craft movement, and the ethnic Kachin insurgency and the Burma Communist Party conflict after Myanmar's independence in 1948 sounded the death knell for the road.[4]

So far as the China Syndrome is concerned, the question arises as to how the threat poses a strategic challenge to India, especially in relation to the northeast. China's "long-term strategy" is clearly "to become the dominant economic and military power in the Asia-Pacific region" and a major power internationally. China's foreign and defence policy initiatives are quite obviously designed to "marginalise India in the long-term and reduce her to the status of a sub-regional power" by increasing Chinese influence and leverage in the Southern Asian region. Hence the "potential for military conflict will always exist" and will, in fact, increase as the armed might of China increases. Srinivasan states that China views the Indian Ocean as strategically important for its future trade relationships; in particular its oil imports from the Persian Gulf. Therefore, it has been making moves to establish its ability to control the key shipping lanes, for example, the Straits of Malacca. This has led China to establish strong relationships with Myanmar, and as a fringe benefit, its Cocos Islands outposts help them keep a close eye on India.

As part of its overall strategic imperatives, China has also embarked on building up a blue-water navy, capable of projecting its force far into the Pacific and Indian oceans. The other imperative for China in developing a blue-water navy is the goal of completing one leg of its triad of nuclear weapons delivery systems—nuclear submarines that can roam the oceans and act as an undetectable second-strike force.[5] Hence, China's aspirations for a "blue water" status for the navy, acquisition of mid-air refuelling capability, deep penetration strike and strategic lift transport aircraft for the PLA Air Force are endeavours aiming to create a modern fighting force capable of undertaking swift offensive operations in areas away from China's borders. Moreover, Competitive elements are inherent in the relationship as both countries compete for foreign investments and markets for their products in the next 15 to 20 years. China's growing power and influence in Asia is a strategic challenge for India as, eventually, Indian and Chinese economic interests will clash, particularly in the South-East Asian markets.

India continues to be viewed as one of the target countries with which border conflicts are a probability. This is an outcome of a clash of strategic interests between India and China in the 21st century. China claims that the reunification of Arunachal Pradesh is a sacred duty for its military. In fact, a potentially conflict prone situation exists between the two sides due to the varying perceptions of the precise locations on the ground and on the map of several points on the Line of Actual Control (LAC) in Ladakh, Uttar Pradesh and Arunachal Pradesh.[6] As such there has hardly been any progress in the long-standing territorial dispute between the two countries, and this is hindering long-term stability. China has been hesitant to resolve border dispute with India, while it has been quick in doing the same with Russia. False maps of the Indo-Sino border have been regularly published by China. A very recent publication, China 2002, of the People's Republic of China, by New Star Publishers, Beijing, shows an administrative map of present China.[7] The Indo-China-Tibet boundary or the McMahon Line in the east and the boundary (Aksai Chin) along Ladakh in the west remained a boundary by usage and understanding. The result was that the precise boundary was not demarcated leading to border skirmishes in 1962 and the Chinese penetration into the Sumdurung Chu Valley of Arunachal Pradesh in 1986.

While border incidents due to patrols, misreading maps or losing their way do occur of and on, China has clearly laid stress on the doctrine of "active defence", "limited war under high technological conditions" and the creation of "rapid reaction combat units" with a focus on her periphery. The redefinitions of China's "strategic frontiers", coupled with military modernisation programmes, are rapidly transforming the force projection capabilities of China's armed forces in the sea, air and on land. In recent years, China has also engaged in upgrading logistic and infrastructure facilities in the Indo-China border areas.[8] For instance, China has substantially upgraded the military logistics infrastructure in Tibet by actively building new roads, supply lines and airfields close to the Indian frontier. China has deployed 15 fighter squadrons in Tibet and has increased the strength of the troops from 1.5 lakhs to 4 lakhs over the years.

While China professes a policy of peace and friendliness towards India, its deeds clearly indicate that concerted efforts are underway aimed at the strategic encirclement of India. For the last several decades, China has been engaged in efforts to create a ring of anti-Indian influences around India through military and economic assistance programmes to neighbouring countries, combined with complementary diplomacy, Pakistan, Bangladesh, Nepal and Sri Lanka have been assiduously and cleverly cultivated towards this end. China has gained strategic advantage over India by progressively making India's neighbours dependent on her to a large extent for their defence supplies. This has helped China "to keep India strategically 'engaged' through its neighbours." The large-scale supply of cheap small arms, such as rifles, hand grenades, rocket launchers, pistols, ammunition and even SAM-7 surface to air missiles, to regimes inimical to India, is an ingenious method of indirect involvement, as these small arms are eventually supplied by agencies such as the Inter-Services Intelligence (ISI) of Pakistan to insurgent groups in Jammu and Kashmir and the north eastern states of India.[9]

The conduct of nuclear tests by India was essential to balance the strategic disadvantage *vis-a-vis* China. India has broken China's nuclear monopoly in Asia. The China-Pakistan nexus in the nuclear, missiles and military hardware fields poses both economic and military threats and this is apparent in the letter Prime Minister Atal Bihari Vajpayee sent to US President Bill Clinton and other world leaders to explain the rationale for the tests made by India on May 13, 1998. To quote:

> I have been deeply concerned at the deteriorating security environment, specially the nuclear environment, faced by India for some years past. We have an overt nuclear weapon state on our borders, a state which committed armed aggression against India in 1962. Although our relations with that country have improved in the last decade or so, an atmosphere of distrust persists mainly due to "the unresolved border problem." To add to the distrust, that country has materially helped another neighbour of ours to become a covert nuclear weapons state. . . . And for the last ten years we have been the victim of "unremitting terrorism and militancy" sponsored by it in several parts of our country. . . .

Diwanji argues that instead of trumpeting the Chinese threat, the present government could have resorted to other measures like preparing India's armed forces, strategic plans, increase defence allocation, improve indigenous abilities and to tackle Chinese assistance to militants in the north east or that of Pakistan's in Kashmir. India requires a stronger paramilitary force, better intelligence and most important, a less dissatisfied population that does not fall prey to the ISI machinations, which in actual are more difficult to tackle because it would mean going against the very people you turn to for votes.[10]

This nuclear and missile issue, while exposing the depth of the China Syndrome, also explains its direct links to the Low Intensity Conflict (LIC) or Proxy War, as the defence analysts maintain, that has been growing in intensity since 1990 along the border, not only in Jammu and Kashmir, but also in the north east, in the form of Pakistan's Inter-Services Intelligence (ISI) activities. It has been established that the Weapons of Mass Destruction (WMD), which pertain to macro-security capability of a state, have emboldened Pakistan to increase the LIC against India. Fig. 6.1 explains "the conflict continuum," how the spectrum of conflict stretches from High Intensity Conflict (HIC) at one end to Low Intensity Conflict (LIC) on the other. At the high end of the continuum are nuclear war, global war and total war and at the other end are guerilla war, revolutionary war, terrorism, insurgency and so on.[11] After Pakistan tested the nuclear bomb (May 1998), the covert capability turned overt. There is no denying the fact that China has been arming Pakistan with both conventional weapons as well as nuclear and missile technology. On the other hand, it has issued public denials and pledged to improve relations with India.

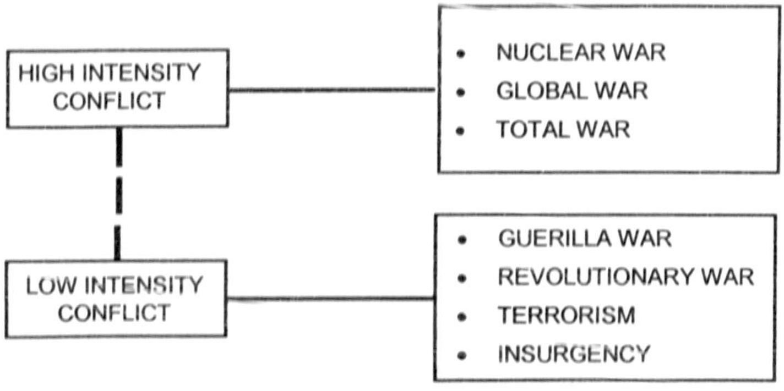

Fig. 6.1: The Conflict Continuum

It is also important to note, especially in relation to the reconstruction of the Stilwell Road, of which some 1000 + km pass through Myanmar, that military collaboration between China and Myanmar has a direct bearing on India's security. "China's increasing involvement in Myanmar, which not only impinges on India's trade and maritime interests but also has adverse geo-strategic implications in the long run." The expansion of Chinese influence into Myanmar is of particular concern to India as it gives the Chinese the potential to deploy their sea power in India's maritime areas of interest, and to eventually directly threaten India's eastern flank. China's sale of sophisticated military technology to Pakistan, Bangladesh and Myanmar, and the possibility of it acquiring naval bases, and overland and air routes to such bases, are areas of great concern for India's security. The objective of the Chinese presence in Coco islands and other Myanmarese naval bases is to keep track of India's missile test-firing ranges.

Such being the bases of the China Syndrome, "the revival of the Stilwell Road could spell more danger to India from the security point of view." This brings us to the issue of the practicality and feasibility of its reopening. Funds may be allotted by the World Bank and other international organisations but the strategic aspect must be underlined. Das in Stilwell's Folly states that the road does not have any economic viability and seen in this perspective, he pointed out that even illegal trade does not operate through this route.[12] Another question could be raised here: If at all it leads to economic prosperity, what if Indian markets are transformed into "dumping grounds" for Chinese goods? After all, after 50 years of planned and large-scale economic restructuring, China's economy has grown at an unprecedented rapid speed. Fig. 6.2 shows the increases in the Gross Domestic Product (GDP) over the years. Much has been written on the invasion of the Chinese "dragon" into the Indian market. A newspaper reads: "After cracking all other industries, the Chinese dragon has hit the Indian crackers market this Diwali with imported guns, bombs and sparklers ruling the trade". In spite of the ban by the Supreme Court, demand for Chinese

```
1978   ==  3,624.1
1985   ====  8,964.4
1990   ========  18,547.9
1995   ========================  58,478.1
2000   ============================  89,403.6
2001   ===============================  95,933.0
```

Fig. 6.2: Increases in the Gross Domestic Product (Unit: 100 million yuan)

crackers, which have 127 decibel noise level, was very high and a survey reported that this was so because of the cheap cost.[13] The level of this danger could be alarming when China has even captured the Ayurvedic market at the international level.

What if this road is used as an effective passage for "the massive transfer of Chinese population that has been the hallmark of Beijing's 'imperialist' policy in the last two decades" in Tibet and Xinjiang. Chinese Han are today a majority in Tibet, (with 7.5 million Chinese *versus* 6 million Tibetans). Srinivasan explained that China needs *lebensraum* for its surplus Han Chinese population, and has therefore settled such large numbers of them in Tibet that Tibetans are now a distinct minority in their own land.[14] Over the past 40 years, the transfer of population and cultural cleansing has continued unabated on the Roof of the World and it is bound to increase with the opening of a railway line from the mainland to Lhasa. The situation is similar in Xinjiang, where the Han population equals Uighur Muslims in the former Eastern Turkestan.[15] To quote Srinivasan: ". . . China has throughout its history been looking for land to dump its excess population—this has caused wave after wave of Chinese migration into Southeast Asia."[16]

The extension of such a policy in the northeast would not be a far-fetched idea when Chinese maps include the entire Arunachal Pradesh in China and since the economists as well as intellectuals in India believe in rapid economic development through the Stilwell Road, that economic hub itself would provide enough cover for the quiet implementation of such a policy. There has been an unprecedented economic growth in China, especially after her accession into the World Trade Organisation (WTO) on December 11, 2001 as its 143rd member.[17] However, despite such exponential economic growth, the present Chinese unemployment situation could also affect the policy of transfer of population. Massive retrenchment from state-owned companies have resulted in China's unemployment level reaching 4 per cent this year (25 million) despite the economy maintaining a robust growth of around 8 per cent. Zheng Peiyan, Minister of State for Development and Planning Commission, said that massive overhaul in the state enterprises had resulted in closure of more than 50,000 companies. The situation got worse each year with the entry of up to 10 million, fresh graduates in the employment market. He perceives this problem as "major" which could have a great impact on social stability in China.[18] At the same time, it could also imply problems for India with respect to a process of demographic inundation.

The development of motorable roads and railway lines to Lhasa as part of the Chinese policy of "Development of the West [of China]" could pose as a grave threat to the security of India, especially after the Government of China have admitted that the railway line will 'strengthen the borders'. A train to Lhasa is of tremendous importance to Beijing, as Arpi observes: "This will complete a pincer movement ultimately encircling India". Moreover, the Chinese now have rail access upto Kashgar in Xinjiang as well as in the south to Burma and the Indo-China peninsula. The train will be able to bring men and armaments dangerously close to the Indian border[19] and the Stilwell Road could be an added advantage in this process.

Another security danger that Arpi projects is that of "the waters from Tibet, the source of most of Asia's great rivers. The control of these rivers is of great strategic importance for the subcontinent." One example is the floods that occurred in the spring of 2000 in Arunachal and in the Kinnaur area in July 2000, which washed away many Indian strategic roads and bridges, especially along the Sutlej in Himachal Pradesh. There are good reasons to believe, he stated, that these floods were not natural calamities, but "human-triggered" and that it was unfortunate that it was hardly reported in the press.[20] The Tibetan website also documents how the water table in Tibet (which feeds many of

Asia's rivers: the Indus, the Ganges, the Mekong, and the Brahmaputra) is threatened with nuclear waste by the Chinese.[21] These factors are vital to the strategic importance of the region as a whole.

"The Stilwell Road is no pragmatic solution for the economic development of the region" and, in fact, it would only promote strategic problems to greater dimensions. The irony of the present situation is that while we are here discussing the problems and prospects of the reopening of the Stilwell Road, as recent as 10th November 2002, Mizoram Chief Minister, Zoramthanga, exhorted the Central Government to show urgency in fencing the borders. To quote: "Unless barbed wire fences are erected immediately, Mizoram will explode under the weight of drug addiction".[22] The problem here is not a mere serious social problem but one that is connected with greater strategic implications which could be an important point for consideration on the question of the development of the Stilwell Road.

Mizoram borders, the heroine producing Golden Triangle region, Laos and Myanmar share an unfenced 710 km border with Myanmar and Bangladesh. Indian Intelligence officials state that there are atleast 90 methamphetamine and amphetamines, like proxyvon, diazepam and codeine production plants along the Thai-Myanmar border, of which 20 are located in the Sagaing division in Myanmar, adjacent to the Indian states of Manipur and Mizoram. Intelligence report maintains that the flourishing drug-manufacturing business in Myanmar is directly linked to the continuing conflict between the military government and the armed ethnic forces fighting for autonomy. While Myanmar's military junta turns a blind eye to drug production and trafficking as a way of ensuring peace among ethnic minority groups, who have been restive for decades, the drug lords, who are rebel leaders, have turned to drug trafficking to finance their military campaigns. Since the 1960s, the Kachin insurgent army has been conducting a bitter guerilla war and the Stilwell Road runs through the Kachin state. The Myanmar army units posted beyond the Pangsau Pass are air-lifted during their change of guard and also they visit the Nampong market to procure their provisions. Hence, trade in commercial terms "is not feasible *via* the Stilwell Road because of the economics, insurgency and the mystique of the Lake of no Return."[23]

When Myanmar as the buffer zone cannot guarantee the "sanitization" of the road, of making the road free of insurgent activities, is the reconstruction of the road practical? By way of comparison, one may point to the small stretch of the National Highway 53, which connects Silchar and Imphal, a distance of approx. 110 km only, which has become the bone of contention among atleast 30 insurgent groups such as the NSCN(IM), NSCN(K), PLA, PREPAK, Kuki Revolutionary Army, etc. to name a few. As such the road has not been developed as even the Border Roads Organisation (BRO) refuses to undertake its development unless 'sanitization' is guaranteed. If such problems become difficult hurdles, the development of the Stilwell Road, that passes through Myanmar for a greater portion, is definitely not possible. Moreover, beyond the Pangsau Pass into Myanmar, a 140 km stretch of the road no longer exists.

In the final analysis it must be understood that the strategic importance of the Stilwell Road has been overemphasised *vis-a-vis* the existence of other alternatives, and more so, in relation to the prognosis and treatment of the China Syndrome, which carries great dimensions of regional, national and international implications. Stilwell did attach great military value to the road and even believed that it would be "the most potent winning factor" in the war against Japan, while others, the British in particular doubted "the overwhelming war-winning value of this road" and saw it as a liability rather than an asset. It was not worth the expenditure in men and resources, as it was unable to carry the weight of supplies that China required. Also, that lorries plying the road consumed a tonne of fuel to deliver each tonne of cargo to China. Only two major convoys travelled over the road to Yunan before the end of the war made it redundant and very soon fell into disuse and disrepair. Gokhale rightly remarked: "It seems incredible that a road built at such cost could have such brief relevance".[24]

The China factor in the north east is apparent in the unresolved territorial disputes and the low intensity conflicts and this adds a significant element of suspicion and unpredictability in the Indo-China relations. The internal security threat can be overcome, as Diwanji argues,[25] by resorting to measures like preparing India's armed forces, strategic plans, increasing defence allocation, improving indigenous abilities and for tackling Chinese assistance to militants in the north east or that of Pakistan's in Kashmir, India requires a stronger paramilitary force, better intelligence and, most important, a less dissatisfied population that does not fall prey to the ISI machinations, which in actual are more difficult to tackle because it would mean going against the very people the political leaders turn to for votes. Analysts feel that by not resolving the boundary disputes China wants to keep India under strategic pressure.[26] In effect, Garver states, if China wishes to demonstrate solidarity with Pakistan, or express anger over Indian policies towards Tibet, the People's Liberation Army (PLA) moves threatening Arunachal Pradesh could be very effective. In fact, this state of affairs multiplies the effect of China's coercive threats. Just as the existence of a strong, anti-India Pakistan siphons Indian forces from India's frontiers with China, so the existence of the unresolved dispute over the eastern Himalayas siphons Indian forces away from India's frontiers with Pakistan.[27]

We cannot ignore China's emergence as a major world power, with widespread economic and security interests, which is a reality, and which has to be accepted. In fact, any attempt to isolate or contain China is unlikely to succeed and such an attempt will also have adverse repercussions.[28] In recent years, India-China relations have acquired maturity and substance. Due to their dominant positions and status in Asia, India and China cannot remain immune to the logic of collective self-interest. It is in the mutual interest of both countries to work towards building a strong, prosperous, self-confident and self-reliant Asia. However, India must be militarily prepared to deal with China from a position of strength. However, it is important to seriously consider the impact of China's rising power in Asia and the manner in which that power may be used by China to further its national interests.

Hence, so far as the external security threat is concerned, India, perforce, has to seriously consider how purely security considerations have determined China's initiatives towards South Asian countries and balance China's power effectively through a strong economic uplift and develop strong relationships with the neighbouring countries of the South Asian Association for Regional Cooperation (SAARC), the Association of South East Asian Nations (ASEAN) countries and the Central Asian Republics (CARs). Despite the present thaw and improvement of relations between India and China, China would continue to remain the primary strategic challenge in political, economic and military terms.

NOTES

1. *Current Affairs*, Directorate General of Military Training (MT 2), Army Head-quarters, compiled and prepared by 76 INF BDE, 2001, p. 181.
2. F.M. William Slim, *Defeat into Victory*, Palit and Dutt, Dehradun, 1971, pp. 248-50.
3. Surendra Baruah, *The Stilwell Road: A Historical Review* in http// tinsukia. nic.in; also, Nitin Gokhale, "Stilwell Road to Nowhere" in *Outlook Traveller Magazine*, Dec. 2001. The figures of the distances vary in different write-ups.
4. K. Das, Stilwill's Folly, *The Sentinel*, Guwahati, Assam, Nov. 10, 2002; For details of early routes, see S. Bora, *The Stilwell Road: A Saga of the Past and a Hope for the Future* in the NEIHA Proceedings, Twentieth Session, 2000.
5. Rejeev Srinivasan, "The Danger from China" in *Rediff Specials*, June 15, 1998.
6. Gurmeet Kanwall, "China's Long March to World Power Status: Strategic Challenge for India," *Strategic Analysis*, Feb. 1999, Vol. xxii, No. ii, pp. 1713-28.
7. *China 2002*, New Star Publishers, China 2002.
8. *Current Affairs, op. cit.*
9. G. Konwall, *op. cit.*
10. A.K. Diwanji, "The China Syndrome," in *The Rediff Specials*, May 27, 1998.
11. *Fundamentals, Doctrine and Concepts*, Indian Army. HQ ARTRAC, Aug. 1998, pp. 56-61.

12. K. Das, *op cit.*
13. *The Sentinel*, Guwahati, Assam, Nov. 11, 2002.
14. R. Srinivasan, *op cit.*
15. Claude Arpi, "Indo-Chinese Relations: Great Leap Forward", in *The Rediff Specials*, Jan. 11, 2002.
16. Srinivasan, *op cit.*
17. *China 2002, op. cit.*, p. 72; also *China's Foreign Trade*, No. 298, Feb. 2002, Lu Feng, PRC.
18. The Sentinel, *op cit.*
19. Claude Arpi, *op cit.*
20. *loc cit.*
21. R. Srinivasan, *op cit.*
22. The Sentinel, *op cit.*, Nov. 10, 2002.
23. K. Das, *op cit.*
24. Nitin Gokhale, *op cit.*
25. A.K. Diwanji, *op cit.*
26. *Current Affairs 2002*, United Academics International, Hyderabad, India, 2002, p. 88.
27. John W. Garver, "Probability of another War between China and India" in *the Rediff Special*, Nov. 2002.
28. G. Konwall, *op cit.*, pp. 1713-28.

7

INTERNAL SECURITY AND ECONOMIC DEVELOPMENT IN NORTH EAST INDIA

M. KAR

Socio-political Scenario

Man's struggle for existence had started with the search for means of sustenance of various groups more or less in an isolated manner. In course of time there developed the idea of communities existing as members of a compound and composite organism. Today this applies to all sections of people everywhere in the world. In common parlance a society means people living under certain varying conditions *en route* to a future existence in a more secure, well organised and better composite life. In other words, human society is an evolving and dynamic phenomenon. A society can develop through joint efforts in properly framed economic and various other social programmes and efficient implementation thereof. This means people's participation, companionship and comraderie for a common cause in every sphere of life and activities maintaining individual liberty of avocation. Social harmony and security are the *sine qua non* for emergence of a healthy society.

People's participation can be ensured only by a peaceful environment ensured by the State. It should not be disturbed by political skulduggery, fundamentalism, religious bigotry, sectarianism, communal perceptions and prejudices *vis-a-vis* social problems. Healthy inter-community and intra-community relations must be developed and nurtured on the basis of peace and harmony.

In a multi-ethnic, multi-cultural and multi-religious or composite society of this part of India, divergences of various interests and perceptions are not unlikely. But a synchronous and amicable solution to the problems can be possible only if the universal interests are given the topmost priority. It has to be remembered that since ancient times the society has been basically divided into two groups, the haves and have-nots, again subdivided into upper and lower or stronger and weaker sections apart from caste, creed and religion. The weaker sections, irrespective of similarities and divergences are the worst sufferers of discrimination, deprivation, poverty and even dehumanisation. Therefore, they need greater attention to create a balance in the society. They should be free from fear psychosis. Only equality and fraternity can make them part and parcel of the society.

Economic development is considered to be the foundation of a society even though the ideals and values of life cannot be measured in terms of money. As a constituent unit of the Indian society, the people of North East India today face the same problems of development and progress to a better worldly life. This study aims at understanding how far the basic ingradient of a healthy society, namely, internal peace and security prevails in the daily life of the people who alone can work for the success of the planned universal economic development and self-sufficiency.

There is a widespread and strong feeling that such an environment is very much, if not altogether absent in North East India. It appeared that investors, entrepreneurs and industrialists were not even willing to visit the area. The situation is such that anyone is hesitant to make any big economic plan and invest in it. Therefore, the Chief Ministers of these States had to go all the way to Mumbai last year to coax the leaders of the economic world to deliberate on the issues of development. Any concrete result is still awaited. It is well known to everyone that a large chunk of the national wealth, men, money and material, is wasted on the question of internal security, naturally economic development taking almost a back seat.

Hindrances to the economic progress can be traced to the failure of the States to ensure socialist, secular and democratic as well as wholly people-oriented planning and proper implementation thereof. This is the result of interaction of the following factors.

1. Lack of healthy, imaginative, selfless, well-informed and well-intentioned leadership. Rather a large number of those in power includes persons allegedly corrupt facing various charges and many of them are communal and self-seeking indulging in horsetrading, defection and other political games.
2. Inefficiency or sometimes inability and unwillingness to govern or lackadaisical actions and lack of social commitments.
3. Lack of social peace and individual and collective safety and security in different spheres of life.
4. Almost all-pervading corruption in every sphere of life.
5. Well organised ethnic, linguistic, cultural and religious adversities. These are often engineered by the Governments or the so called leaders frustrating grandiose plans for economic development. In other words, inter-community and intra-community relations are not congenial to the creation of properly modern economic infrastructures in the region.

Genesis of Instability

Between 1826 and 1900 the British imperial power had committed a forgery by bringing the entire region under one administrative umbrella. They ignored the pluralistic character of the people of the society engaged in fighting against one another for power and domination. Under the alien rule, these people nearly completely surrendered their political rights and identities, but their ethnic, linguistic, cultural and social identities remained subdued or paralysed. India's struggle for freedom on the one hand generated a sense of oneness and on the other a consciousness of their distinct identities with respect to non-tribals in general expressed through political parties and groups. The state policy of the foreign rulers as well as the preaching of many Indian nationalist leaders both during the struggle for freedom and after, very much prompted and engendered the resurrection and emergence of separateness in respective caste, creed, language, religion and other aspects of life. Such consciousness took the form of mutual hostility and urge for isolated development. It became a competition for prosperity for one community at the cost of another through deprivation and suppression. In other words communalism of a new dimension appeared.

Our teachings of oneness was never truly put to practice even in free India. The concept of development according to genious was limited to the tribal people while for others it was left to the dictated terms of the State. This first wrought a complete cleavage between tribals and non-tribals both with respect to society and polity. These expressions became powerful, well organised and assertive often through violence. Then began the process of more vigorous expressions of divergences than the concept of unity in diversity and the demand for separate states for almost every ethnic group and community for satisfying the so called people's aspirations on community, language and other divides. This became the general pattern of political life in free India. Mainly the spirit of separateness, advocated by politicians in their own interests lead to the creation of 29 full-fledged States and six Union Territories. Then also began the demand and armed struggle for independence out of independent India, especially in the North East, the Nagas being the pioneers of the demand, followed by the Mizos. The people of Meghalaya, however, achieved statehood without violence and bloodshed. After long militant expressions of separation and violence the Mizos came back to the mainstream having a separate state. Now the Muslim League's geo-politics of India before 1947 has almost taken the form of ethno-politics and chauvinism. On all India level, once again the two nation theory and on a microlevel in this region, the multinational expressions are on the rise.

One result of the spirit of isolation and resentment against hegemony was the Balkanisation of Assam and creation of as many as five smaller states between 1 January, 1963 and

20 August, 1987. The inept attitude and approach of the Assamese elite and their successive governments and especially their linguistic chauvinism, big brotherly attitude as well as the absurd theory of the 'sons of the soil' played a dominant role in disintegration, of course, in the name of ethnic identities and aspirations. But the problem still remains in the region. The socio-political life in Assam is disturbed by insurgency of varied characters. The Bodo Movement is already very well known. In Meghalaya, a separatist movement seems to be gaining ground mainly on the basis of ethnicity and geo-politics. Some sections of the Tripura Tribes want not only freedom but also expulsion of non-tribals. Manipur is not free from the troubles. The militants themselves are divided everywhere on sectorial leadership and killing of the cadres of one group by those of another is a daily routine. The Nagas would not be satisfied only with independence but also demand Naga-inhabited territories of the neighbouring states of Arunachal, Assam and Manipur. Militancy has appeared in Aruncahal Pradesh also. Chakma refugees are unwanted there. Border disputes often vitiate the inter-state relations in the region. Liberation armies are galore and there is the threat of further balkanisation. Though the troubles centre mainly round ethnicity, often the minorities are the targets of violence and discrimination and treated like enemies and pariahs. It is forgotten that even a majority community is a minority beyond its geographical location.

The Trouble Shooters

Particularly the upper echelons of society are leading the divisive activities making groups or communities unwilling to live and let live together. They do not realise that geographical and ethnic isolation or separation are no longer possible in he present world. Any part of the population wishing to live in that manner will only decimate it quickly. Living together does not mean that their distinctive social characters cannot be protected and maintained. It should be recognised that a majority in a democratic set-up has a much greater share and say in a state and its social affairs. Therefore, they have a far greater obligation to protect and safeguard the minorities for social assimilation. Then, of course, the latter can be reasonably expected to reciprocate the sense of belonging to the society as a whole. Contrary to this, we have in the States a minority phobia, expressed through the fear of being numerically swamped, though our own Census figures do not reflect such a picture. Take for instance the case of Meghalaya. The population of the State in 2001 was 23,06,069. According to Government estimate (2000), 74.39 per cent of them were Christians, the Scheduled 'tribes' having an overwhelming majority of 85.63 per cent of the population in 2002. There were 11.68 per cent Hindus and 3.64 per cent Muslims. The Anti-foreigner Agitation in Assam had raised the cry that there were more than 50,00,000 illegal migrants, mostly Muslims, to that State. The Assam Gana Parishad Government which took office after great fan fare in 1985 found 8,692 such persons liable to expulsion and actually expelled 1,190. The Story goes on.

The Motives

The conflicts are mainly motivated by vote-bank politics and counter-actions against rivals. These are nurtured, publicised and put to practice and play by fundamentalists. The perceptions and purposes being narrow-minded and opposed to universal upliftment and progress, they divide the people into "we" and "they". The expressions of conflicts of interests and demands are apparently inocuous and given the nomenclatures like reservations, ethnic aspirations, identities and so on, the most curious being the slogan of being swamped by the minorities. Take for instance the demand for jobs and educational facilities. The spirit is, "give us employment" and not "others" or "give us first preference not in terms of merit but ethnicity only". Sadly enough, even the talented and meritorious among the tribel people still remain satisfied to be classified as backward. The demands and grievances are sometimes real but often imaginary. Under tainted and self-seeking leadership, these easily turn sectarian resulting in ill feelings and distrust exhibited through repeated communal flare ups before the eyes of the flippant authorities.

Communalism

The worst bane of society is the premeditated, well-planned and well-organised repeated violence against minorities. These take the diabolical forms, namely, mass murders, arson, loot, ethnic cleansing, deprivation of the right to settle in a place of choice, opposition to granting of trade licences, franchise etc. Assam has a long history of such evils. Between 1947 and 1985, about a dozen holocaust and anti-minority pogroms were recorded. No clear picture of anti-violence State programme and action, if any, was made public though thousands of people were killed, many more thousands were displaced and properties worth huge amounts were destroyed. One of the most sanguinary elections was held in 1983. On that occasion alone 17,000 people were the victims. More than 4,000 people lost their lives. Lakhs of people had to take shelter in camps. These facts are only indicators of the social ills.

Shillong was one of the most peaceful places as observed by me during the period 1953-1978, half of my fifty years' life in the city. Its long history of 114 years of synchronous co-existence of different communities and groups of people was blackened and tarnished in 1979 by communal violence. Thus before the birth pang of Meghalaya was over, it was invaded by the same social virus. Along with Assam agitation, the city went in flames during the Durga Puja festivals and remained under night curfew continuously for two months. The state was then under the stewardship of a top leader of the State Demand Movement.

Government Inaction

Daily television and radio newscasts as well as newspapers give us details of gory activities creating social instability and fear psychosis amongst people in general and particularly the minorities. Over the last fifty years, the Government of Assam and the Government of Meghalaya since 1979, had set-up about half a dozen Inquiry Commissions to investigate the series of communal violences. But the reports were not made transparently public with any policy declaration to meet the scourge. As the society as a whole suffered, the people were entitled to know what exact measures were taken to punish the culprits and to ensure the safety and security of the citizens and their families. The perpetration of such atrocities and the negligent and often partisan attitude of the state authorities have shaken each and every community, locality and inter-community relations. A sense of insecurity prevails. Such persistent feelings destroy personality and devotion to work which is a part of the struggle for existence. Our leaders seem to be interested only in their own safety and security.

It is important to remember that even within a community the benefits of development go mainly to the upper stronger or creamy layer of the people. Literacy rates and educational facilities are much less among the poorer sections. As a result of such inequalities and discrimination even intra-community relations like those among different communities are strained and peace is disturbed. For instance, in an area in Shillong inhabited almost wholly by a single community, public expression of insecurity was made recently. Development is not possible in an atmosphere of violence and mutual hatred. Records reveal that in many cases our Government played the role of silent spectators and allegedly some of the leaders were involved.

The Result

The apprehensions of social and personal insecurity, the spirit of ethnic separatism with active communal perceptions and propaganda raise important questions. If India has innumerable kinds of "sons of the soil" on state basis, what and where is the soil of India, *Sare Jahan Se Achchha Hindustan Hamara* and Mother India that is Bharat? Should we not remember and recognise that a constant stream of thoughts and unifying actions, through the ages, enriched and sustained the common heritage of mankind? How far does the present social structure reflect unity in diversity of which we are so proud? Is the concept of peaceful and secular co-existence in a multi-faceted and progressive society falling down? Is not India the product of co-operation and partnership of all the so called "sons of the soil", "indigenous" and "outsiders"? Are not concrete remedial measures to eradicate the social evils and reconstruct North East India the most urgent call of the day?

Working of Destabilisation

Social conflicts and anti-government agitations in these states as elsewhere also take the form of bundh, boycott, curfew, road blockade and strike and implementation thereof often through coercion and violence. The results are:

- disruption of communications, educational institutions, administration;
- loss of innumerable man-days of work;
- lowering and hampering of production of goods and trade and commerce;
- loss of state revenue as well as corporate and individual family income;
- destruction of public and private properties and most importantly, intolerance to opposition in exercise of democratic right to differ; and
- disruption and decay of the spirit of co-operation, often absence of public interests and common causes behind those activities.

In Meghalaya the main advocates of these methods are the Khasi Students' Union and the Federation of Khasi Jaintia and Garo People's Union. During these activities the state power is virtually allowed to be taken over by the organisers. It may also be noted that such programmes are usually fixed for Fridays or Mondays so that the employees, especially those under government, may enjoy breaks for three days, the last two days of the week being usual holidays. All this is done in the name of democratic rights browbeating or even physically assaulting those who do not agree. The agitations mainly centre round the so-called foreign nationals, swamping of the sons of the soil by outsiders, non-tribal traders and most surprisingly even against the extension of railways to Meghalaya. During the years from 1987 to 1991, generally between April and November, *bundhs* in Meghalaya became the characteristic feature of life, sparing, of course, the month of December. On every occasion the whole state was paralysed and the organisers claimed the bundhs to be successful. The picture in Assam was not different and no less disappointing. The so-called anti-foreigner agitation is too well known to need narration. Those six years formed a period of no peace, no work, no fraternity and no development. The legacy continues almost unbroken. For instance, according to news reports, between 16 February and 29 December 2000, 13 organisations enforced bundhs on 13 occasions for a total loss of 276 hours.

Physical violence has become a mind-set as a remedy to private or public grievances. Demonstrations of various kinds often take violent forms and result in destruction of public property. Easy money is being aimed at and earned through extortion, kidnapping and threat to life and killings, even children not being spared. Greater consciousness of community distinctions are being more emphasised and propagated not in terms of unity in diversity but as adversaries. The gender bias against women folk, an indispensable workforce and makers and shapers of families and society, is well known. Even the much lauded matrilineal societies are not free from the bias. The state machinery remains indifferent and silent at the beginning of troubles of various kinds. Then in taking actions, if any, it puts the blame on anti-socials, as a skin saving strategy. Such conflicts, agitations and government attitude are anti-development and destructive of work culture apart from internal security.

The Crime Profiles

No less disturbing and threatening have been the extent of various crimes recorded in Assam and Meghalaya. The statistics given below are indicative of the decay penetrating the social structure.

Assam (1997-2002)

Murder	8,868
Dacoity	4,228
Snatching	5,065
Burglary	18,459
Theft	39,038
Total	75,658

Murders constituted 12 per cent of the total crimes committed during the last six years. Number and nature of other offences and convicts are not readily available.

Meghalaya (1996-1998)

Murder	448
Rape	112
Riots	146
Kidnapping	71
Dacoity, Robbery, Burglary and Theft	2,557
Other Crimes	2,336
Total	5,670

Altogether 13 categories of crimes were recorded, eight per cent were murders. Figures of culprits punished were not published. Between 1981 and 1991, in Shillong only, altogether 18 categories of crimes were recorded, the total number being 9,566. Persons murdered were 969. There were 119 cases of rapes, 657 riots, 144 kidnappings and various other offences. Murder accounted for 10.13 per cent of the total. A total of 11,004 persons were convicted, the nature and extent of punishment were perhaps not published.

The Perpetrators

The largest number of convicts during the later period in Shillong belonged to the age group of 15-24 years accounting for 44.18 per cent of the total. The share of the next group of 25-34 years was

36.09 per cent. In other words, 80.27 per cent of the convicts belonged to the young generation. No comments are perhaps called for.

Our discussion so far was not to disparage the society. But it must be pointed out that a numerically insignificant section of people has put to ransom and destabilised social harmony and the essential ingradients for development in any sphere of life. The last quarter of a century not only broke down the composite thinking to a great extent but also frustrated and forestalled economic development causing a sinister set-back to progress. Healing of the wounds, it appears, has been left to times.

Under these circumstances, it was perhaps inevitable that no new major industries came up in the states since 1947. Tea, Petroleum and Coal industries established in Assam during British rule are facing economic crisis.

Nothing can be done without Central Aid which, however, is not properly and timely utilised. The entire region is backward and the pace of development is slow. There are 155 large and medium and 20,377 small scale industrial units in the states. The output of the units are respectively 2 and 1.2 per cent of the national total. Employment is less than 1 per cent of the population. People below poverty line in Assam accounted for 36.09 per cent of its population in 1999-2000.

Political Scenario

Unprincipled political rivalries, the so called coalitions of mostly of groups and defectors, the resulting chaos, confusion and inefficiency of successive governments became hindrances to development. Those coalitions only aimed at acquisition of individual power and pelf through capturing the guddi with hardly any thought for the masses of the people, living largely below the poverty line defined and determined by the upper sections of the rulers. Politics has become the politicians' shopper stops. This is evident from the toppling games which have become most of the leaders' whole time occupation. Internecine conflicts and rivalries come to light everyday. Closest friends of today become the worst enemies tomorrow. Deprivation or loss of Cabinet berths only can expose corruptions. Specially, since 1978 till 2001, Assam had 10 Chief Ministers, six of them between 12 March, 1978 and 18 March, 1982. Changing loyalties and sides have become the characteristics of the time. Meghalaya does not lag behind. In the last four years we had two Chief Ministers. The sixth incumbent in its history who took office in 2001 will run the government only for a fortnight more, that is, upto 26 February, 2003. What real work can be expected from such combinations, especially when these are infested with personal aims and ambitions as press, media and proceedings of legislatures reveal? In this State, out of 60 legislators, 28 are Ministers. Comparatively, however, Assam has a small Cabinet of 27 Ministers out of 126 M.L.As. A good many of them enjoying headship of this or that committee with various perks and benefits.

Human Resource

Management and utilisation of human resources for industries and economy as a whole cannot be separated from development. But whatever trained and trainable man power there is in various sectors of the economy is not properly utilised as indicated by the large scale unemployment of the young people, the main workforce. Employments could open up only with fast growing industries and other sectors. Training in values of life apart from material pursuit is a must. Also the foremost need of the hour is the creation of an atmosphere of social peace, tranquillity, fraternity and liberty of co-existence.

We now have a glimpse into the economy of Assam and Meghalaya, based on opinions and views of experts and official statistics.

Assam has a revenue of Rs. 6,649 crores. The Government spends Rs. 3,125 crores or 47 per cent on salaries and pensions of its employees. This amounts to Rs. 260 crores a month. "From the first day to the last, the Government is preoccupied in finding the resources for this and there is hardly any scope of thinking about development plans." Increase in revenue was 0.04 per cent during 1999-2000. In 2001 the State could amass an income of

Rs. 1,424.54 crores. That meant that it would not be able to meet the expenses on education alone which amounted to 2,613.46 crores. "This is only an example. The Government runs like this."

In terms of the Assam Accord of 1985, the Planning Commission had appointed the L.C. Jain Committee to look into the development issues. Its report was discussed but without result. So was the fate of the reports of Dinesh Goswami and the guidelines prepared for investors in Assam by the Koopers and Librend Adviser in 1995. The following year a committee was formed under Jayanta Madhav to prepare another blueprint for development, but the Government of Assam did not attach importance to the study of the report submitted by him. Then came the Sukla Committee and another under H.N. Das. These plans and reports expose the nature and commitments of the political leadership of the state. What leadership the people of Assam are dreaming for? Jayanta Madhav had also observed that development would not be possible without peace and tranquility. Further, inspiring, ideal and capable leadership were the need of the hour. Till now not only the state is suffering from grave financial crisis but also is so encumbered by political issues and power equations that there is hardly anytime to devote to universal economic development. The Live Registers of Employment Exchanges show that 19,00,000 people are unemployed in the State. Eighty-eight per cent of the people live in rural areas. Assam has a population of 2,66,38,407. Ninety per cent of the rural people live below poverty line and a total of 55 lakh children belong to those families. To summarise, Assam's economy suffers from the following deficiencies:

1. Lack of congenial atmosphere;
2. Static infrastructural facilities;
3. Sickness of industrial units;
4. Lack of entrepreneurship;
5. Increasing rural poverty;
6. Large scale and all pervading corruption;
7. Lack of transparency in administrative policy and its implementation;

8. Illiteracy;
9. Unemployment etc.

The overall Budgetary position of the State of Meghalaya is depicted below:

Table 7.1: State Finance: Overall Budgetary Position

(*Rs. in lakhs*)

Particulars	1997-98 (Actuals)	1998-99 (Revised Estimates)	1999-2000 (Budget Estimates)
1. Opening Balance	(–) 5,917.72	(–) 4,434.41	(–) 6,434.63
2. Total Revenue			
(a) Receipts	69,675.17	93,974.80	1,01,817.83
(b) Expenditure	68,510.93	91,524.04	1,07,571.86
(c) Surplus (+) or Deficit (–) on Revenue account	(–) 1,164.24	(+) 2,450.76	(–) 5,754.03
3. Total Capital			
(a) Receipt	16,880.23	26,189.91	30,505.05
(b) Expenditure	16,561.16	30,640.89	39,648.72
(c) Surplus (+) or Deficit (–) on Capital account	(–) 319.09	(–) 4,450.98	(–) 9,143.67
4. Overall Surplus (+) or Deficit (–)	(–) 1,483.31	(–) 2,000.22	(–) 14,897.70
Closing Balance	(–) 4,434.41	(–) 6,448.63	(–) 21,332.33

Table 7.2: Revenue Receipts of the State of Meghalaya

(*Rs. in Lakhs*)

Heads	1997-98 (Actuals)	1998-99 (Revised Estimates)	1999-2000 (Budget Estimates)
1. Shares of Central Taxes	28,677.00	29,705.00	29,705.00
2. State Taxes	7,355.14	8,637.75	10,041.24
3. Non-Tax Revenue	2,984.61	6,518.89	6,807.00
4. Grant-in-aid from the Centre	30,658.42	48,317.91	54,353.83
5. Additional Resources Mobilisation	31.00	795.25	910.76
6. Total Revenue Receipts	69,675.17	93,974.80	1,01,817.83

Table 7.3: Revenue Expenditure of the State of Meghalaya

(Rs. in lakhs)

Heads	1997-98 (Actuals)	1998-99 (Revised Estimates)	1999-2000 (Budget Estimates)
1. General Services	23,624.79	29,757.49	38,739.02
2. Social & Community Services	25,364.10	35,989.99	38,214.86
3. Economic Services	19,522.04	25,776.56	30,617.98
4. Total Revenue Expenditure	68,510.93	91,524.04	1,07,571.86

The figures in the three preceding Tables 7.1, 7.2 and 7.3 speak for themselves and therefore no further comments are called for.

Now we have an idea of employment in the State.

Table 7.4: Employment in Public and Private Sectors

(In Nos.)

Sector	1996-97	1997-98	Percentage of Increase/Decrease
Public Sector:			
1. Central Govt.	15,088	16,787	11.26
2. State Govt.	36,410	39,023	7.18
3. State Quasi Govt.	8,090	7,965	– 1.55
4. Central Quasi Govt.	7,200	7,296	1.33
5. Local Bodies	2,308	2,366	2.51
Total	69,096	73,437	6.28
Private Sector:			
1. Larger Establishment	5,692	6,005	5.50
2. Smaller Establishment	2,018	1,879	– 6.89
Total	7,710	7,884	2.26
Grand Total	76,806	81,321	

In 1997-98, the Private Sector had a mere 9.7 per cent of the total number of employees. In 2002, the numbers were 70,763 and 9,330 respectively.

Agriculture Sector

Total cropped area increased from 2,38,681 hectares in 1994-95 to 2,62,830 hectares in 1998-99 or 2.2 per cent per year. During the same period, rice cultivation rose from 1,04,045 hectares to 1,05,402 hectares, i.e., 0.26 per cent per year.

The following statistics give a glimpse into the employment situation in the State, during the period from 1995 to 1998.

Table 7.5: Employment Exchange Statistics

	1995	1996	1997	1998
Registration	3,816	8,677	11,108	7,401
Vacancies notified	489	631	628	294
Placement	190	131	271	191
Number on the Live Register	27,584	27,888	34,349	33,460

During the period of four years 782 persons were employed. Out of 33,460, job seekers, there were 18,195 Educated Applicants recorded in the Live Registers of the 10 Employment Exchanges. Their levels of education and numbers are shown below:

Table 7.6: Levels of Education and Numbers of Job Seekers

1.	Secondary	9,597
2.	HSSLC & PU	5,616
3.	Graduates:	
	Engineering, Agriculture and Medical	177
	Arts	1,862
	Science	427
	Commerce	482
	Education	113
	Law	2
4.	Post Graduates:	
	Engineering	9
	Agriculture	7
	Education	20
	Arts	104
	Science	101
	Commerce	11
5.	Diploma holders	387
	Grand Total	18,915

During the last five years, there was hardly any new economic progress. Population of Meghalaya in 1991 was 17,74,778 and literacy rate was 49 per cent. The population in 2001 was 23,06,069 and literacy rose to 63.31 per cent, i.e., at the annual rate of 2.4 per cent during 1991-1997.

Development Plans and Implementation

We are not going into the detailed study of the Five Year Plans and other State and Central Government Schemes. Instead, some instances of lapses, inefficiency and inactions are given. More than twenty years ago, the Government of Meghalaya had conceived the idea of upgrading the Shillong Polytechnic. The North Eastern Hill University had endorsed the plan but no action was taken. The latest news in this respect is no less frustration. On 6 December last, *The Telegraph* writes as follows:

> A Rs. 53.2 crore World Bank assisted technical education project is slipping out of Meghalaya's grasp because of the Government's failure to complete the necessary ground work. Almost two years have elapsed since the project was sanctioned, but Meghalaya has done nothing to improve the infrastructure required for its implementation. Four other north eastern states chosen for similar venture—Arunachal Pradesh, Mizoram, Nagaland and Tripura, have done no better.

The project was launched on 17 January 2001. It envisaged the establishment of Polytechnics in Tura and Jowai and upgradation of the one existing in Shillong. But the 'progress being tardy', the World Bank threatened to withdraw the project from Meghalaya. The Central Government also warned that the project would be "curtailed" if the State Government did not act promptly. Even earlier they had told the authorities that the funds would be diverted to the "better performing States". out of a grant of Rs. 4.75 crores for the year 2002-03, only a sum of Rs. 5.10 lakhs had been utilised till September last year. The Education Secretary reportedly said that he "knew nothing about the project" except that tenders had been floated several months ago. The

Director of Higher and Technical Education reportedly "declined to comment on the progress " of the scheme.

According to the same newspaper dated January 24, three Central Ministers "have come down hard on the State Government charging it with misutilisation of Central funds". One of them also complained that it implemented only 18 per cent of the Centrally Aided Schemes, like the grandiose one, the Greater Shillong Water Supply Scheme for which an amount of Rs.95.4 crore was sanctioned. The pre-election propaganda and rhetoric apart, there is a verisimilitude. Many years ago, the scheme had earned notoriety for squandering crores of rupees. Further, the same source claimed on 9 February last that "The state governments of the Northeast have failed to spend Rs. 23 crore allotted over the past year under various schemes by the Union Ministry of Social Justice and Empowerment. The Joint Secretary to the Ministry said that "utilisation of funds in the current year is not very healthy either". Strangely, however, she admitted that "This is due to ignorance of the Ministry's schemes in the region and non-submission of projects." Complaints and counter complaints are the essential ingradients of India's political life today. Passing the buck and the condemnation of hindrances to development created by "them" are the mutual practices today. Whatever that may be, it is the people who suffer. If work culture is adversely affected, whatever the plea may be, and camouflaged under political wrappers, the society is bound to tread backward economically as well as in every other walk of life. Concrete measures and not perfunctory committees and commissions usually constituted as diversionary and consolatory strategies, are of immediate necessity for the rejuvenation of the work culture and the society as a whole.

The purpose of this discourse was to trace and define some of the ills and evils of North East India. Diagnosis of ailments facilitates remedial measures. This was corroborated by the proceedings of a National seminar sponsored by the Indian Council of Social Science Research, North Eastern Regional Centre. The theme was "Coming out of Violence: Resolving Ethnic Conflicts in North East India". It was held at the Gauhati University on

12 and 13 November 2000. The consensus of the seminar is summarised below:

1. In his inaugural address, the Vice-Chancellor of the University, Dr. G.N. Talukdar, emphasised that all communities of the region must learn how to live together with each other to change the prevailing atmosphere of violence. The ethnic clashes led not only to violence affecting the social fabric but also prevented development activities. He also pleaded that our education system should be designed for inculcating a sense of co-operation and tolerance to the needs of other communities.
2. In his keynote address, Prof. Imtiaz Ahmad of the Jawaharlal Nehru University observed that the intensification and proliferation of violent and seemingly unmanageable ethnic, communal and linguistic conflicts have become a "prominent", perhaps the "predominant" problem of the day. Further, the conventional way of dealing with ethnic conflicts was a combination of repression and militarisation. But "the foremost need is for greater sensitivities to the economic, political, social and linguistic concerns of minorities in state policy even in normal times rather than the tendency to take such policies out of mothballs only in a state of crisis". He also emphasised that "defamatory propaganda about cultural and linguistic resistance" as well as the policy of repression was likely to be harmful in the long run.
3. Prof. D.R. Symleih, Director, ICSSR, North Eastern Regional Centre advised that the role of teachers and scholars should be given due importance in checking violence.
4. Prof. Monirul Hussain, of the Gauhati University urged upon the educationists and the youth to take the path of understanding and find solutions that would not harm the interests of others in the society.

The 47th Conference of the North Eastern Council was held at Guwahati on 14 November 2002. It was attended by the

Governors and the Chief Ministers of the states for discussing the issues concerning development. The deliberations "veered away from its main issues" as the member states insisted that unless the law and order scene was conducive, all other issues were "irrelevant". The Governor of Meghalaya reportedly said that the Council should take up the issue of security *vis-a-vis* development in a serious manner.

Progress can be achieved only by progressive minds, non-sectarian planning and timely and successful implementation thereof. Socio-economic development for self-sufficiency must go hand in hand with peace and harmony. We must make sure that the society as a whole and not "we" or "they", is to prosper. In other words, we should not debit the poor to credit the rich.

NOTES

1. Government records and Newspaper Reports on various Inquiry Commissions.
2. Report on Assam Elections 1983.
3. Datta Roy, B., and S.K. Agnihotri (Eds.), *Dynamics of a Tribal Society*, Articles by Mrinmoyee Banerjee, Rakhal Kumar Purkayastha and others.
4. Proceedings of Lok Sabha and Newspaper Reports.
5. Phukan, Adeep Kumar, Bhavisyat Assom (Ed.), *Assomor Arthaniti, 2002* (in Assamese and English).
6. Government of Meghalaya (Pub): (i) *Pocket Statistical Hand Book of Meghalaya, 2000*, (ii) *District Level Statistics 2000*, (iii) *Where Do We Stand in 2000, Meghalaya in North East India and The World.*
7. Personal Observations and Collections, 1953-2003.
8. Proceedings of the Annual Sessions of the North East India History Association.

8

PROBLEMS OF ETHNICITY AND SECURITY IN NORTH EAST INDIA

P.C. DUTTA

Introduction

The contemporary world has witnessed on increasing assertion of rights and privileges on the basis of '*religion*', '*ethnicity*' and '*nationality*'. India is no exception to it. 'Ethnicity' and 'Security' are relative concepts and in the context of North East India (NER) it is clearly visible that both the terms are closely connected. The question of 'security' in the region is basically the outcome of various ethnic insurgencies developed from time to time. Thus when the question of security of a region arises, it would obviously preceded by what is called a threat perspective. Unless a region or a country feels threatened there is hardly any reason why it should try to secure itself. Further, security of a region cannot be understood only in terms of military power. In common parlance the security problem of a region is the problem of physical protection of the common people from external military threats but in the present age of globalisation, it has become traditional and outdated idea. The term 'security' carries different meaning for different people. In the context of present age, weak political system leading to perpetual domestic unrest which includes ethnic strife and economic underdevelopment may feel insecure. Thus the concept of security is closely related to economic backwardness and ethnic strives too. Since last few decades, NER have been suffering from internal disturbances leading to various ethnic movements as a result of which economic underdevelopment is clearly visible. As ethnic struggle is against the established authority the ethnic insurgency invite the external power for the fulfilment of their objective.

The geographical location of the region also provided a congenial atmosphere for the insurgent groups to establish link with the neighbouring foreign countries because the region is surrounded by one-third of country's international border linked with the countries like China, Myanmar, Bangladesh, Bhutan. There is continuous help from those countries to the ethnic insurgent groups. As more than 100 major ethnic groups are existing in the region, the bifurcation of the region is a continuous process and obviously give birth to different insurgent groups. Sometimes they are so violent that even it threatens the security and economic development of the region.

A review of the sub-nationalist movements in Assam have resulted in the formation of different states and ongoing movements of the Bodos, Bengalis, tribes of Karbi-Anglong, Koach Rajbanshis etc. Are very much in the air and day will come when they will secede away from the Assamese main stream (Dutta 2001).

Keeping the above in view the present study is designed to analyise the different ethnic insurgent groups and their linkages with neighbouring foreign countries threatening the security of the region in particular and the country in general. Further, attempts have been made to go into the root of the insurgency and their primordial loyalties in the region. Again, the ethnic movements of the region do not always reflect the ethno-cultural aspiration of the people for which case has been taken to analyse how temptation to earn quick money, lust for power, material gains, through drug smuggling etc. Encouraged different insurgent groups which ultimately cause a threat to the region. The study is concluded with viable suggestions for the policy makers to take as precautionary measures and to check the growth of insurgency in the interest of the region.

A plenty of literatures have been published to relate the terms 'ethnicity' and 'security'. For the purpose of the study the literatures which are partially followed in this paper are:

Ghose (1998) stated that insurgency is a phenomenon similar to revolution, a struggle against the established authority and try to keep good relation with external powers for fulfilment of certain goals. The oppressed group or insurgent groups get the status of a peripheral group or communities and the conflict has assumed the form of centre-peripheri conflict. 'Periphery' can be defined from different perspectives. Firstly, the socio-cultural periphery, where people at the periphery have feelings of psychological insecurity and emotional alienation. Secondly, politico-administrative periphery, where people have a feeling of being left out of the power-sharing mechanism. Thirdly, economic-periphery, where they have deep rooted sense of economic deprivation. A combination of these three perspectives lead to the geo-political periphery, where the deprived people look for assistance from forces across the border and sometimes strive for physical alienation leading to secessionism.

Faizul (1996), in his study, stated that national security may be defined in terms of military power. The security problem of a state is the problem of physical protection of the state from external military threats. The traditional idea of the 'security' relates to the actual security of the state especially against threats from other states. He further stated that the concept of security carries different meanings for developed and developing countries. The problem of security to the third world countries is substantially different from the security problem faced by the developed world. The weak political system leads to perpetual domestic unrest including ethnic strife and the problem of economic under-development. Thus economy and society play an important role in the national security of these developing states along with political and territorial security.

Hussain (1995) argued that ethnicity *per se* does not endanger security. However, the liberation movements of different ethnic groups may threat to the security of the dominate elite and not to the society as a whole or nation as a whole. The study of Das (1998) is vital and references can be made in this paper for the author's socio-political interpretation of ethnicity and security.

Bandyopaddhyay and Chakraborty (1998) discussed another aspect of the problem of security in the region due to migration which led to an increased pressure on land and increase in the number of sub-holding and landlessness among the indigenous population and the problem of security emerged with both migrants and local people feeling degrees of insecurity out of this.

Mishra (1998) referred another aspect of migration that is forced migration and internal displacement for which security becomes a question for Chakmas, Santals and other tribals of the region.

The study of Das (1998), is appropriate as India can best be described as a multinational state. The idea of a 'mainstream' is absolutely absurd in this context. At the cultural level, the idea of a great Indian tradition which essentially means a Brahminic, Aryan and Sanskrit dominated tradition faces great challenges from the so called little traditions. People of NER have increasingly aligned themselves with the Indo-Burman and Mongolian cultures and heritage. Thus it creates an atmosphere of bloody ethnic turmoil leading to a threat to the security of the nation from inside and outside also. The author further mentioned that the ethnic conflict is closely related to elite competition and is both horizontal and vertical that is *vis-à-vis* immigrants and tribals at the intra-state level, and with the centre at the second level.

Another study made by Bhowmik (1998) in which discussion have been made on external linkages of ethnic movements in the region and growing involvement of neighbouring foreign countries in promoting insurgency in the NER by creating a problem of security.

Baruah (2002) stated that what Amalendu Guha called the 'little nationalism' has not acquired another level because below the little nationalities still smaller communities are articulating their interests. The relatively larger communities of NER have acquired nationalities consciousness and small ethnic groups with district cultural markers are in the process of acquiring community consciousness. In a situation scarcity of opportunities, the interest of the elites or dominate sections of individual communities came into serious conflicts with those of other communities.

These interests are being manifolded in secessionist demands, demand of households, and attempts at ethnic cleansing.

In the contemporary sense ethnicity has come to acquire its importance only when states to organise in national terms. The national communities were contrasted with other groups within the states, who had cultural traders that distinguished them from the mainstream '*nation*'. In India these cultural groups are often identified as ethnic communities or groups and their project perceived as ethno-nationalist, ethnicity not only remains an important part of the reality but also the source of a series of major problems which endangers security.

Referring Paul Brass, Baruah (2002) in his article stated that nationality formation involves passing through three stages—the ethnicity, implying an existence of cultural markers recognised easily but their political significance unnoticed, the community awareness, implying evolution of political consciousness of cultural identity and the urge to imply it for furthering community interests and the nationality, involving right to self-determination. Many of the so called ethnic groups of NER have already crossed the stage of ethnicity and have entered the stage of community and the others have entered the stage of nationality formulation. Peoples like the Assomiya, the Bengalis, the Khasis, the Bodos, the Mizos, the Nagas and recently even the Karbis appear to have become nationalities, demanding the political right to control their own affairs.

Just after the Sylhet referendum a large number of Hindu and Muslim infiltrators came to the present Barak Valley of Assam and settled down permanently. The immigration was taken easily by the local Muslims with an intention to outnumber the Hindus in the valley. . . . Thereafter, a series of communal disturbances have taken place in the valley by which socio-economic progress of the valley has been greatly hampered (Dutta & Pradhan, 1998).

From the above study of literatures, it is clear that the authors have taken their own stand on the problem of security from different points of view which can be applied in the context of present study on "problems of Ethnicity and threat to security in North East India."

The North Eastern Region of India (NER) comprises, at present, seven full-fledged states like Assam, Nagaland, Meghalaya, Mizoram, Arunachal Pradesh, Tripura and Manipur, poetically called "seven sisters". Before independence, the region consisted of one province of Assam, two native states like Manipur and Tripura and one centrally ruled area known as North Eastern Frontier Agency (NEFA). Within a span of 40 years in the post-independence period, the region has been splinted several times and yet the region is not free from the threat of further split with the most dominant tribes like Bodos, Karbis etc. What really has been the root cause for all these separatists and militant activities is the moot question is that requires serious question of the policy makers and political masters. During the fateful discussions prior to the transfer of power in 1946, the Congress leadership agreed to accept the British Cabinet Mission Proposal of grouping in May 16, 1946 under which Assam as then existed was to be placed in group C which was by another name *Jinnah's Moth-Eaten Pakistan* as he called it. But Mr. Gopinath Bordoloi who understood the serious implications of the scheme hatched by the British Government in collusion with the Muslim League. Finally, with the blessings of M.K. Gandhi, Assam remained with India and the dream of M.A. Jinnah never fulfilled. However, the problem of NER still remains in a different manner even after 55 years of independence, with the vital problems of ethnicity and economic backwardness causing the problem of security in the region. Lord Wavell, the Viceroy of India expressed Assam's cause for discussion on the eve of All Fools' Day, i.e., on April 1, 1946. The allusion to independence, her unjust exploitation by the Centre, the fear of further Muslim migration, the hegemonic aspiration over the tribals, and desire to over power the Bengalis in short, an intricate cobwebs of "exist and voice" that would subsequently lead to disturbance of the security scenario of the North East. People of the region can fight against poverty or backwardness but it is too difficult on their part to fight against the problem of security arose out of ethnicity which has given the rise of different insurgent groups.

CAUSES

The roots of ethnic division in the region dates back to the British times when the colonial government imposed a system of government known as '*non-regulated system*' over this area with the purpose of maintaining the exclusive culture and tradition of the tribal people.

The important causes responsible for the rise of different ethnic problems threatening the security of the region may be discussed as:

Problems of Infiltration

Infiltration into the region is considered as a major factor contributing growth rate of the population in the region. The population of the region according to 1991 census was 316 lakhs and in 2001, the figure raised to 385 lakhs, showing 25.3 per cent of decadal growth rate. The share of population of NER to the total population of India was as low as 1.70 per cent in 1901, since then it has been steadily increasing and reached at nearly 745 thousand in the census year of 1991. The share of migrants from Bangladesh was between slightly more than 70 per cent to slightly more than 87 per cent in pre-independence era. In the post-independence era it reached at 94 per cent in 1951. However, the share was around 89 per cent in the census year of 1991 and it again shows an increasing trend after 1991 (Dutta, 2002). The phenomenon of migration is instrumental in creating not only social tension but also jeopardising the security of the region, in particular and the century in general. The phenomenon of migration and its socio-economic effects has attracted the attention of many social scientists, political personal and journalists who tend to focus on social, political, economical and cultural factors. The influx to the region changed the ethnic composition of the population and raised a feeling of threat to the cultural identity of the local people. Inadequate safeguards were taken to protect them for economical advanced section of the people. When the economic development, language, culture etc. were at stake, a section of youth embarked on a violent struggle by forming different insurgent groups in the region like ULFA in Assam, NSCN in Nagaland, MNF in Mizoram and a host of others. NER witnessed the worst type of insurgent activities since independence by making the situation of the entire region extremely volatile.

There are as many as 15 to 20 lakh Bangladeshi illegal infiltrators entered into India during the period 1971-99. According to the Report of the Joint Secretary of Indian Home Ministry, Mr. G.K. Pillai, at the time of visiting Indo-Bangladesh international border, on 18th August, 1999, at Southern Assam's Karimganj and Hailakandi, approximately every year 3 lakhs illegal Bangladeshi nationals crossed the Indo-Bangladesh border and reached Indian territory for permanent settlement in NER, West Bengal and its surroundings. On the other hand, former Indian Chief Election Commissioner, Mr. T.N. Sheshan was quoted in the *New York Times* (12th November 1995) as saying that there are still more than one Million migrants on the electoral rolls of Assam. The American research team indicates that 20 million Bangladeshis are at present in India out of which 20 lakhs came in 1971 alone.

Dutta & Roy (2000) argued that the potential cause of the high population growth in Assam, in particular is due to the high influx of people from Bangladesh. This is due to easy entry routes all through 94 km. Virtually uncared for international border line. . . . This situation definitely act as a drag and pulls down all sorts of development efforts in the state.

Whatever the reasons behind the huge number of Bangladeshi nationals presence in India, observers said that the overall effect of their presence in India and in the NER in particular is the shattering of the socio-economic balance in the region. The observers further said that the infiltrators not only occupied Char-areas in the riverine-belt, but also led grow up unauthorised settlements in government lands, agricultural lands, grazing reserves and forest areas by illegal felling forest products indiscriminately. This indiscriminate felling of trees ultimately resulted in environmental problems and destruction of the ecological balance (Chatterjee, 2002).

Geo-cultural Affinity

The problem of security in NER and its linkage with the neighbouring foreign countries has history of its own. So far as ethnicity is concerned, the region has been inhabited mainly by Mongoloid ethnic groups. The Khasis of Meghalaya are believed to have come from Kampuchea as a section of them speak a form of Mon-kher language. The Tai-Ahoms migrated from Thailand *via* Myanmar to Assam 600 years ago. There are also Garos in Meghalaya, Nagas and Mizos in Nagaland and Mizoram. Many Nagas still refer to their own region as "Western Nagaland", referring to areas with Naga communities in Myanmar as "Eastern Nagaland". Such ecological, geographical and cultural affinities have given rise to links with tribes and communities across the Indian Frontier. Many of the tribes feel that they have much more in common with peer groups across the border than with India. So far as political history of the region is concerned, British Frontier Policy was designed to keep the tribal areas isolated from the mainstream of politics of the plains and a sense of isolation and exclusiveness developed. Colonial encroachment created artificial boundaries and some group of people were found in different countries. The Simphos of India have their counterpart in neighbouring countries like Jimphos of Myanmar, Southern China, Thailand and Laos. The Mizo-Kuki-Chin group of tribes are found in Meghalaya and Mizoram and many of the tribes in Arunachal Pradesh and even the plains of people, the Meitheis, have their counterparts across the border. Therefore, instead of national spirit, a sense of regional nationalism grew in the hills.

Fear Psychosis among Tribals

After independence, efforts were made by the leaders of the nation for achieving national integration and removing imbalances created by the imperialist rule in India. However, the national leadership was not able to appreciable the life and living conditions of the tribal masses in NER. As a result of which Nagas, Mizos and other tribes tried their level best to separate themselves from the mainstream of Assam out of fear that merger with Assam would destroy traditional self-governance, swamp their economy and disrupt their socio-cultural life. The national outcome of all these were a new awakening among the tribal people of the region which began a quest for a new ethnic identity and the search for the same during the last few decades has given birth a secessionist tendency which ultimately has given birth to insurgency with the help of the foreign nations. As a result the security of India's North East is being threatened.

Political Parties and Security

The biggest distortion in politics of India today is the polarisation on communal lines, a development for which the so called secular parties of the country bear the heaviest responsibility. Indian National Congress pondering to Muslim religiosity, characterised by the Friday school holiday with daily 2 hour prayer break in Kerala, like the Shahbanu Case, was a decision on communal line which harms the concept of secularism. Communalism is favoured by the political parties for electoral and political ends by creating a havoc with the objective of security and national integration. The political parties show less interest in healing communal wounds or ending communal divisions than using them for partition ends. In a few states including Assam of NER, the Congress party depends heavily on the Muslim block votes for capturing power. The past records of the party show that for the sake of electoral gain, the party can openly seek the help of Muslim block even by entering into certain agreement with the influential Muslim leaders. In 1980 election, Smt. Indira Gandhi approached the Imam of Jama Masjid, Syed Abdullah Bukhari and entered into an agreement with Imam on the basis of 10-point programme to secure the support of Muslim votes. Such a move on the part of Congress (I) or any other party shows the seeds of separation by threatening security and integrity of Indian Union. In one of election campaigns, the president of Assam Pradesh Congress Committee remarked, "so long as Alis and Kulis are with the Congress, it has nothing to fear". Then in 1983-Assam Assembly election, when Assamese people boycotted the poll,

Smt. Gandhi visited Assam and her visit was confined to old Cachar and some minority pockets predominantly inhabited by illegal immigrants so that they will cast their votes in favour of the Congress party.

The IMDT Act of 1983 having several pro-alien clauses passed in the parliament by the Congress (I) in absence of any M.P. from Assam and the same was imposed on Assam with sole intention of safeguarding the minority votes. The Congress' over concern for the minorities had caused the Congress party clearly in last 2 to 3 Lok Sabha elections. In 1992 when the then Chief Minister of Assam declared in the Assembly that about 30 lakh illegal foreigners had entered Assam in 1987 alone a section of minority Congress legislators and fundamentalist leaders threaten to withdraw the support from the government if the statement is not withdrawn forthwith. Even the Assam Muslim Forum threatened to dislodge the Saikia-Government in five minutes if the statement is not withdrawn. Ultimately, obviously under duress he had to retract his statement. When Union Home Minister Mr. S.V. Chavan told the Rajya Sabha on August 13, 1994 that in the NER, the migrant population from Bangladesh in some areas are larger than the local population, the Congress government ignored the statement for the fear of antagonising the minorities on whom it depends heavily for its survival. Again, the Defence Ministry through a press release on February 1, 1994 had expressed deep concern, at the spread of Muslim fundamentalism among the Muslim organisations operating in the region and advised the government to curb the activities of these organisations. Instead of waking up to this alarming situation, the Saikia-government reportedly reached in anger and rather lodged a strong protest with the centre, branding the defence wings advised as unwarranted comments on the sensitive issue. From the fact that meaningful many ultras belonging to several Muslim fundamentalist militant outfits like MULTA operating in the states of NER were nabbed with some who surrendered, one can infer that defence wing's advice and vital information involving the nation's security correct and timely.

Recently, the Assam police is reported to have stressed links between the world's most wanted terrorist Osama Bin Laden and militant outfits operating in the North East. Even, the military intelligence in a report has identified O.B. Laden and Dawoud Ibrahim as likely sources of funds for terrorist activities in the North East. This report also reveals that at least 11 Muslim Fundamentalist outfits including Harkat-ul-Muzahideen are active in Assam.

Now, whether any issue, no matter how sensitive the issue should be kept concealed or unattended, when the issue endangers the nation's security. Was it not aimed at pleasing the minorities by the political parties at the cost of security of the majority?

The AGP government of Assam continued to appease the Muslims by making them as their vote bank too. To reduce the Hindu Bengalis into minority in Assam, the Government of Assam is still trying and the process of Assamisation has not stopped. Leaving the post-independence period aside, the Government of Assam has been trying to suppress the Bengalis on the language issue in different ways even after independence for which communal riots took place in different points of time and shaded harmonious communal imbalance has been observed in the State of Assam and as result vital ethnic issues are still in a hanging position.

Again party in power at the centre at present cannot be escaped from the accusations as NER is deliberately ignored by the Central Government so far as the problem of security is concerned. Since the formation of the present government attention has always been paid to secure Kashmir border leaving NER a free entrance of the cross border terrorists. Further, after the inauguration of the new Islamic constitution in Bangladesh and declaration of an Islamic state anti-India feelings have been aggravated among the people of Bangladesh. At the same time, after the formation of the new NDA government with the domination of having ideology of *Hindutwa* as main partner. Anti-Indian feeling in Bangladesh is not only confined within the people but also within the government of that country and the NER has been chosen as their epicentre for which the innocent people of this region are victim of the situation.

Change of Government

Change of government in neighbouring countries also adversely affect the security scenario of our country in general and NER in particular. The creation of Bangladesh made a radical change in the security scenario of NER. India was in advantageous position by recognising Mujibur Rahman's government of Bangladesh in 1971. However, the situation of early eighties undergone a radical change in nineties and at present when Awami League in Bangladesh replaced by military generals. It has already been established that former military rulers and Bangladesh National Party (BNP) government provided the rebels form NER with shelter and support. Most rebel leaders of different insurgent groups who have since been arrested, carried Bangladesh passports. Although in 1992, the Bangladesh Rifles handed over 3 top Manipur rebel leaders to the Indian Border Security Force (BSF) during the reign of Begum Khaleda Zia but she did not take any concrete steps to crack down the anti-Indian forces completely in their country. However, with the coming of the Awami League government in Bangladesh, Dhaka cracked down some anti-Indian camps in that country for which more than 300 rebels of different groups including ISI fled that country. Again, with the coming of BNP-government in Bangladesh, the security scenario of NER in India is in constant danger due to the support and shelter provided by the present government there to create disturbances in the border areas of Indian Union.

Enemy's Evil Eye

While the Government of India remains focused on the Western front, where a massive deployment of troops has taken place, Pakistan's notorious I.S.I. is concentrating its attention on enlarging its subversive network in the NER. The series of massacres in the states of NER in last few years suggest the revival of terrorist activities by different extremist groups under different banners or labels. Further, as the entire nation's attention currently riveted on Pakistan, which refuses to stop its trans-border terrorism and handed over the 20 most wanted terrorists to stand trial in India for their crimes, the various insurgent groups in the NER are developing a feeling that their demands are being neglected. As most of these insurgent groups are trained, funded and armed by I.S.I., it suits the Pakistan subversive agency to step its activities in the region in order to divert the Delhi's attention and to establish more cells for continuing subversive activities. New Delhi has been slow to react to the designs of Pakistan in this highly sensitive areas and has neither implemented a viable political policy nor undertaken serious measures to combat the same. Delay is dangerous, and hence, NER is going to be another Kashmir under Indian Federalism in near future.

Complexity and Ethnic Intolerance

The Indian state is always looked down upon by the insurgent groups of the region as an external agency which is against their indigenous traditions and culture. The fact is clearly emphasised when ULFA raised its slogan against Indian administration and dubbed it as colonialism of New Delhi (Delhibad or Delhism).

Ethnic intolerance is becoming increasingly clear from the demands of many of the community based youth organisations of the NER that they want all others to leave their homelands. There are attempts at most of the hill states to monopolise admissions to good schools, colleges, and of course, universities and also to corner all jobs for so called local candidates. Business by non-indigenous communities are becoming almost impossible in these states. Each of these states has taken measure to ensure that non-indigenous residents do not purchase the landed property in the states. Both legal and illegal means are adopted to ensure the monopoly of the indigenous (Baruah, 2002). The attitude of intolerance by indigenous people towards non-indigenous is clearly visible in the region from the violent activities of different youth organisations like AASU in Assam, NSF in Nagaland, AAPSU in

Arunachal Pradesh, KSU in Shillong. Recently, in Mizoram, there are attempts at totally denying any political rights to the non-indigenous.

So far as communal militancy of Assam is concerned, the earlier affinity between Assamese Muslims and Assamese Hindus get strained in recent years and religion has united most of the Muslims of Assam, irrespective of the mother tongue (Dutta, 2002).

It may be said that ethnic conflicts in Assam were due to the excess repressive attitude of the Government of Assam from time to time. Had the leaders of Assam been liberal to all the ethnic groups and sympathetic to safeguard their language, customs and culture, ethnic movements in different parts of Assam would not have taken place and this is also true for all other states of NER.

Excess of Security Forces

North East India had faced insurgent activities since independence as consequence of which security forces of different categories had been deployed in 'seven sisters' that caused Wonton Violation of Human Rights and also threatened the security of the common people of the region. So far as history of conflicting situation in the region concerned, traditional loyalties and ethnic affinities demand for separation and self-determination, combined with mobilisation of popular sentiments to further group causes etc. had been some of the important causes for the rise of insurgent groups, terrorism, extortion, kidnapping etc. which facilitated intervention of security forces in the region from time to time to restore peace and order. Many a times NER was declared a "Disturbed Area" under the *Armed Forces Special Power Act* of 1958. Several army operations, namely 'Sher-E-Dil','Tiger Heart', 'Rhino', 'Rhino-II', 'Operation Blue Bird' etc. marked in the region since the beginning of disturbances. A reign of terror was let loose by the army in the name of flushing out the extremists. As a result of which anybody could be arrested without referring to police authority. The civil administration was totally paralysed. The security forces remained active even after the completion of the combing operation. Several lawyers and human right activists who helped the victims were arrested and retained. The relatives of the victims were also threatened and tortured by the security forces. Women and young girls were raped, private properties were looted and destroyed by these forces. Under the circumstances, the situation was further deteriorated and provided fuel to the fire of extremism. Instead of inviting the extremists into the negotiating table the government wanted to suppress the act of terrorism with heavy hands. As a result of which it created a situation of tension and turmoil in the region by threatening the normal life of the common people.

Economic Underdevelopment

In the context of the present age and weak political policies, the concept of insecurity emerged out of ethnic conflicts is closely related to economic underdevelopment and NER has provided ample opportunities to the social scientists and reformers to have a discussion on it. Initially it was economic deprivation, disparity, exploitation and lack of development which created congenial condition for the rise of ethnic conflicts leading to insurgency in NER.

From economic point of view, unequal distribution of wealth and resources caused a regional disparity in our country and the states of NER are the victim of the situation for which they are always lagging behind. Exploiting the socio-economic problems of the region various divisive forces raised their ugly heads under the banner of regionalism to gain the support of the mass people. But sometimes their activities are so serious that cause a threat to the security of the region and the economy of the region worsened further.

Dutta and Choudhury (1995, 1996) observed in his study that poorest section of the society in Assam has been badly affected. The results revealed that the extent of degree of inequality in the level of living in the states of NER is much more than what is taken to guide some of the decision making elements in connection with resource transfer from centre to these north eastern states and more particularly in Assam. An important cause of regional tension which led to popular agitations and at times militant activities as such regional disparities in economic and social development which will exist within some of the states of Indian Union and all the states of NER. Thus regional disparity gives birth to the ugly force of regionalism in the region by threatening unity and integrity of the nation (Dutta, 2001).

It is not worthwhile to mention that a sizable population in the North East living along the Bangladesh and Burmese border regularly smuggle large quantities of drugs like heroine etc. from across the border to the rest of India. There have been reports of the Indian security forces being bribed to turn a blind eye to the smuggling activities and the militant groups are indifferent to all these activities as they receive their self-imposed taxes and commissions from the smuggles which they used to procure arms and ammunition from across the bordering states. Thus drug trafficking has become a matter of security concern for the north east India in particular and our nation in general. As a result of smuggling of different commodities and illegal trades, the economy of the region is at the continuous jeopardy.

Inter-Tribal Conflicts

Inter-tribal conflicts out of extreme ethnicity has given rise to militarism and war like situation in the region by creating an environment of natural hatredness among them. This has created lack of trust between the tribal communities and other people living in the areas. The demand of the Naga insurgents for "Greater Nagaland" virtually set Manipur on fire. This was followed by widespread violent protest in Manipur. Border disputes between Assam and Nagaland and the concept of "Greater Nagaland" has not only created a conflict situation among the states of NER but also a vertical conflict between Central Government and the states of NER. While the Central Government is in quest of solution to the problems of NER, the states become anti-Centre as they are not ready to accept the solution made by the Centre by reducing their territories into further sub-division.

SECURITY SCENARIO

After inauguration of 51st police games at Bhiwani in Haryana on 7th November 2002, Central Home Minister Mr. L.K. Advani, told PTI, "After the change of government in Bangladesh, there has been an increase in the activities of the Al-Quaeda and I.S.I. there." He voiced serious concern over growing activities of ISI and Al-Quaeda in Bangladesh and asked the International community to threat the Pakistani Intelligence Agency at par with terrorist outfits like the Taliban. Asked whether Dhaka's support to the militant was covert or overt, he said, covert. All insurgent groups of NER are getting refugees there. Asked whether, the government has taken up the issue of insurgent groups and Al-Quaeda activities with Bangladesh, Mr. Advani said, Dhaka has been told that these were areas they would have to think about seriously. He further said the recent massacre in Assam was carried out by terrorist based in Bhutan. However, he stated that Bhutan was not supporting the insurgent groups though it was not taking enough action. Stressing on the importance of modernising police forces in the country, he said the Centre has raised the outlay for it considerably from the earlier allocation of Rs. 100 crores.

The increasing menace of terrorism has gripped several parts of the country and India's North East is badly affected by the same. The situation is same in all the 14 border states of the country. Turn North, South, East and West, the frightening scenario that a security threat looms large on India's horizon. It has become a fashion of the politicians of our country to blame easily all these activities to Pakistan. However, only to blame Pakistan is not enough without any concrete step. The fact is that ISI spread its tentacles across the country. It is extending all support to local insurgent groups as well as some fundamentalist Muslims by way of training, sophisticated arms and ammunition and money. They left sufficient evidences to prove their attacks on Indian soil (Kaushish, 2002).

So far as NER is concerned ISI activities can be guessed not only from the side of Bangladesh but also from the bordering areas of North Bengal. Only recently the outlaw ULFA and the Democratic Front of Bodoland killed 40 people in Assam with clear ISI backing. They set up terrorist camps in adjoining countries which enjoy a pours border with India, like Nepal, Bhutan, Myanmar and Bangladesh. Just after killing of 40 people in Assam, India's Foreign Secretary handed over to the visiting Director General of Bangladesh Riffles a list of 99 camps set-up by the ISI to train Indian terrorists. Of these, 25 are to train the National Liberation Front of Tripura, followed by All Tripura Tiger Force (20 bases), 18 are the National Socialist Council of Nagaland (IM). The list also includes 10 training camps runs by Peoples Liberation Army (PLA), 17 by United Liberation Front of Assam (ULFA), 2 by National Democratic Front of Bodoland (NDFB), 2 by Muslim United Liberation Tiger of Assam (MULTA), 3 by Achik National Volunteers (ANV), 1 by Chakma National Liberation Front (CNLF) and 1 by Dima Halong Daogah (DHD).

The areas pin-pointed to show existence of these camps are Naikhongchari, Alikadam and Ruma in Bandarban district, Kaukhali, Nanirchar, Baghaichari and Dhiginala in Rangamati district, Kamalganj and Srimangal in Maulavi Bazar district and Chunarughat in Habiganj. Again NSCN (IM) is running its camps in Sajek in Khagrachari district, Langdu and Baghaichari in Rangamati, Kulaura in Maulavi Bazar, Zakiganj in Sylhet, Ruma, Alikadam and Thangchi in Bandarban district, Dhiginala in Khagrachari and Baghaichari in Rangamati. The PLA is training its insurgents at Dhiginala, Kamalganj, Kulaura, Chunarughat, Sylhhet and Sherpur. The ULFA insurgents are being trained in its camps at Baghaichari, Sylhet, Teharpur in Sunmaganj district, Srimangal, Mymensingh, Chilanganj in Sherpur district, Chilchari, Companyganj and Rauhmari in Kurigram. The NDFB is running its camps in Khagrachari and Tangail districts while CNLF has its one camp in Baghaichari. The camp of MULTA exists in Chittagong and Coxbazar while DHD camps situated at Kulaura. ANVC run its camps in Tangail, Mymensingh and Sherpur.

Although verbal assurance had been given by the Bangladesh Rifles Director General to India's Home Secretary, Mr. N.

Gopalswami that his country would not allow its territory to be used by anti-India forces, the results are yet to come.

The local people of Bangladesh are helping these terrorist groups as they are assigned by them in kind and cash. What is more dangerous is the support they solicit from Muslim places of worships and the seat of religious education like the Madarssas specially, the unregistered ones which are slowly but surely turning into time bombs for national security in general and security of NER in particular. Recently, the Madarssas across the country, specially in the border states, are known to have become fertile training centres for militants. An authoritative source estimates the number of madarssas at 50,000 in the country. The situation of NER is favourable to the militants helped by the Muslim fundamentalists as it is bordering with Bangladesh.

The figures available with the Home Ministry show a sudden spurt in Mosques and Madarssas in India's border states, specially Indo-Nepal, and Indo-Bangladesh borders. It is observed that in border states the growth rate of Muslim population is higher than the national average of 32.76 per cent. The studies of Border Security Force (BSF) and the Intelligence Bureau (IB) revealed that a total of 1050 have came up along the Bangladesh border. The number of unregistered Madarssas was also found to be equally high. The IB report has identified 208 Madarssas and 450 mosques in 10 districts along the Indo-Nepal and Indo-Bangladesh border. The fundamentalists bring with them a communal mind set which goes against the secular character of India. These madarssas are heavily funded by foreign sources. A recent Home Ministry's Report says that Rs. 2000 to Rs. 3000 crores are being funneled to these madarssas, mainly through hawala channels while officially merely Rs. 40 crore have been received under the Foreign Contribution Regulation Act (FCRA) from the gulf countries. According to an IB document, nearly all the Madarssas receive funds through the Jeddah-based Islamic Development Bank and the Habib Bank, Pakistan.

The period in Assam following the agitations show the prospering Marwari Businessmen and other investors became the main targets of the ULFA as a result of which they started fleeing some of them relocated their establishments to other states. The state's economy thus started loosing out on huge financial investments that were earlier coming to them form other parts of the country.

North east states have invaluable natural resources, breathtaking, scenic beauties and good weather—a combination of which can spell a rapid economic development by way of local cottage industry, a sound market economy and a vibrant tourist industry. But the fear in the minds of potential tourists made them stop from visiting these areas. The local inhabitants also miss out an opportunity to interact with the people form outside and thus get a broader understanding form the country as a whole and *vice versa*.

Insurgency adversely affects the healthy social environment because of deteriorated law and order situation in the region. Because of the fear of armed terrorists as well as security forces, the common men had to consciously restrict their movement. "*Carfews*", "*Bandhs*", and "*strikes*" paralysed the good social atmosphere and no neighbour will come forward to sympathise and suggest the victims of the situation. Such an atmosphere apart from not being viable for proper economic and social development amounts to virtual hell to this region.

Residing in disturbed areas leaves its impact on the minds of the youths of the NER for which in someway or the other, the quality of education that they set suffers. Unemployed youths become victims of this worst situation. Out of frustration they are forced to join insurgent groups because of the feeling that they become a burden on their respective families. Most of these youths who join insurgent groups die, and those who return home in most cases fail to become normal for the rest of their life.

Insurgency has the greatest influence in the minds of the people of NER so far as drug addiction and other related practices are concerned. Most of the youths in the region are acting as the agents of foreign dealers in narco-terrorism. In Manipur, it is believed that the main cause behind the spread of AIDS is because of the sharing of needles used for injecting drugs rather than any other reason. Further, money is extracted from the innocent people by making them drug addicted towards anti-people and anti-national activities.

The huge resources wasted to combat insurgency and to restore peace and security could have been used for development of the region. As a result North East economy is always lagging behind.

Approximately 17 per cent of India's total budget spents to meet the expenditure on India's internal security. Regarding the generation of illegal funds in Assam only it was said that illegal trade of PDS quota in the state generated Rs. 60 lakhs per month. In actual practice the entire PDS quota of the state is diverted to the open market by the ULFA and SULFA providing no security of food to the common people. Similarly, 70 per cent of funds for the rural development goes to the coffers of the ULFA. The same is more or less true in case of all other states of NER. Thus under the above circumstances, rural development, food security and development in other fields are unthinkable in the region.

In the current financial year, the Government of India has allocated nearly Rs. 89,000 crores out of the total expenditure of Rs. 4,10,310 crores for security which represents 22 per cent of the total expenditure of the Indian government. For internal security, Government of India spends Rs. 25,000 crores which has been increasing in budgetary allocation every year.

A free and responsible press is the basic requisite or precondition for the success of a democracy. However, a good number of media persons engaged in different means of communication system of the region are not free from business and are not properly highlighting the problems of security in due channels. Sometimes the problems and issues of the region are misinterpreted and the people of other regions of the country are not well aware of the situation. Hence, appeal should be made to the media persons to act in a positive manner.

Conclusion and Suggestion

The study reveals that the problem of ethnicity and ethnic crises and conflicts have given rise to the different terrorist organizations in the region by jeopardising security of the common people.

Where there is problem, there is solution to the problem. The security problem of NER is no exception to it. As per the figures available in the web-site launched by the Department of Development of NER of Union Government, the level of violence in the region is gradually coming down and a bright future is clearly visible. As many as 1,963 incidents of violence involving insurgents were reported in the region in 2000 and the figures come down to 1,339 in 2001 and to 760 upto July 15, 2000. As per records available, 584 extremists, 164 security personnel and 907 civilians were killed in the region in 2000. The figures came down to 572 extremists and 600 civilians in 2001, while up to July 15, 2002, 355 extremists, 67 security personnel and 284 civilians were killed. So far as Assam's case is concerned, the level of violence has not came down considerably and the number of security personnel killed by extremists registered a sharp decline in the last two and a half years. As per reports 536 incidence involving insurgents were reported in Assam in 2000 and the figures came down to 458 in 2001 and to 232 up to July 15, 2002. As many as 321 insurgents, 76 security personnel and 419 civilians were killed in Assam in 2000. During 2001, the respective figures came down to 282, 80 and 248 respectively while up to July 2000, 184 militants, 8 security personnel and 119 civilians lost their lives in insurgency related violence. The Union Government had started talks with 4 insurgent outfits like NSCN(IM) and NSCN(K), BLT and one faction of United Peoples Democratic Solidarity (UPDS) led by Haren Singh Bey.

From the above trend it is amply clear that the progress of talks with the insurgent groups already started and this is the beginning of the end. For a concrete result following suggestions may be made both for the policy makers and the insurgent groups of the region to restore normalcy by leaving militarism and the path of violence.

One must agree with the views of Sri Atal Behari Vajpayee when he was addressing the Director General of police and Inspector General of police at Vijnan Bhavan, New Delhi on September 30, 2002. He appeared to the police leadership for remaining apolitical, neutral and free of sectorian, regional or any other kind of biasness. To him closer interaction between the central and the state police and intelligence should be initiated. Referring to the north east, the Prime Minister not only encouraged the police force engaged in the states of NER to combat terrorism but also stated that the government is trying to speed up all-round economic and infrastructural development in the states of NER to bring the attention of the different insurgent groups of the region. Hence, it may be suggested employment of security forces is not the right way to bring solution to the problem of security in the region. Economic development, infrastructural development, removal of poverty, providing food security to the people of the region, and other social welfare measures in all spheres of life should be the concern of the government by which the insurgent group may be distracted and may not get any co-operation and sympathy from the common masses of the region.

Historically NER is deliberately neglected by the political masters sitting at New Delhi. The same should not be repeated in the present day context of the security scenario. For any further negligence the government must pay heavy price and there is every possibility that NER may be out of control of the Indian Federation in future. Hence quick implementation of the plans for all-round development and security measures in the region are urgently needed. At the same time respective state governments should whole heartedly co-operate with the Federal Government for the actual development and restoration of normalcy in the region. Hence all the governments of the region be appealed not to misappropriate the actual funds allotted for the developmental activities by leaving their traditional accusation against the centre to divert the attention of the common people and to create anti-centre environment of the region. At the same time Union Government should disbursed the sanctioned outlay properly.

The rise of sub-nationality at the cost of nationality created common heartedness among the different tribes and communities for individual or sectoral gains by creating an environment of suspicion. Hence, a composite north eastern society through amalgamation of several tribes and communities with a strong single nationality leaving narrow primordial loyalties is need of the situation to make north eastern culture strong and long lasting.

There are limitations in crushing insurgence by force alone. The unlimited solution is always political. Dialogue and reconciliation between the government and the insurgent groups must start as soon as possible after they have been subdued and convinced. If LTTE like organisation in Sri Lanka can come to the negotiating table by dropping the demand for Tamil-Eelam why not insurgent groups of NER? The department of Development of NER of the Union Government, on its newly launched Website, gave a detailed account of the security scenario in the region and said that the Government of India categorically rejects violence as a means of achieving any objective. At the same time, the Centre made it clear that the government believes in solution of problems through negotiation and the doors are open to all insurgent groups of NER to come for talk. Thus all the insurgent groups should come forward in this regard for the actual benefit of the society and over all development of the region.

The solution to the problem can be made by following a humane approach by which the hearts of the people of the region should be nurtured. They should be made to understand that the destructive nature of the foreign hands will have no enduring benefits for them. Such type of activities would hinder their progress in socio-economic, educational and cultural spheres of life and as a result they cannot cope with the main stream of Indian society and would always lag behind.

The sacrifices of the younger generation in different movements in NER for either statehood or otherwise and subsequent incidents have distinctly displayed the fundamental weakness of civil society in the region. The majority of the youth, in the region today are averse to hard work and face competition. They are now busy in making quick fortunes through extortions, kidnapping for ransoms, shot-out and murder leaving the actual work to the others. The words like honesty, sincerity, security, integrity and righteousness have no meaning among the majority member of the region's civil society, particularly amongst the younger generation. Glorifying terrorist organisations by the politicians and the political parties, electronic media and the inability of the police force to tackle the same have been leading to gradual erosion and degradation of moral values and induces the youths to crime for easy money. Consequently, shackled by fear, the law abiding citizens do not open their mouths and silently suffer. Thus time has come and a peoples approach is the need of the hour. Unless and until the common people of the region are well aware of the situation with high consciousness normalcy cannot be restored and the society will suffer from insecurity.

REFERENCES

Bandyopadhyay, S. and D. Chakraborty (1998), "Migration to the North Eastern Region and the Problem of Security" in *Perspectives on India's North East* (ed.) Sanjukta Banerji Bhattacharya and Rochna Das, Bibhasa, Kolkata, 1998.

Baruah, A.K. (2002), "Ethnic Homelands—Insecurity of the Non-indegenous" in *The Assam Tribune*, May 12, 2002.

Baruah, A.K. (2002), "Inter-Community Conflicts in NER", *The Assam Tribune*, September 15.

Bhattacharjee, A. (2001), "The Crisis of Ethnic Identity in Assam", *The Assam Tribune*, May 29.

Bhaumik, S. (1998), "India's North East-Archilles' Heel or Welcome Bridgehead", *op. cit.*, 1.

Chatterjee, S.S. (2002), "Infiltration Problem in North East", *The Assam Tribune*, August 14.

Das, R. (1998), "Ethnicity and Security—The North East Indian Scene", *op. cit.* 1.

Dutta, P.C. (2000), "Issues and Problems of Ethnicity in Assam of North East India", paper presented in the *Seminar on Ethnic Issues, Secularism and Conflict in North East India, NEICSSR*, 25-26 April, Shillong.

Dutta, P.C. (2001), "Regional Disparity and Its Consequences in NER", paper presented in the *33rd Regional Science Conference of Regional Science Association of India*, October 19-20, held at NEHU, Shillong.

Dutta, P.C. (2002), "Ethnic Issues and Social Tension in North Eastern Region (NER) of India" paper presented in *Regional Seminar Organised Jointly by Indian Statistical Institute, Kolkata and Department of Statistics, Gauhati University*, March 2-3, Guwahati.

Dutta, P.C. (2002), "Population Growth and Environmental Crisis in North East India—Problems and Remedies" in *Development Priorities in North East India*, (ed.), B.J. Deb, Concept Publishing Company, New Delhi.

Dutta, P.C. and B.C. Pradhan (1998), "Certain Aspects of Social Movements in the North Eastern Region—A Case Study of Barak Valley" in *Social Movements in North East India* (ed.), M.N. Karna, Indus Publishing Company, New Delhi.

Dutta, P.C. and H. Choudhury (1995), "Per Capital Household Consumption Inequalities in the North-Eastern Region of India", *Indian Journal of Regional Science (IJRS)*, Vol. 27, No. 1 & 2.

Dutta, P.C. and H. Choudhury (1996), "A Note on Inter State Variation in Per Capita Non-Food Household Items of Consumption in the North East India", *IJRS*, Vol. 28, No. 2.

Dutta, P.C. and N. Roy (2000), "The Impact of Cross-Border Human Traffic: A Case Study of Karimganj District" in *Border Trade North East India and Neighbouring Countries* (ed.), G. Das and R.K. Purkayastha, Akansha Publishing House, New Delhi.

Faizul, F. (1996), "Insecurity and Islandness—The Maldives Perspectives", paper presented at the *International Seminar on "Newer Sources of National Insecurity in South Asia"*, organised by the Regional Centre for Strategic Studies (RCSS), Colombo held on 7-11 November, Paro, Bhutan.

Ghosh, L. (1998), "Insurent Ethnicity and External Linkage in North East India—A Study of Nagaland", *op. cit.*, 1.

Hussain, S.A. (1995), "Ethnicity and Security of Bangladesh", in *South Asia's Security—Primacy of Internal Dimension* (ed.), Iftekharuzzaman, Vikas, New Delhi.

Kaushish, P.I. (2002), "Sitting on Power KEG", *The Assam Tribune*, November 19.

Mishra, O. (1998), "Forced Displacement in India's North East", *op. cit.*, 1.

9

PERSPECTIVE OF SECURITY AND DEVELOPMENT IN THE NORTH EASTERN REGION

B.B. KUMAR

The security and development are, to a large extent, related phenomena. The development work suffers if the security scenario is bad. On the other hand, lack of development, or lopsided development as we find in the North Eastern region, creates alienation and complicates the security problem. Here, it needs mention that the North Eastern region of the country suffers due to the lack of development on the one hand and the acute problems of the internal and the external security on the other.

Eight out of the ten Special Category States of the country are from this region. These states, including Sikkim, receive 90 per cent grants and 10 per cent loans for development from the Centre, whereas other states receive only 30 per cent grants and 70 per cent loan. In spite of most liberal funding from the Centre, the benefits of development have not percolated to the lowermost strata of the society in these states. The states have failed to deliver.[1]

This region of the country is one of the least developed and the most problematic. It is geographically isolated from the rest of the country and is linked through a narrow stretch of land near Siliguri. In many ways, this region is the least understood part of the country. This is the most densely administered part of the country today. Nagaland, Meghalaya and Mizoram were carved out from Assam. Manipur, Mizoram, Sikkim and Tripura had only one district each; Nagaland and Meghalaya had two each. Populationwise, all the states, except Assam, are small. Similarly, only Assam and Arunachal Pradesh have larger areas. The facts mentioned above bring the following two points to sharp focus:

(i) dense administration does not ensure increased capacity to govern and to deliver good;
(ii) liberal funding alone is not enough to ensure development.

Bigger states were replicated in the North Eastern region. The same thing is happening in Uttranchal, Chhattisgarh and Jharkhand today. The states of this region developed oversized state machineries, which consumed most of the resources. Naturally, very meagre fund was left in these states after the payment of the salary, perks and the pensions. Moreover, the leakage of the resource and wasteful expenditure continued unabated. No serious efforts were made by the state governments to mobilise the resources locally. The non-plan and revenue expenditure swelled; the plan and capital expenditure dwindled. The increased wage bills of the state governments, after implementation of the recommendations of the Fifth Pay Commission, resulted into further worsening of the situation. They are practically at the verge of bankruptcy, as many state governments are not in a position now to make timely payment of the salary to their employees.[2]

The increasing quantum of loans from the Centre and other sources and its servicing is becoming day by day burdensome. There is every danger of the states falling in debt-trap. The situation in the states in other parts of the country, however, is not better. The basic malady is the same everywhere. But the difference that other states get far too less development fund from the Centre, cannot be ignored. Needless to say that the development scenario is not at all satisfactory. The development is pushed to the margin. Attempts were made to save the states from this mess. Many state governments signed "Memorandum of Understanding" (MOU) with the Centre. But, the follow up actions are being taken up only half-heartedly.

It needs mention that liberal funding is necessary in the North East. The Government of India has directed its various ministries to spend 10 per cent of the development funds in the North East. It has also decided to have non-lapsable pool of resources for the region. The newly created Department of Development of North Eastern Region has started functioning. However, that is not enough. The economy of the North Eastern states must be managed differently. It is essential to ensure fiscal discipline and efficiency at any cost, as many problems in the region emanate from improper use of the resources. It is necessary to promote entreprenurship and self-employment. The vast potential of growth in certain sectors, such as tourism, should be fully utilised. The economy should be planned in such a way that the last man of the society is also benefited. It should increase productivity and revenue earning capacity of the states, so that the states become viable units of the Union. Rural development schemes should be worked out in such a way that the production structure of the economy gets adequately strengthened.

The flight of capital away from the region is taking place due to the disturbed situation. It is not possible to arrest the outflow of the capital from the region and the inflow from outside without restoration of the peace. Obviously, peace and normalcy is vital for the development of the region. The border trade should also be imaginatively planned and promoted.

A sad part of the development scenario in the North East is that the recommendations and observations of various commissions and studies have not been implemented. Complaints about the mis-use of funds and rampant corruption abound. Funds received by the states under the Prime Minister's package for numerous schemes and projects, for many other regular schemes and programmes, specially for rural development, and that received under the annual plans, are not properly utilised. Often, there is fund diversion. As often reported in the media, "bureaucrats, politicians, bank managers, contractors and their cohorts siphon-off major portions of the funds, consequently leaving very little—and at times nothing—for the poor.[3] As a result of the diverted funds, there is exponential increase in the construction and luxury business, particularly in the urban areas.[4] As per a recent survey by the Federation of Industries and Commerce of the North Eastern Region (FINER) 604 multi-storied buildings, housing residential and commercial appartments, with an investment of Rs. 1,200 crores have been constructed in Guwahati city alone during 1995-2000. Fourty new restaurants, besides the ones that are part of the larger hotels, had come up in Guwahati during that period, and 'Guwahatians' spend Rs. 1.3 crores on dining out per month. There is phenomenal growth in sectors like transportation, hotels, tourism, greeting cards, health care, courier services, travel agencies and computer education in Assam in the last 3-4 years.[5] The rise in the "disposable income" among a section of the urban and rural population has resulted in the same. The boom in the sectors mentioned above has been fuelled, as per the survey report of the FINER, by the World Bank-assisted Assam Rural Infrastructure and Social Project (ARIASP)'s Rs. 273.5 crores and the funds flowing out of the Prime Minister's package of Rs. 10,271 crores.[6] Here, it is difficult to differ from the opinion expressed by one of the most experienced seniormost officers of Assam "that such a high level of investment and conspicuous consumption has been provisioned by the funds siphoned-off from developmental projects and schemes."[7] The phenomena mentioned above is not restricted to only Assam. The same thing has happened in other states of the region.

Extortion in the North East by numerous insurgent groups is a well-known phenomena. The biggest extortionist outfits are the NSCN (both Isaak Muiva and Khaplang groups of National Socialist Council of Nagaland) and ULFA (United Liberation Front of Assam). NSCN was instrumental in the formation of many insurgent outfits in different parts of the region. The NSCN provides arms and training to various outfits and the latter shared extortion money collected by them with the former. ULFA, now, has entered into the same kind of relationship with the KLO (Kamtapur Liberation Organisation) in North Bengal. Various terrorist insurgent outfits collect huge money by extortion. As per the Governor's report dated 26th November 1990, estimated extortion by ULFA by that date was approximately Rs. four to five billion.[8] This gives an idea about the quantum of funds flowing to the terrorist economy in the region where scores of terrorist outfits are operating.

The main source of the fund flowing to the terrorist economy is the development fund from the Centre to the States. This is a well-known fact. Venkaiah Naidu, the then Union Minister for Rural Development in a meeting of the Rural Development Ministers of the North Eastern States at Shillong on 14th June 2001, like other Central leaders warned against such flow of funds. He said, "the Centre would stop disbursing rural development funds to those States, where a bulk of the funds go to the coffers of the extremist outfits".[9] The funds to the coffers of the insurgent outfits flow not only from the government establishments, but also from the commercial and industrial houses. A tea company paid Rs. 1.35 crores to the erstwhile Bodo Security Force; another tea company had shown Rs. one crore as unexplained 'expenditure on security' in their audited balance sheet. Small businessmen, corrupt/uncorrupt government personnel, bureaucrats, politicians, contractors, tea planters, bank executives, and even teachers and petty government employees purchase their security by paying to their coffers. The channels of the fund-flow are well-known.[10]

The insurgency in the North East leads to vicious cycle of cause and effect. There is not only siphoning-off of the resources due to the extortion, but also the resource-crunch due to increasing security-related expenditure. There is flight of the capital from rural to urban areas as the people feel less secure in the villages. Outwards flight of the capital from the region, as stated earlier, also takes place due to security reasons. All these lead to the resource crunch and under-development. It also promotes unemployment and feeling of alienation. This, in turn, helps insurgency.

Opinions advocating linkages between insurgency and unemployment and under-development are freely expressed. Here, two things need special mention:

(i) Most of the educational institutions of the region,

including Central Universities, like those in the rest of the country, churn out army of unemployed and unemployable degree-holders. These institutions give proto-type education and prepare youth mostly for unproductive white-color jobs.[11]

(ii) There is a limit up to which the present kind of employment can be given and in the North East that limit is already exceeded.

In the given situation, the unproductive jobs shall have to be reduced. The change in the present system of education is over-due. Much of the problems of the region and that of the nation may vanish if the system of the education is changed without further delay. A break from the colonial tradition of scholarship is over-due now. It is expected that our institutions and intellectuals shall awake from long slumber and work for vibrant academia. They would provide liberal education to our youth which liberates.

As stated earlier, development and security are linked together. Development is highly retarded in absence of peace and security. One of the reasons of the retarded economic development is the insurgency and lack of peace in the region. Our politicians are self-centred and myopic. They lack vision. They often sacrifice national and social interest for petty short term personal and political gains. Most of the problems of the country today are due to the diseased politics of the country. Many insurgent outfits used to gain strength through clandestine support network of politicians and overground from organisations, and also with the ill-gotten money acquired mainly through extortion.[12] It was, after all, the tacit support of the first AGP government of Prafulla Kumar Mahanta which was primarily responsible for allowing ULFA to become a large outfit.[13] It was described as "one of the classic examples of culpable inaction on the part of a State government" by the former Assam Governor D.D. Thakur.[14]

The shortsightedness of the Indian politics is also responsible for large-scale illegal migration of the Bangladeshis in the North East, West Bengal and elsewhere in the country. They get protection due to vote-bank politics of our country. Today illegal

Bangladeshi immigrants dominate a large number of the constituencies of our country, especially in Assam and West Bengal. There is change in the demographic texture of the Indo-Bangladesh border. Today, the Bangladeshis dominate at least upto 5 to 10 kilometres inside the Indian territory in West Bengal. In Assam, the number of Muslim majority districts have risen to four. Pakistan's Inter Services Intelligence agency uses such Bangladeshi dominant areas for promoting infiltration and subversion. These foreigners share our scarce development funds and practically push the border of our neighbour inside our territory. They act as the carriers of communal virus and thereby promote and intensify communal divide and conflict. The implications of their participation in our electoral process is equally dangerous for the security and development of the region and the country.

The ISI helps in the net working and spread of the terrorist/secessionist organisations. The spread of KLO and ULFA in North Bengal, their extortionist activities and using the corridor for slipping into Bhutan and Bangladesh is going to have serious adverse impact on the security and development of the country east of Siliguri bottleneck. The demand for separate Simanchal state in Muslim dominated North East Bihar was raised sometimes back.[15] As per a recent newspaper report, ISI is also taking interest in that issue.[16] This is going to add a new dimension to the alien's issue and give depth to the problem to the west of the corridor. It is a worrisome affair that even the names of Bangladeshis are included in the voters's list before their arrival in India.[17]

The North Eastern region faces greatest danger due to the presence and inflow of aliens. The destabilisation plans of the ISI and the Fundamentalist-producing institutions, presence of terrorist training camps in our neighbourhood in Bangladesh, and Bhutan, need serious attention of the Central and State Governments.

North East has seen the upsurge of violence, ethnicity and State demands during last 50 years. Somehow, the wrong signals emanated from the Central Government's actions that the 'Violence pays' and 'Social distancing pays'.[18] Nothing was done to counter these myths by the Central and the State Governments. Steps were not taken to prevent the elitist mis-use of the resources. Often, *ad hoc* measures were taken without thinking about the repercussions. We expect more mature actions from the Centre and the States now to effectively handle the problems of underdevelopment and that of the internal and external security in the North East.

NOTES

1. *Dialogue* (Quarterly), New Delhi, Vol. 4, No. 1, July-September, 2002, Editorial, p. 7.
2. *Ibid.*, pp. 7-8.
3. H.N. Das, "Insurgency and Development: The Assam Experience", in *Faultlines Writings of Conflict and Resolution*, Vol. 10, January 2002, New Delhi, Institute of Conflict Management, pp. 65-66.
4. *Ibid.*, p. 66.
5. *Ibid.*
6. "Assam's Economy: A Fresh Perspective, Federation of Industries and Commerce of North Eastern Region (FINER), Guwahati, 2001"; quoted by H.N. Das, *op. cit.*, p. 66.
7. H.N. Das, *op. cit.*, p. 66.
8. South Asia Terrorism Portal; India; States; Assam; Backgrounder; www.satp.org.; quoted by H.N. Das, *op. cit.*, p. 67.
9. *Sentinel*, Guwahati, June 15, 2001.
10. Ajai Sahni, "The Terrorist Economy in the India's North East: Preliminary Explorations", *Faultlines*, Vol. 8, pp. 127-48.
11. *Dialogue*, Vol. 2, No. 1, Editorial, p. 10.
12. H.N. Das, *op. cit.*, p. 69.
13. *Ibid.*
14. *Ibid.*, quoted By H.N. Das.
15. B.B. Kumar, *Small State Syndrome in India.*
16. *Dainik Jagaran*, February 2, 2003.
17. Pinaki Bhattacharya, "The Shiliguri Corridor", in *Faultline*, book 10, p. 121.
18. *Dialogue*, Vol. 4, No. 1, p. 8.

10

IMPACT OF MILITANCY ON ECONOMIC DEVELOPMENT OF NORTH EAST INDIA

PRANAY JYOTI GOSWAMI

North East India witnessed a large number of militant groups and their number is increasing decade after decade more particularly since independence. Some of the influential groups are: The faction of the National Socialist Council of Nagaland led by Thuingaleh Muivah and Issak Chisi Swu (NSCN-IM) in Nagaland, United Liberation Front of Assam (ULFA), Bodoland Liberation Tiger Force (BLTF) in Assam; United National Liberation Front (UNLF), People's Liberation Army (PLA), People's Revolutionary Army of Kangleipak (PREPAK), Kuki National Army in Manipur, Tripura National Volunteers (TNV) in Tripura etc. (Baruah Sanjib, 2002).

The militant groups of the North East are mostly ethnically based, even though their political projects are not always exclusionary and may even be pluralistic. The names of some militant groups suggest agenda to liberate homelands, many of the organisations simply proclaim the names of ethnic groups that the organisations seeks to defend, e.g., the Karbi National Volunteers, Tiwa National Revolutionary Force, Hmar Revolutionary Front or Zomi Revolutionary Volunteers. Manipur's UNLF and PLA do not refer to Manipur by name, but another organisation PREPAK refers to Manipur's historical name Kangleipak.

There are in addition, a large number of Islamicist militant organisations mostly in Assam.

According to one count, Manipur tops the list of militant organisations in the region with 35, Assam is second with 34 and Tripura has 30, Nagaland has four and Meghalaya checks in with three militant organisations. The number, of course, can change quickly and they are not proportionate to political challenge that militancy present in particular state.

Affects of Militancy on Economic Development

The militancy in North East is responsible for slow economic development in this region in different ways.

First, it imposes additional financial burden on the state. The State Governments have been spending huge amount of money in counter insurgency operations, which could be spent for the economic development of the state.

Secondly, there is loss of valuable lives due to militants attack, counter insurgency operation and also due to internal clash among different militant groups. For example, 823 militants belonging to different groups have been killed during counter insurgency operations between January 21, 1997 and December 31, 2000 in Assam. 5827 militants have surrendered to the authorities during the same period in Assam. Again rivals have killed as many as 1,548 people, including 333 security personnel (Hussain Wasbir, 2001). In 2000, in separaté attacks between October and December, a total of 109 Hindi speaking people have been massacred by armed militants in different parts of Assam. In Assam in the year 2000, the number of militants killed was 327 as against 65 security personnel and in 2001, the figure stands at 283 militants as against 59 security personnel. In the current year upto April 2002, the number of militants killed has been 98, while two security men lost their lives (Misra, Udayan, 2002).

Thirdly, there is the loss of production due to the bandh called by the militants or other organisations. The militants of North East called bandh on 15th August, 26th January almost every year. Again, when militants killed civilians without any reasons; Bandhs are also called by different organisations in order to condemn the brutal attacks of militants.

Fourthly, the development work is also halted due to the insurgency. For an example:

(a) In Nagaland threats from the NSCN(IM) and the Khaplang faction had forced ONGC to call a halt to its activities in Nagaland in 1994 (*The Telegraph*, Guwahati, 11th November, 2002).

(b) The Broad-gauge line from Badarpur to Lumding is also affected by insurgency. Two camps of Rail contractors were burnt by the militants recently (*The Dainik Yugashanka*, 2nd December, 2002).

(c) In Madhura quarry, the suspected DHD group burnt 27 trucks. For a few days, many workers did not work into the quarry and remained unemployed (*The Dainik Yugashanka*, 5th September, 2002).

(d) The collection of raw materials (Bamboo) for H.P.C. Panchgram from N.C. Hills also becomes difficult due to insurgency problems (*The Dainik Yugashanka*, 13th August, 2002).

Fifthly, insurgency imposes additional burden on the State. In order to maintain peace in the state, additional force is to be deployed. This requires extra expenditure on the part of the Government, which could be utilised for developmental work.

Sixthly, due to militancy problem, the forest officials do not regularly visit the forest. As a result sometimes jungles are cleared by the anti-social groups. Sometimes, displaced people for the survival also cleared the jungle. This creates an ecological problem in the region.

Seventhly, the problem of capital plight is also connected with the militancy problem. If law and order situation in a part of the region is not sound, the capital of the disturb region will be used in other region where law and order situation is sound. For example, in Assam, credit deposit ratio of the Banks is much lower than other parts of India because entrepreneurs do not like to invest in this region due to internal disturbance. The Banking sector transfers something like Rupees five thousand crores from this region to other regions for investment (Jayanta Madhav, *EPW*, 6-12 February, 1999).

Eighthly, due to insecurity, at night time no business transactions takes place in many hill stations of North East. This reduces trade, savings and investment in the region.

Ninethly, there is also adverse effect of militancy on tourism. The number of foreign tourists visiting Kaziranga is gradually decreasing due to un-sound law and order situation.

Tenthly, there is an adverse effect of militancy on Tea Industry. The Tea Industry has probably suffered the most during the past few years in Assam, when militant organisation gained in strength. In fact there is the reports of extortion of money from the Tea gardens, the murder of Tea garden officials. For example, in Cachar district the militant once kidnapped Asstt. Manager of Thaligram-Pathimara Tea Estate, Mr. Rajat Benarjee. Later, in counter insurgency operation Rajat Benarjee was killed (*Yugashanka*, 20-8-1999). In the same garden a Tea garden worker injured due to the attack of militants (*Yugashanka*, 10-1-1992). On 23-1-1992, the militant killed one person, catches fire in five houses in that area. A little girl Harshika, daughter of an Assistant Manager of Kalain Tea Estate was kidnapped in 2002. After about three months, however, she was released.

During 1991, due to militant activities the two major buyers of tea from the state have been compelled to withdraw its operation from Guwahati tea auction centre. Though the Brook Bond and Lipton returned to the scene later on, their purchase of tea at the Guwahati Auction Centre is learnt to be below the normal for many months. This has affected production also (*News of North East*, a monthly compilation of clippings, June 1991).

The psychological effect on militancy cannot be under-estimated. The people who witnessed the killing, rape etc. will suffer from trauma. They will become mental patients. For example, after witnessing the killings and torture, the guard of Thaligram-Pathimara Tea Estate one day fired on a passer-by who was going to his home with a stick. The guard has seen the stick as rifles and fired (*Yugashanka*, 12th November 2002). The physical and psychological damage to children who witnessed killings, rape or sexual abuse at the time of insurgency and counter-insurgency operation is very serious. The fact that the entire generations are growing up in an atmosphere of hatred, fear today is bound to affect the social climate and development prospects many years ahead.

Again in many places, the insurgent groups impose taxes on the people. The collecting capacity of militants is much better than the state governments. For example, the State Government of Nagaland collects house tax @ Rs. 5 per house whereas the underground collects the same tax @ Rs. 110 per house. Other taxes collected by the underground are in the form of tax on development expenditure—five to ten of expenditure and Income Tax on salaried government employees @ 25 per cent of one month's salary (Ravi Duggal *et al.*, Nagaland : Issues in Governance, *EPW*). This imposes additional burden on the people. It is also reported that some of the militant organisations imposes taxes on goat, cows etc. also.

Sometimes when some militant organisations impose underground taxes on the people, other militant organisations forbid them to pay the tax. For example when Revolutionary Peoples Front, Kuki National Front imposes taxes on the people of Jirighat area of Assam, United National Liberation Front forbids the people to pay the tax (*Yugashanka*, 5th November, 2002).

In order to maintain peace in the state additional forces is to be deployed. This requires extra expenditure, which could be utilised for developmental work.

Due to insurgency problem, the quality of developmental work also deteriorates. In the Badarpur-Lumding broad-gauge line, it is reported that bridges are not being constructed as per the standard laid down by the railway authority. Again due to militancy there is also the delay in the completion of work, which ultimately raises the cost of the project.

Many militant groups try to draw the attention of the Government and the public to their demand by destroying national property. Incidence of blast in Oil pipeline, sabotage the railway line are being taking place in Assam.

Again, one of the reasons of internal displacement is militancy. There is an adverse effect of internal displacement on people's health, education and livelihood. Forced displacement often disrupts family life, community support and social norms. The disruption of family life leads to *inter alia* to reduce parental supervision of children, low school attendance and a surge in juvenile crimes, psychological trauma, personal bereavement and all the hardships that go with life in addition to economic and social disruption.

There are many refugee camps in Assam. For example, due to ethnic clash with dominant Mizos in Mizoram, many Reangs took shelter in Hailakandi district in Assam and Tripura in 1997. Many people in the refugee camps died due to starvation and insanitary condition. For example, in six refugee camps of Tripura 2480 died in 2002. Some of the Reangs entered the deep forest of Barak Valley and they are maintaining their livelihood miserably. In Kokrajhar area also there are many refugee camps.

Causes

Now the question arises what are the causes of militancy in North East India? There are many causes of militancy. According to some, economic underdevelopment is the root cause of militancy. A few days ago George Fernandes said, "unemployment problem aggravates militancy problem" (*Yugashanka*, 11 November, 2002). To some, immigration is the root of militancy. In order to preserve the identity, culture etc. sometimes people also go on the path of militancy. For example, in Tripura the rapid growth of non-tribal population during twentieth century made the tribal very much alert regarding their rights, identity etc.

Failure of the state to provide basic services is another reason for the growth of the militancy.

In many cases internal conflicts have solid roots in International politics.

Other major international influences on internal conflicts include corporate interest in primary commodities, the destabilising effects of structural adjustment programmes and organised crime networks.

Next, the cleavages associated with internal conflicts have many possible bases, from ethnicity and religion to class, ideology and economic interest. In some cases at least, ethnic conflict is a convenient camouflage for economic plunder, leadership contests or other old fashion struggles for power and privileges.

The adverse impact of conflict on human well-being also includes wide ranging material and psychological deprivations associated with entitlement failures, health crisis, physical violence, forced displacement and related processes (Dreze, Jean, *EPW*, April 1, 2000 p. 1181).

Conclusion

Militancy problem in North East is very complex. So it needs to be considered from different angles. The following suggestions are put forward in order to solve the problem:

1. Encourage free, frank and open debate on the issues of the North East within and outside the region; let the population understand the issues in their perspective and in totality.
2. Willingness on the part of the Government of India to discuss unconditionally with all major insurgent groups.
3. Sincere efforts are required on the part of the Central and State Governments to strengthen the functioning of tertiary level institutions like panchayats, autonomous districts/ village councils.
4. Identity and security which are such emotional issues in the north east can be assured through various means which need to be explored. Land alone need not be only means of security (Jayanta Madhab, *EPW*, 6-12 February, 1999, p. 322).
5. Identity cards should be issued immediately to all citizens in order to check immigration problem.
6. Ecological diversity, which in turn comprises organic and cultural diversity, could perhaps provide the buffer system that would absorb the shocks of social tensions in this turbulent region (Gupta, Abhik).

REFERENCES

Baruah, Sanjib, "Gulliver's Troubles: State and Militants in North East India", *EPW*, October 12-18, 2002, pp. 4178-4182.

Dainik Yugashanka, 5th September, 2002, 13th August, 2002.

Duggal, Ravi, "Verma Raj etc. Nagaland: Issues in Governance", *EPW*.

Goswami, Pranay Jyoti, *Internal Displacement in North East India with Special Reference to Barak Valley*, the Paper was presented in a Seminar in Assam University, Silchar in 2002.

Gupta, Abhik, "Social Tension in North East India—An Ecological Perspective". In *Human Rights & Insurgency—The North East India*, edited by R.R. Dhamala and Sukalpa Bhattacharjee.

Hussain, Wasbir, "Election under the Shadow of the Gun", *EPW*, Feb. 3-10, 2001, pp. 442-444.

Kumar Sanjoy, "Creation of New States: Rationale and Implications", *EPW*, 7th September, 2002, p. 3705.

Madhab Jayanta, "North East: Crisis of Identity, Security and Under-development", *EPW*, February 6-12, 1999, pp. 320-22.

Misra, Udayan, "Assam, Roll call of the Dead", *EPW*, Sept. 14, 2002.

The Telegraph, Guwahati, 11th November, 2002 [The outlawed NSCN (Issak-Muivah) has warned the ONGC official of dire consequences if it resumes drilling operations in Nagaland].

11

ECONOMIC DEVELOPMENT, PEACE AND SECURITY IN THE NORTH EAST

SUKHENDU MAZUMDER

The entire North East India, as is evident from its geographical location, presumably, is placed on the top of a live volcano where the eruptions are quite common and a regular feature to witness within the shape of insurgency in different pockets coupled with infiltration from Bangladesh and other neighbouring countries. Therefore, it is a matter of grave concern that unless we are able to check such activities of the cessionist groups, not only the peace of and tranquillity of the region will be disturbed but at the same token—the economic development and such other developmental measures will be jeopardised.

Economic development, in anywhere of the globe, needs political stability and an all-round healthy atmosphere within the territory. But, if the same is often challenged from the outside and the political unrest within if often mounts up causing irreparable damage to growth process, then surely, the country as a whole suffers. And, this is how, the people of the North East in particular face tremendous pressure and often undergo untold sufferings. In resultant, the efforts rendered, fail to achieve the desired outcome and everything goes to the dogs. Hence, it is very much felt that concerted efforts towards peace and amelioration should be showered by the people, NGOs, the State Governments, and the Central Government.

It is a pity that India has a vast border-line with many countries and that too is full of hilly tracts and rivers which cannot be manned and managed that easily and yet it needs constant vigil and tight watch round the corner. The Indo-Bangla border alone runs for 4096 kms. Perhaps, Bangladesh, the country, which has been born out of India's help, is the breeding ground of all insurgent activities and a safe training ground too! Strategically the Indo-Bangla border can be divided into three primary segments—the South Bengal Frontier, the North Bengal Frontier and the Tripura-Mizoram-Cachar segment.

The relevant issues connected with the peace and security and economic development of the entire North East region have been studied and the following are submitted:

NSCN(*IM*)—Nagaland and Manipur Issues

Right now the single issue of the NSCN (*Issak-Muiva*) encompassing the entire Nagaland and Manipur is a mind-boggling one and sincere efforts are on from both the outfit and the Central Govenment authorities to pave the way for an amicable solution and a lasting peace. However, there are hurdles enough that need a careful and a very very delicate touch to give it a shape. The NSCN wants the Naga dominated areas of Assam, Arunachal Pradesh, Manipur etc. to be included to form the new state of Nagalim or Nagaland. But the same is being resented by many factions and the state govenments too. For example, a new youth organisation of Manipur, the MFYF (Manipur Forward Youth Front) has threatened that in case of division of the state of Manipur, the party members may sacrifice their lives in thousands! Another organisation, represented by the Kuki community in Manipur has appealed the Prime Minister and the Dy. Prime Minister not to sign any agreement with the NSCN(*IM*) faction. Even the NSCN (Khaplang) the other group in Nagaland, is not in favour of any peace talk with the NSCN(IM) group! And in another part of the globe, the Naga National Council (NNC) President, Adinno Phizo, the daughter of late Naga Supremo, Zapu Phizo, expresses her anguish from London saying that the approach of Government of India to settle the Naga issue involving the NNC is 'absolutely non-serious'. She feels that the NSCN(IM) does not have the mandate of the Nagas and the NNC will challenge the outcome of the peace-talk between the Central Government and the NSCN. It seems, in case of settlement her party would challenge it vehemently. The lady, in an exclusive interview with the North East Sun (*North East Sun*, Dec. 1-14, 2001) says, "We will raise this issue at various international platforms including the UN bodies. We will not call it a settlement at all. However, it is very difficult to say whether the NNC still commands a strong following in Nagaland. But it cannot be denied that till today, the older villagers in Nagaland have soft corner for the NNC.

Another group from Manipur, the United Committee Manipur (UCM) has alleged that the Centre has been adopting the policy of appeasing the Nagas at the cost of Manipur. But the NSCN(IM) has strongly refuted the allegation and warned the repercussion in no uncertain manner saying, "It is unfortunate that one of the Manipur's valley based voluntary organisation, the so-called UCM has desperately expressed their discontented feelings towards the Indo-Naga Peace Process. It is high time for all concerned to deviate from hostile attitudes, which will unnecessarily create undesirable relation in future." (*The Telegraph*, 9-10-2002).

Even in the State of Nagaland, the present Govenment of S.C. Jamir does not want the ban on the NSCN to be lifted and efforts have been intensified to extend the ban on the outfit [the ban is imposed under the provision of the Unlawful Activities (Prevention) Act]. Again in Manipur, the story is more or less the same. The Govenment of Manipur does not want to withdraw the arrest warrants against the NSCN activists and has opposed the idea to bifurcate the state for the creation of greater Nagaland. But the NSCN has a considerable following in the hill districts of Ukhrul, Tamenglong, Senapati and Chandel which is, of course, power to reckon with. The general secretary of the NSCN Thuingaleng Muiva himself belongs to Ukhrul District of Manipur. It is also confusing but understood that the Centre has been assuring the state government that there would be no division of the state of Manipur.

It is hoped that the efforts so far made would certainly pay dividends. However rigidity on the both sides is witnessed but things cannot remain dormant for an uncertain period. Moreover, the outfits have, by now realised, the public support and sympathy is on the wane and they cannot win their mission by armed struggle.

Assam

In Assam, the Bodo and Karbi issues have been troubling the people and the administration for some time and presently, some newly formed Ismalic foundations on the line of ISI, Al-Qaeda and some inspired by the activities of Osama Bin Laden (e.g., the Islamic Security Force of India, i.e., ISFI) are in the news. The peaceful Barak Valley too is not totally free from disturbance these days. In this part of Assam, two tribal groups, viz., the Barak Valley Hill Tribes Development Council and the Barak Valley Hills People's Union have demanded an autonomous district council for South Assam's Tribal Community.

The Bodoland issue has been strongly opposed by the Non-Bodos and an organisation called the Sanmilita Janagosthiya Sangram Samiti (SJSS), a confederation of 18 non-Bodo organisations has threatened to go on agitation provided the ABSU (All Bodo Student's Union) and the BPAC (Bodo People's Action Committee) revive movement for the Bodoland State. The same, if created, would be on the dead bodies of the non-Bodos! The SJSS is dead against the formation of BTC even (i.e., Bodoland Territorial Council) since the creation of the same under the Sixth Schedule of the Constitution, may give birth to a Bodo State.

But some positive and significant development is also visible. Some underground outfits in Assam are showing their willingness to enter into the formal dialogue. The UPDS (United People's Democratic Solidarity), a stronghold in the Karbi Anglong District has begun a dialogue with the Centre. But the Islamic Militancy in Assam is damaging the social fabric as they are pushing the illegal migrants inside India and especially in the North Eastern states. It is urgently required that we keep close watch on such activities and check their activities. The activities of the ISFI has been detected one recovery of some vital documents, which were distributed in the remote areas of Darrang District in Assam. Out of 34 insurgent groups in Assam, there are more than dozen Islamic or Muslim outfits actively engaged. They are, Muslim United Liberation Front of Assam (MULFA), Muslim United Liberation Tigers of Assam (MULTA), Muslim Security Council of Assam (MSCA), Islamic Liberation Army of Assam (ILAA), Muslim Volunteer Force (MVF), Muslim Liberation Army (MLA), Muslim Security Force (MSF), Islamic Sevak Sangh (ISS), Islamic United Reformation Protest of India (IURPI), United Muslim Liberation Front of Assam (UMLFA), Revolutionary Muslim Commando (RMC), Muslim Tiger Force (MTF), Harkat-ul-Mujahideen, etc. There should be constant vigil and check on the activities of such militant groups.

Meghalaya and Tripura

Meghalaya has some problems to deal with the demand of Garoland and with Bangladesh border there has been illegal border trade and influx of migrants and cheap labour. Though the ANVC (A'CHIK National Volunteer Council) is ready for a peace talk but the party wants the creation of Garoland comprising the following area which include Garo Hills Autonomous districts of East, West and South Garo Hills. It also includes Garo inhabitated areas of Khasi Hills lying close to Garo Hills. It goes beyond this even, as it includes Garo inhabitated areas of Goalpara and South Kamrup District of Assam lying contiguous to Garo Hills. The party wants the separate Garoland autonomous state amending the North Eastern Areas (Reorganisation) Act, 1971. Now it is a question of creating a state cutting the boundaries of other states and hence, the same can be done by the Parliament only. Another outfit, HNLC (Hyhnniewtrap National Liberation Council) also gives bandh calls from time to time to prove its existence.

In Tripura, there has been continuous killing and disturbance of life and influx of *Bangladeshis* to add. The Tripura issue needs a careful handling so that the tribal population there and the non-tribal both can live peacefully and the atmosphere of mistrust and ill-feelings are removed at the earliest for healthy and peaceful co-existence. Because, killings, be it of the civilians or the troops, cannot be accepted. The very atmosphere of hatred has to be removed fast. One such recent killing on October 2 of 20 young soldiers of Tripura State Rifles speaks of the brutality prevailing in the state. It needs sincere efforts to be made to stop and tackle the situation.

Political Issues

The whole of the North East India has been gripped under several problems and each needs head and heart to deal with for lasting peace and an amicable solution. It is, perhaps a lack political will and foresightedness that has been causing things to linger and soaring. Now the Naga-Manipur issue may be settled if patience and sincerity is reflected in the environment. It is good to hear from a senior Naga Hoho leader Hekhevi Achumi when he says, "Yes, we are not expecting miracles to happen. We do not expect that a few rounds of talks inside air-conditioned room in New Delhi will settle the long drawn problem. But we do hope that the warmth inside the room would be reflected in the ground situation."

But the trouble is lying in the influx from Bangladesh to the bordering states of India, including West Bengal. However, the Bangladesh issue is not a new phenomenon, it has been there for a long time and is likely to remain for days to come also. It appears that India does not have a coherent policy to follow and deal things across the border and even with its own people, which, ultimately is resulting into all such chaos and trouble to the people. It is apparent that, Bangladesh, with a sea route only and a small portion of Myanmar in the other side, is supposed to remain a constant threat to India. In addition, it shares a long border of 4000 km, which cannot be sealed altogether.

Outsiders mix with the locals and get married and gradually succeed in their attempt to get them enlisted in the voter's list. The problem is, Bangladesh is a welcome training institution for the insurgent groups and hence, the attitude for lebensraum cannot be allowed at any cost. Our Dy. Prime Minister and DG, BSF both hold the view that there has been considerable increase in the activities of the Al-Qaeda and ISI in India through the Bangladesh gate only. The same has increased after the change in Government there. The Tripura Chief Minister Mr. Manik Sarker has also pointed out the presence of militants in the state. The Intelligence source has also confirmed of foreign ships carrying sophisticated weapons and militants from abroad and deporting them to Bangladesh. It was reported that 150 men who entered Bangladesh were Taliban and Al-Qaeda fighters from Afghanistan. Apart from this, many insurgent groups from the North East are sheltered, trained in Bangladesh and also are sent to Pakistan for training. In fact, all the insurgent groups including PLA, NSCN, NLFT, ATTF, all had camps in Bangladesh.

Suggestions to Combat

It is absolutely necessary to set up fencing all along the border and set up lights in the areas to stop infiltration. No inhabitation to be allowed to settle along the border, atleast there should be 100-150 yards gap between the fence and the nearest human settlement. Electronic devices such as RADAR, FLIR (forward looking infra red) device and balloons to be used to trace the targets. And also, work permits to the Bangladeshis may be given but not the land to work. Another very important issue is, that two separate Acts, viz., IMDT and the Foreigners Act is not required as it may lead to unnecessary harassment of the public. The IMDT Act has to be repealed.

It is hoped that if we combine our best efforts to implement the policies as has been pointed out about, we can change the scenario and peace and economic development may spread every nook and corner of the North East. The border trade in the informal sector can be formalised as there has been vast potentiality lying in the border areas of Moreh in Manipur, Champai in Mizoram. It is expected that we can stop infiltration and strengthen our security of the Nation and at the same time bring peace and development.

REFERENCES

North East Sun, July 1-14, 2002, July 15-30, 2002, December 1-14, 2001, October 15-30, 2002, November 1-14, 2002, September 1-14, 2001, June 15-30, 2001.

Pakem, B., *Insurgency in North East India.*

Ray, B. Datta (ed), *Agenda for North East India.*

Ray, B. Datta and Agarwal, S.P., *Reorganisation of North East India, Since 1947.*

The Telegraph, Guwahati, from 2001 to 2002.

12

MIGRATION IN THE NORTH EASTERN REGION OF INDIA IN THE PERSPECTIVE OF SECURITY AND DEVELOPMENT

SABARI BANDYOPADHYAY

Introduction

The seven sister states—Arunachal Pradesh, Assam, Manipur, Meghalaya, Mizoram, Nagaland and Tripura covers the North Eastern Region of India. The geographical area of the region is slightly more than 2.55 lakh sq.km. which gives residence to 38.50 million people (3.75% of the total population of India), according to 2001 Census. The region's density of population is lowest among the other regions of India. According to 2001 Census of India density of population of the region is 151 per sq.km. whereas the density of population of the Northern region (comprising Jammu and Kashmir, Himachal Pradesh, Punjab, Chandigarh, Haryana, Delhi, Rajasthan), Central Region (comprising Uttar Pradesh, Uttaranchal, Chhattisgarh, Madhya Pradesh), Eastern Region (comprising Bihar, Sikkim, West Bengal, Jharkhand, Orissa, Andaman and Nicobar), Western Region (comprising Goa, Gujarat, Daman and Diu, Dadra and Nagar Haveli, Maharashtra) and Southern Region (comprising Andhra Pradesh, Karnataka, Lakshadeep, Kerala, Tamil Nadu and Pondicherry) are 223, 347, 525, 293 and 351 per sq.km. respectively so the sparsely populated region has attracted the migrants for more than a century from not only different parts of the country but also from neighbouring countries like Bangladesh,

Nepal, Myanmar, etc. The migration plays role in creating tensions in the region. As the influx to the region is large enough to change the ethnic composition of the population and rouse the feeling of the threatening cultural identity among the local people. As a result the region has to face grave situation. Tension in the region has jeopardised the security of the region as well as the country as a whole since the region covers slightly more than 4000 km. of international boundary. Also the jeopardised security may pose as a stumbling block to the development of the region.

There are considerable numbers of studies on migration in India. Mention may be made of several notable works conducted by Zachariah (1964), Mahalingam (1964), Bose (1967), Chakraborty (1968), Mitra (1967), Rele (1969), Piplai and Majumdar (1969), Greenwood (1971), Connell, Dasgupta, Laishley and Lipton (1976), Saxena (1977), Oberai and Singh (1982), Sivamurthy and Kadi (1983), Dasgupa (1984), Chakraborty and Khasnobis (1984), Nair (1985), Pravakar (1986), Gupta, Arora and Agarwal (1988), Premi (1980, 1989), Sarkar (1989), Narayana (1990, 1994), Bhattacharya (1996), Sekhar (1993), Selvaraj and Rao (1993), Dey and Chakraborty (1994), Guha Roy and Datta (1995), Bandyopadhyay and Chakraborty (1995), Chakraborty, Gupta and Bandyopadhyay (1997) and Singh (1998). But the focus of these studies was not on the population movement of North Eastern region.

Important studies have been conducted on the North Eastern region. For example, Sarin (1980), Rustomji (1983), Xexa (1983), Sebastian (1986), Saikia (1986), Agarwal (1988), Bandyopadhyay and Chakraborty (1998) have made considerable contributions in this field. Besides, these studies, researchers like Dass (1980), Sharma (1980), Guha (1977, 1991), Choudhury (1982), Goswami and Gogoi (1984), Goswami (1984), Pathak (1986), Baruah (1986) have also done research concentrating on one state, Assam. All these studies though have made significant contributions, but lack in completeness as they remain confined either to a single state or to a single objective. The present study is concerned with the phenomenon of migration in the North Eastern region in the perspective of security and development, considering a long period from 1901-1991. The chapter is organised as follows. In Section I, there will be a brief discussion on the various components of the migrants. Section II will discuss the migration in the perspective of security and development. Section III will conclude the chapter.

SECTION I

COMPONENTS OF MIGRATION IN THE NORTH EASTERN REGION

The concept of "Migration" is actually the net product of two dimen-sionally opposite ideas, viz., "Immigration" and "Emigration". The people who inflowed during a particular period to the place of enumeration is termed as "immigrants", whereas those who outflowed from the place of enumeration is termed as "emigrants". Here we shall confine ourselves mainly within the immigratory movement. So the following discussions regarding the migration of the North Eastern region of India has concerned with the immigratory movements in the region. From the Census data we have observed that the share of migrants to the total population of the North Eastern region of India varies throughout the period 1901-1991. The proportion has steadily increased from around 17 per cent in 1901 to slightly more than 23 per cent in 1931. But from 1951 onwards it is declining. It was 15.62 per cent in 1951 and 5.36 per cent in 1991. The population of the region is recorded as 38.50 million in 2001 Census. So we may expect the region would have get around 16 lakh migrants, if not more according to the 2001 Census.

We have divided the total migrants in the North Eastern region into three groups.

(i) Migrants in the North Eastern region from outside India. The people who undertook migratory movements as "Foreign migrants".

(ii) Migrants in the North Eastern region from the rest of India. The people who undertook migratory movements to the region from rest of India. Here we shall refer these migrants as the "Migrants from other states of India".

(iii) Migrants in the North Eastern region from within the region. The people who undertook the migratory movements to the North Eastern region from within the region. In our study, we shall refer these migrants as "Intra-regional" migrants. Here we have ignored the intra-state movements of the people of each state of the region.

Table 12.1 presents trend of various components of total migrants to the region during 1901-1991. From Table 12.1, it is evident that foreign migration is very important component of the total migration to the North Eastern region of India.

From Table 12.2, it can be observed that the foreign migrants, who came to the region were largely from Bangladesh, Nepal and Myanmar (erstwhile Burma). Starting from 1901 it can be observed that the majority of the foreign migrants were from Bangladesh. The share of the migrants from Bangladesh was between slightly more than 77 per cent to slightly more than 87 per cent in pre-independence era. In post-independence era it reached at 94 per cent in 1951—the highest among all the periods under consideration. From 1961 onwards the share started to decline and became around 89 per cent in the Census year of 1991. It is also clear from Table 12.2, the Bangladesh was followed by Nepal in sending migrants to the North Eastern region of India. Among the foreign migrants to the region slightly more than 10 per cent to slightly more than 26 per cent came from Nepal in pre-independence era. But in post-independence era it is observed that the share of the migrants from Nepal has declined and remained slightly more than 5 per cent to about 8 per cent. In the Census years of both pre- as well as post-independence eras, the proportion of the migrants from Myanmar was considerably very low.

It is observed from Table 12.3, the number of migrants who came from other states of India varied between 0.5 million to around 0.8 million during the pre-independence era. But it declined to around 0.4 million in 1951 and reaching slightly more than 0.5 million in 1991. From Table 12.3, it is also observed that in the pre- as well as in the post-independence eras most of the migrants

Table 12.1: Different Types of Migrants in the North Eastern Region of India during 1901-1991

Year	1901	1911	1921	1931	1951	1961	1971	1981(a)	1991
Migrants From									
Foreign Countries	1,17,923 (16.48)	1,78,494 (21.65)	3,55,213 (28.58)	8,09,000 (48.05)	11,09,319 (68.77)	12,91,294 (69.36)	16,29,678 (69.23)	5,72,587 (63.83)	8,33,753 (49.34)
Other states of India	5,49,781 (76.83)	6,14,058 (74.50)	8,55,999 (68.87)	8,35,861 (49.64)	4,37,053 (27.09)	4,98,422 (26.77)	5,62,502 (23.90)	1,32,658 (14.79)	5,65,431 (33.46)
Intra Region	47,910 (6.69)	31,736 (3.85)	31,673 (2.55)	38,909 (2.31)	66,818 (4.14)	71,910 (3.86)	1,61,718 (6.87)	1,91,818 (21.38)	2,90,607 (17.20)
Total	7,15,614 (100)	8,24,288 (100)	12,42,885 (100)	16,83,770 (100)	16,13,190 (100)	18,61,626 (100)	23,53,898 (100)	8,97,063 (100)	16,89,791 (100)

(a) Without including the data for Assam.

Note: Figures in parentheses are percentages.

Source: *Census of India*-1901, Table XI; 1911, Table XI; 1921, Table XI; 1931, Table VI; 1951, Table D-IV, 1961, Table D-1; 1971, Table D-I, 1981, Table D-1; 1991, Table D-1.

Table 12.2: Foreign Migrants to the North Eastern Region of India During 1901-1991

Countries Migrating	1901	1911	1921	1931	1951	1961	1971	1981(a)	1991
Bangladesh@	91,096 (77.25)	1,25,621 (70.38)	2,74,492 (77.28)	7,06,452 (87.32)	10,44,843 (94.19)	11,75,789 (91.06)	14,89,873 (91.42)	5,13,149 (89.62)	7,45,414 (89.40)
Nepal	21,268 (18.04)	47,463 (26 59)	70,053 (19.72)	88,269 (10.91)	57,266 (5.16)	1,00,210 (7.76)	1,24,364 (7.63)	48,377 (8.45)	45,892 (5.50)
Myanmar	1,666 (1.41)	2,292 (1.28)	7,395 (2.08)	7,749 (0.96)	3,674 (0.33)	4,571 (0.35)	5,507 (0.34)	4,931 (0.86)	5,824 (0.70)
Other Countries	3,893 (3.30)	3,118 (1.75)	3,273 (0.92)	6,530 (0.81)	3,536 (0.32)	10,724 (0.83)	9,934 (0.61)	6,130 (1.07)	36,623 (4.39)
Total	1,17,923 (100)	1,78,494 (100)	3,55,213 (100)	8,09,000 (100)	11,09,313 (100)	12,91,294 (100)	16,29,678 (100)	5,72,587 (100)	8,33,753 (100)

The data for 1941 are not available.

(a) without the data of Assam.

@ We have estimated the figures for Bangladesh during 1901-31 by identifying those areas which were included in present Bangladesh and for the years 1951-1971 data of Pakistan is taken as an approximation because we have assumed that most of the migrants who came from Pakistan to the region were from the contiguous East Pakistan (now Bangladesh).

Note: Figures in parantheses are percentages.

Source: *Census of India* 1901. 1911, 1921, 1931, 1951, 1961, 1971, 1981, 1991.

Table 12.3: Migrants from Other States of India to the North Eastern Region of India during 1901-1991

States	1901	1911	1921	1931	1951	1961	1971	1981*	1991
West Bengal	60,707	84,363	1,23,520	1,71,249	26,485	59,467	78,308	20,760	1,16,796
	(11.04)	(13.59)	(14.43)	(20.49)	(6.06)	(11.93)	(13.92)	(15.65)	(20.64)
Bihar(a)	3,13,509	3,63,474	5,28,620	4,46,419	2,08,608	2,63,483	2,68,421	49,320	2,42,008
	(57.02)	(59.19)	(61.75)	(53.41)	(47.73)	(52.86)	(47.72)	(37.18)	(42.80)
Orissa	33,139	—	—	—	89,051	53,486	33,005	4,609	14,222
	(6.03)				(20.38)	(10.73)	(5.87)	(3.47)	(20.52)
Uttar Pradesh	58,820	53,594	44,062	45,298	33,904	48,934	83,000	23,351	75,188
	(10.70)	(8.73)	(5.15)	(5.42)	(7.76)	(9.82)	(14.76)	(17.60)	(13.30)
Madhya Pradesh	56,684	75,319	98,200	90,150	10,643	11,887	15,296	1,532	8,788
	(10.31)	(12.27)	(11.47)	(10.79)	(2.44)	(2.38)	(2.72)	(1.15)	(1.55)
Rajasthan	9,101	11,397	15,349	21,554	17,629	23,467	32,685	6,601	35,701
	(1.66)	(1.86)	(1.79)	(2.58)	(4.03)	(4.71)	(5.81)	(4.98)	(6.31)
Maharashtra	5,910	1,096	1,330	6,043	4,838	1,897	2,556	1,230	3,996
	(1.07)	(0.18)	(0.16)	(0.72)	(1.11)	(0.38)	(0.45)	(0.93)	(0.71)
Punjab	6,049	3,389	2,872	5,990	5,681	14,788	12,711	3,857	9,338
	(1.10)	(0.55)	(0.34)	(0.72)	(1.30)	(2.97)	(2.26)	(2.91)	(1.65)
Other States	5,862	22,326	42,046	49,158	40,213	21,013	36,520	21,398	59,464
	(1.07)	(3.64)	(4.91)	(5.88)	(9.20)	(4.22)	(6.49)	(16.13)	(10.52)
Total	5,49,781	6,14,058	8,55,999	8,35,861	4,37,052	4,98,422	5,62,502	1,32,658	5,65,431
	(100)	(100)	(100)	(100)	(100)	(100)	(100)	(100)	(100)

(a) Included the data of both Bihar and Orissa for the Census year of 1911-1931. * Without Assam.

Note: Figures in parentheses are percentages.

Source: Census of India 1901, Table XI; 1911, Table XI; 1921, Table XI; 1931, Table VI; 1951, Table D-IV; 1961, Table D-I; 1971, Table D-I; 1981, Table D-1; 1991, Table D-1.

came from the state of Bihar. The percentage of the migrants from Bihar to the region was around 57 per cent during 1901 and declined to 43 per cent in 1991. We have clubbed data for Bihar and Orissa for the three successive census years 1911, 1921, 1931 which present that these two states together send about 53 per cent to 62 per cent of the migrants in the pre-independence period. Even in the post-independence era the migrants from Bihar and Orissa, constituted a large portion of the migrant population from other states of India to the region. Besides Bihar and Orissa, among other states (outside the region) West Bengal and Uttar Pradesh were the other major states from where the migrants made their way to the region, in the pre- as well as in post-independence era. The percentage share of the migrants from West Bengal and Uttar Pradesh among the 'migrants from other states of India' to the region was around 11 per cent each in 1901 but reached to nearly 21 per cent and nearly 13 per cent respectively in 1991.

Let us study from which states of the region migrants made their way to the states of the region. We have tried to construct intra-regional "Immigration-Emigration" matrices [given in Tables 12.4(a) and 12.4(b)] though there is gap in state-wise data in the Census years. From the intra-regional "Immigration-Emigration" matrices it is observed that most of the migrants who came to Assam from other North-Eastern states were from Meghalaya in most of the Census years. From the matrices it is also evident that Assam is the major state from where migrants came to the other North Eastern states.

SECTION II

MIGRATION IN THE NORTH EASTERN REGION IN THE PERSPECTIVE OF SECURITY AND DEVELOPMENT

The immigration to the region took place from the beginning of the previous century. There were several factors behind this type of migration. Assam became a British protectorate of the East India Company after the Burmese invasion in 1826. The then Government in its revenue earning pursuit declared certain terms

Table 12.4(a): Intra-Regional Migrants in the North Eastern Region of India during 1901-1931

(States of Enumeration)

Year	States Migrating from	Arunachal Pradesh	Assam	Manipur	Meghalaya	Mizoram	Nagaland	Tripura	Total
(1)	(2)	(3)	(4)	(5)	(6)	(7)	(8)	(9)	(10)
1901	Arunachal Pradesh	—	N.A.	N.A.	N.A.	N.A.	N.A.	*	
	Assam	N.A.	—	356 (65.2)	9,589 (96.91)	395 (34.12)	2,463 (64.34)	*	
	Manipur	—	1,524 (9.22)	—	186 (1.88)	561 (55.49)	1,088 (28.42)	*	
	Meghalaya	—	3,963 (23.98)	102 (18.68)	—	101 (9.99)	242 (6.32)	*	
	Mizoram	—	94 (0.57)	—	—	—	35 (0.91)	*	
	Nagaland	—	10,943 (66.22)	88 (16.12)	120 (1.21)	4 (0.4)	—	*	
	Tripura	—	—	—	—	—	—	—	
	Total	—	16,524 (100)	546 (100)	9,895 (100)	1,011 (100)	3,828 (100)	16,106	47,910
1911	Arunachal Pradesh	—	N.A.	N.A.	N.A.	N.A.	N.A.	N.A.	N.A.
	Assam	—	—	1,208 (25.78)	7,787 (97.53)	486 (27.26)	1,266 (68.88)	1,197 (58.59)	11,944 (37.64)
	Manipur	—	1,717 (12.81)	0	113 (1.42)	1,150 (64.5)	503 (27.37)	86 (4.21)	3,569 (11.25)

(Contd.)

Table 12.4(a): (*Contd.*)

(1)	(2)	(3)	(4)	(5)	(6)	(7)	(8)	(9)	(10)
	Meghalaya	—	3,769	57	—	130	63	0	4,027
			(28.12)	(1.22)		(7.74)	(3.43)		(12.69)
	Mizoram	—	74	3,281	15	—	6	760	4,136
			(0.55)	(70.02)	(0.19)		(0.33)	(37.2)	(13.03)
	Nagaland	—	7,830	140	0	3	—	0	8,039
			(58.42)	(2.99)		(0.17)			(25.33)
	Tripura	—	12	0	3	6	0	—	21
			(0.09)		(0.04)	(0.34)			(0.07)
	Total	—	13,402	4,686	7,982	4,897	1,838	2,043	31,736
			(100)	(100)	(100)	(100)	(100)	(100)	(100)
1921	Arunachal Pradesh	—	104	1	0	2	0	0	107
			(0.99)	(0.03)		(0.14)			(0.34)
	Assam	30,773	—	1,639	5,817	345	2,285	1,613	14,772
		(90.81)		(42.05)	(97.93)	(24.56)	(69.41)	(49.74)	(46.64)
	Manipur	89	2,291	—	47	960	944	196	4,331
		(2.63)	(21.80)		(0.79)	(68.33)	(28.68)	(6.04)	(13.67)
	Meghalaya	88	5,460	144	—	44	56	0	5,988
		(2.60)	(51.95)	(3.69)		(3.13)	(1.70)		(18.91)
	Mizoram	56	397	1,835	40	—	7	1,434	3,769
		(1.65)	(3.78)	(47.08)	(0.67)		(0.21)	(44.22)	(11.90)
	Nagaland	78	2,251	277	35	14	—	0	2,655
		(2.30)	(21.42)	(7.11)	(0.59)	(1)			(8.38)

(*Contd.*)

Table 12.4(a): (*Contd.*)

(1)	(2)	(3)	(4)	(5)	(6)	(7)	(8)	(9)	(10)
	Tripura	0	8 (0.08)	2 (0.05)	1 (0.02)	40 (2.85)	0	—	51 (0.16)
	Total	3,384 (100)	10,511 (100)	3,898 (100)	5,940 (100)	1,405 (100)	3,292 (100)	3,243 (100)	31,673 (100)
1931	Arunachal Pradesh	—	128 (0.94)	1 (0.02)	0	1 (0.15)	0	0	131 (0.34)
	Assam	4,988 (91.37)	—	2,087 (42.09)	6,547 (94.03)	449 (33.01)	2,560 (72.19)	1,450 (47.29)	18,081 (46.47)
	Manipur	113 (2.07)	3,849 (28.39)	—	284 (4.08)	832 (61.18)	918 (25.89)	327 (10.67)	6,323 (16.25)
	Meghalaya	142 (2.60)	6,713 (49.52)	183 (3.69)	—	57 (4.19)	62 (1.75)	0	7,157 (18.39)
	Mizoram	90 (1.65)	488 (3.60)	2,336 (47.11)	45 (0.65)	—	6 (0.17)	1,289 (42.04)	4,254 (10.93)
	Nagaland	126 (2.31)	2,768 (20.42)	352 (7.10)	40 (0.57)	19 (1.40)	—	0	3,305 (8.49)
	Tripura	0	Insigni- ficant	0	47 (0.67)	0	0	—	Insigni- ficant
	Total	5,459 (100)	13,556 (100)	4,959 (100)	6,963 (100)	1,360 (100)	3,546 (100)	3,066 (100)	38,909 (100)

* The migrants from undivided Assam are taken as Intra-Regional migrants to Tripura. N.A. Not available.

Note: Figures in parantheses are percentages.

Source: *Census of India*, 1901, Table XI; 1911, Table XI; 1921, Table XI; 1931, Table VI.

Table 12.4(b): Intra-Regional Migrants in the North Eastern Region of India during 1951-1991

(States of Enumeration)

Year	States Migrating from	Arunachal Pradesh	Assam	Manipur	Meghalaya	Mizoram	Nagaland	Tripura	Total
(1)	(2)	(3)	(4)	(5)	(6)	(7)	(8)	(9)	(10)
1951	Arunachal Pradesh	—	1,386 (4.44)	—	9 (0.09)	2 (0.38)	8 (0.38)	—	—
	Assam	8,274 (89.70)	—	—	8,114 (83.25)	147 (28.27)	1,609 (77.36)	—	—
	Manipur	183 (1.90)	2,933 (9.40)	3,806**	402 (4.12)	137 (26.35)	268 (12.88)	330 (3.22)	—
	Meghalaya	235 (2.55)	9,208 (29.52)	—	—	96 (18.46)	119 (5.72)	9,908**	—
	Mizoram	95 (1.03)	1,259 (4.04)	—	574 (5.89)	—	12 (0.58)	—	—
	Nagaland	250 (2.71)	1,904 (6.10)	—	429 (4.5)	4 (0.77)	—	—	—
	Tripura	187 (2.03)	14,504 (46.50)	9	209 (2.14)	134 (25.77)	64 (3.08)	—	—
	Total	9,224 (100)	31,194 (100)	3,815 (100)	9,747 (100)	520 (100)	2,080 (100)	10,238 (100)	66,818
1961	Arunachal Pradesh	—	140 (0.94)	0	11 (0.05)	8 (0.16)	18 (0.44)	0	177 (0.25)
	Assam	5,208 (88.72)	—	6,509 (82.73)	22,284 (93.56)	1,316 (25.78)	3,404 (82.58)	10,127 (98.76)	48,848 (67.93)

(Contd.)

Table 12.4(b): (*Contd.*)

(1)	(2)	(3)	(4)	(5)	(6)	(7)	(8)	(9)	(10)
	Manipur	415	5,010	—	386	343	605	118	6,877
		(7.07)	(33.69)		(1.62)	(6.72)	(14.68)	(1.15)	(9.56)
	Meghalaya	*	*	*	*	*	*	*	*
	Mizoram	*	*	*	*	*	*	*	*
	Nagaland	193	1,943	158	865	14	—	9	3,182
		(3.29)	(13.06)	(2.01)	(3.63)	(0.27)		(0.09)	(4.42)
	Tripura	54	7,779	1,201	273	3,424	95	—	12,826
		(0.92)	(52.31)	(15.26)	(1.15)	(67.07)	(2.3)		(17.84)
	Total	5,870	14,872	7,868	23,819	5,105	4,122	10,254	71,910
		(100)	(100)	(100)	(100)	(100)	(100)	(100)	(100)
1971	Arunachal Pradesh	—	1,415	7	171	15	53	11	1,672
			(0.65)	(0.05)	(0.47)	(0.33)	(0.38)	(0.09)	(1.03)
	Assam	25,325	—	12,856	34,813	2,024	10,100	11,738	96,856
		(95.38)		(89.93)	(94.97)	(45.02)	(71.69)	(95.86)	(59.89)
	Manipur	124	5,640	—	620	265	3,006	222	9,877
		(0.47)	(10.56)		(1.69)	(5.89)	(21.34)	(1.81)	(6.11)
	Meghalaya	525	26,151	199	—	362	569	227	28,033
		(1.98)	(48.98)	(1.39)		(8.05)	(4.04)	(1.85)	(17.33)
	Mizoram	*	*	*	*	*	*	*	*
	Nagaland	399	4,645	308	504	25	—	47	5,928
		(1.5)	(8.70)	(2.15)	(1.37)	(0.56)		(0.38)	(3.67)

(*Contd.*)

Table 12.4(b): (*Contd.*)

(1)	(2)	(3)	(4)	(5)	(6)	(7)	(8)	(9)	(10)
	Tripura	178 (0.67)	15,535 (29.10)	925 (6.47)	548 (1.49)	1,805 (40.15)	361 (2.56)	—	19,352 (11.97)
	Total	26,551 (100)	53,386 (100)	14,295 (100)	36,656 (100)	4,496 (100)	14,089 (100)	12,245 (100)	1,61,718 (100)
1981	Arunachal Pradesh	—	N.A.	104 (0.66)	267 (0.54)	108 (0.70)	279 (0.73)	67 (0.39)	825 (0.43)
	Assam	51,526 (92.72)	N.A.	9,409 (59.38)	42,720 (86.75)	6,210 (40.27)	27,868 (72.52)	15,170 (87.64)	1,52,903 (79.71)
	Manipur	322 (0.58)	N.A.	—	1,341 (2.72)	1,341 (8.70)	7,207 (18.75)	251 (1.45)	10,462 (5.45)
	Meghalaya	2,287 (4.12)	N.A.	503 (3.17)	—	1,320 (8.56)	1,132 (2.95)	1,068 (6.17)	6,310 (3.29)
	Mizoram	218 (0.39)	N.A.	4,048 (25.55)	2,030 (4.12)	—	437 (1.14)	599 (3.46)	7,332 (3.82)
	Nagaland	425 (0.76)	N.A.	456 (2.88)	983 (2.00)	236 (1.53)	—	154 (0.89)	2,254 (1.18)
	Tripura	791 (1.42)	N.A.	1,325 (8.36)	1,905 (3.87)	6,204 (40.24)	1,507 (3.92)	—	11,732 (6.12)
	Total	55,569 (100)	—	15,845 (100)	49,246 (100)	15,419 (100)	38,430 (100)	17,309 (100)	1,91,818 (100)

(*Contd.*)

Table 12.4(b): (*Contd.*)

(1)	(2)	(3)	(4)	(5)	(6)	(7)	(8)	(9)	(10)
1991	Arunachal Pradesh	—	7,500 (7.78)	29 (0.32)	256 (0.51)	75 (0.90)	160 (0.55)	99 (0.49)	8,119 (2.79)
	Assam	72,246 (94.08)	—	6,508 (72.10)	45,592 (89.99)	4,165 (49.78)	21,867 (75.59)	17,902 (87.80)	1,68,280 (57.91)
	Manipur	726 (0.95)	7,500 (7.78)	—	1,302 (2.57)	1,015 (12.13)	5,074 (17.54)	351 (1.72)	15,968 (5.49)
	Meghalaya	2,158 (2.81)	31,749 (32.92)	225 (2.49)	—	698 (8.34)	565 (1.95)	924 (4.53)	36,319 (12.50)
	Mizoram	170 (0.22)	2,790 (2.89)	1,259 (13.95)	1,171 (2.31)	—	177 (0.61)	832 (4.08)	6,399 (2.20)
	Nagaland	437 (0.57)	9,800 (10.16)	306 (3.39)	704 (1.39)	140 (1.67)	—	281 (1.38)	11,668 (4.02)
	Tripura	1,059 (1.38)	37,101 (38.47)	699 (7.74)	1,636 (3.23)	2,274 (27.18)	1,085 (3.75)	—	43,854 (15.09)
	Total	76,796 (100)	96,440 (100)	9,026 (100)	50,661 (100)	8,367 (100)	28,928 (100)	20,389 (100)	2,90,607 (100)

* Included in Assam.
** From other five states.
N.A. Note available.
Note: Figures in parantheses are percentages.
Source: *Census of India* 1951, Table D-IV; 1961, Table D-I; 1971, Table D-I; 1981, Table D-I; 1991, Table D-I.

for granting waste lands for cultivation in 1827. At first it was offered to the Assamese only, but later observing failure the Government decided in 1856 to grant the waste lands to "Europeans, Assamese, Bengalees and others without distinction and cultivation of whatever the grantee might think proper to produce" (Barpujari, 1980). As a consequence, from the time onwards, the cultivation of tea began by European capital in Assam. Assam with its favourable climate for tea plantation and abundant land attracted the Britishers to invest their capital for the production of this important item of consumption, which has a great demand in the U.K. market. In spite of the availability of abundant land and capital, they had to face the severe shortage of labour supply. In Tripura also plantation began after First World War. Local conditions were such as to release working population for tea gardens, in addition to that employment was not so attractive in the tea garden. Therefore, one who had minimum livelihood refused to work there and as a result migration of labour took place from other parts of the country as well as from outside the country. Besides, the immigration of cultivators from Bangladesh (erstwhile East Bengal) began from the start of the previous century. The cultivator-migrants mainly came from the contiguous districts of Bangladesh. The basic cause of migratory movement was the availability of abundant cultivable land. The ryotwari land tenure system in Assam giving the opportunity of new life of cultivator proprietorship, also attracted the migrants. There was further immigration of the Bangladeshi migrants to North-Eastern region between 1931 and partition. Among them were Muslims encouraged by Sadullah Ministry governed the then Assam after 1937. According to Goswami (1984), "It was during this period Sadullah Ministry under pretext of raising the state's agricultural production, engineered the systematic settlement of people in Assam from East Bengal. Though it was protested later in Assam, but in Tripura the cultivator immigrants were welcomed as there was abundant supply of virgin land in the valleys and local people (tribals) were outnumbered by the immigrants."

During the period 1941-51, most of the foreign migrants were compelled to enter into North Eastern region. A large number of

Indian evacuees from Burma (now Myanmar) during the Second World War and the Hindu Refugees from Bangladesh were the main constituents of the foreign migrants during the decade. Besides, in the post-partition era, along with Hindu refugees Muslim farm labourers also came to the region at the same pre-Independence rate if not on a large scale, reversing the general expectations that partition would prevent the influx of Muslim migrants from the newly emerged East Pakistan (now Bangladesh) to the North Eastern region. Also influx of the Bangladeshi migrants to the region took place in connection with the Bangladesh liberation movement. Many people who took shelter never went back. A large number of Chakmas entered Mizoram, Tripura and Arunachal Pradesh.

In addition to the above discussed migrants there were Nepali migrants. Most of them were originally soldiers of Gurkha regiments. Besides, there was the immigration of Nepali graziers which was continuously unnoticed "as they settled only in hill slopes which are not demanded either by the indigenous farmers or immigrants from East Bengal. Some of these are Government wasteland and some belong to the local people. By allowing the Nepalies to settle down the landowners are able to get some income instead of the land remaining unoccupied. The rising demand for milk and milk products and firewood in urban centres encouraged the Nepalies to settle in hill slopes near the line of communication from/to urban market centres" (Goswami, 1984). Thus, we observed that the foreign migrants have moved across difficult geographical obstacles driven by possibilities of better economic opportunity.

Let us focus on the reasons for migration to the region from rest of India. The Britishers had imported thousands of tribal workers from Bengal, Bihar, Orissa, Central India to employ them in their tea plantation. The potential immigrants with their earnest desire to be the master of their land readily accepted the proposal of emigrating from their native land permanently. Besides the above migrants Marwari merchants who were the natives of Rajasthan (formerly Rajputana) also migrated to the North Eastern region to capture trade and commerce. Their migration to the region began to increase gradually and these merchants capture almost all of the business of Brahmaputra valley. The migrants from Punjab were mostly contractors, skilled mechanics, carpenters, motor *mistries* and motor drivers. These people were attracted to the province by the Assam-Bengal Railway. They concentrated principally in Lakhimpur, the most developed industrial district in Assam.

After Independence, the development and other economic activities geared up in North Eastern region. For instance, along with wood-based industries several cottage and small scale industries were started flourishing. Besides cultivation of 'coffee' as was encouraged to be a potential exportable commodity. All these activities required a large number of labourers. But local population specially in Arunachal Pradesh, Nagaland, Manipur, Meghalaya and Mizoram were too small and scattered to provide sufficient labour.

Most of the intra-regional migrants preferred to go to the adjacent states. Assam got maximum migrants from the other states of the region and also it is the major state from where migration took place to the other states of the North Eastern region. Thus, we observed that the migrants have moved across difficult geographical obstacles driven mainly by possibilities of better economic opportunity.

With the passage of time the presence of migrants become undesirable to the local people. They began to feel that inadequate safeguards were taken to protect them. So their position worsened. They were threatened to be overwhelmed by a process of cultural absorption. Besides, the migrants competed with the local people in every appointment to different services. As a consequence, a section of youth have embarked on a violent struggle. The demand for expulsion of the 'foreigners' started at Assam in the early sixties. This demand with the passing of time had spread to the other states and has made the situation more grave. The rival groups wage battle against one another to safeguard their distinct identities and languages. The Centre put up a legal barrier in the form of the Illegal Migration Determination by Tribunal Act (IMDT) to determine the foreigners. But this Act is not above the controversy. Also "the Assamese efforts to assimilate non-Assamese into their political and cultural framework have largely resulted in the breakup of Assam into discrete cultural political units. Because one by one each of the major non-Assamese groups pressed the Central Government for the creation of a separate political structure apart from Assam, the Nagas pressed for Nagaland, the NEFA tribes for Arunachal, Khasi and Garos for Meghalaya and the Mizos for Mizoram" [Weirner, 1978]. Even after the formation of different states carrying from Assam it is still on an 'ethnic time bomb'. Because the tribal states in the region are ethnic states (although uniform ethnicity is absent in some of them) but not linguistic states like other parts of India. The All Assam Students Union (AASU) demanded the reservation of all Lok Sabha and Assembly seats in Assam for indigenous people of the State. . . . AASU leaders also demanded the reservation of all Government jobs for indigenous Assamese, imposition of Article 370 of the Constitution as well as the introduction of the Inner Line Permit System in Assam [*The Asian Age*, 1st July, 1999].

"The Hindu Security Task Force (HSTF) and Gorkha Task Force (GTF) are the latest entries in Assam's ever-going list of armed outfit. . . . The HSTF's professed goal is to "safeguard Hindutva" and propagate the "one nation, one culture" theory through armed struggle, intelligence sources said. The group has identified Bangladeshi Muslims and agents of Pakistan's ISI as enemy. The force. . . , has already trained in the use of firearms about 20 cadres at camps in Borangabari in Sonitpur district and Ramghat in Arunachal Pradesh. The GTF, on the other hand has been formed to protect the interest of Gorkhas living in Assam. Formation of the HSTF has come as a cause for worry. . . . Because there are atleast two armed Muslim fundamentalist outfits—the Muslim United Liberation Front of Assam (MULFA) and the comparatively new Muslim Liberation Tigers of Assam (MULTA) active around. . . . The MULFA and MULTA share objective of protecting Muslims, their religious place and property. But the MULTA additionally aims to secure 30 per cent reservation of jobs for the community and reservation of seats in the Assam Assembly for the Barak valley.

Also two armed ethnic groups which have been around for a while and have been steadily growing in stature are the Bengali Tiger Force (BTF) and Birsa Commando Force (BCF). The BTF works in tandem with the Bodo Liberation Tigers. The BCF seeks to protect the rights of the Adibasis. [*The Statesman*, 21st Jan., 1999].

In Arunachal Pradesh the Chakma and Hajong refugees are facing the wrath of the locals who want their eviction. "Anti-Chakma sentiments though simmering since 1972 when Arunachal was carved out as a separate state from Assam, gained in intensity with the rising Christian influence in the polity, according to observers. But the fact remains that the Arunachali opinion has been consistently in favour of the removal of the refugees who allegedly have been grabbing far more land than allotted to them as settlers and encroaching the forest. The souring of relationship with the locals apparently hardened the Arunachal Government's stance on the granting of citizenship to the Chakmas. The Centre on its part had been equally consistent in its stand that there was no question of removing the refugees from Arunachal Pradesh and that they would be granted citizenship" [*The Hindustan Times*, 28 Dec., 1995].

In Mizoram the "foreigners" are mainly Chakma tribals from Bangladesh and Chin tribals of Myanmar. Differences have been surfaced between the Centre and the Mizoram Government regarding the cut off date to determine the entry of aliens into the state. It was alleged that the Chukkas are trying to change the state's demographic pattern by a policy of gradual settlement across western Mizoram bordering Bangladesh [*The Statesman*, 26th Oct., 1999].

The activities of Bru (Reang) National Liberation Front are also a jolt to the peace process of Mizoram. Zoramthanga's (the Chief Minister) refusal to repatriate 40,000 Reang refugees living in Tripura camps since October, 1997, on the ground that they are not permanent settlers, has complicated the issue. No official explanation has been given as to what forced them to leave the

State. The fact Reangs constitute the second largest ethnic group in Tripura should serve to emphasise that if the refugees are not taken back the Mizoram-Tripura border will remain tense, a prospect neither side will relish [*The Statesman*, 16*th* Jan., 2000].

Another ethnic violence that has shaken the region is the Naga-Kuki rivalry. "Naga-Kuki rivalry dates back to 1845 when the British authorities had, after taking overwhelming control over the hills in the region stated using the fierce 'New Kuki' tribesmen against the Nagas to counter the latter depredations. The New Kukis were given rehabilitation by the British in the North Cachar hill region, apparently in a move on putting up a defence line against Naga hostiles" [*The Statesman*, 9th February, 1996].

In Tripura, Mizo-Reang conflict also caught our attention. The Mizos are known to have a traditional rivalry with the Reangs, generally employed as manual labourers in Jhum land by the better off Mizors. "Tripura's North Eastern fringe adjacent to Mizoram is dominated by a Mizo population of over 5,000. Besides them about 4,000 Reangs identified as the primitive tribes in Tripura live in the lower ridges. In December 1995, the Reang insurgents, belonging to the Tripura Resurrection Army (TRA) served quit notices asking many of the Mizos to pack up and leave the Jampui hills. Mizo owners of the orange plantations were asked by TRA to pay 'subscriptions' at rates ranging from a Rs. 30,000 up to 2,00,000 each. About 3,000 hectares of land is now under orange farming by the Mizos in 13 Jampui hamlets" [*The Statesman*, 9th February, 1996].

"Ethnic terrorism continues to devastate Tripura. Yet the long violence between tribals and non-tribals in the state is finally creating forms of resistance within the tribals themselves. This is only ground for hope in the face of civil society having come to a brutal standstill in the state. Ever since the indigenous People's Front of Tripura wrested control of Tripura Tribal Area Autonomous District Council in May, 2000, . . . the NLFT (the IPFT's militant wing) and the All Tripura Tiger Force have been ceaseless in their attacks on the non-tribal immigrants." The insurgents demand autonomy—expressed through massacres, arson, abduction, extortion and religious conflict—has resulted in a non-tribal backlash, the formation of the United Bengali Liberation Front. Hence, the familiar and seemingly unstoppable vicious circle. But the tribal Chakmas of Tuichakma village has been standing firm in their attempt to break this circle. They have unanimously organised a resistance movement" [*The Telegraph*, 21st November 2000].

"Non-Manipuris settled in Manipur have threatened to impose a "tax" on Manipuris settled outside the state to send a message to the underground "tax collectors" who extract huge sums from them every month . . . if the situation in the state for non-North Eastern does not improve, it (a Silchar-based group called North East Indian Democratic Organisation) would impose 'taxes' to the tune of Rs. one lakh per year for residing elsewhere in India" [*Hindustan Times*, 22nd March, 1999]. North East Indian Democratic Organisation has a good following among south Indian professionals who are forced by circumstance to live in the region, particularly the Tamilian population of Manipur, who have been residing in the state for generations, but have to increasingly pay to the "underground" to live on and conduct their profitable border trade. In Manipur there are 12 "invisible governments" who demand that non-Manipuries above three months of age pay up Rs. 100 per head annually as "immigrant permit fee". They are called "Mayangs" (foreigners) whose locus standi in Manipur is at the mercy of the "underground". Apart from threatening ordinary Manipuris residing in other parts of India. NEIDO has threatened to target children and relatives of known underground leaders, who are receiving education or doing business in other states.

In the recent past "people's anger at the extension of the ceasefire with NSCN(IM) (on June 14, the ceasefire was extended by another year from August 1, 2001) and to all Naga-dominated areas (the Naga inhabited areas outside Nagaland are Manipur, Arunachal Pradesh and Assam) in the Northeast erupted in Imphal in June, 2001 on a scale that was unprecedented even for a state like Manipur that has seen insurgency related violence for decades. Thousands of angry people burnt down the Assembly building, the Speaker's bungalow, the Chief Minister's secretariat and offices of the Congress(I), the MSCP, and the MPP. They were about to torch the Chief Minister's official residence when the security forces opened fire. Thirteen persons including five teenagers were killed. Manipuris have a deep-rooted fear that any political settlement with the NSCN, they will have to cede territory to a "Greater Nagaland" now called "Greater Nagalim" (There are four Naga-inhabited districts in Manipur: Ukrul, Chandel, Tamenglong and Senapati)" [*The Hindu*, 24th June 2001].

It is clear that peace has eluded the region now-a-days which is a matter of great concern to us. The presence of migrants in the region mostly contributed to such widespread unrest raising the powerful assimilationist and nativist sentiments and backlash separatist agitations. Such unrest in the region has resulted in alarming changes which not only has endangered the security of the region itself but also of the country as a whole by hindering the development of such strategically significant region of the country. As "the region is a beehive now of some 70 highly motivated insurgent organisations which have pinned down about 2,00,000 of our military and paramilitary troops engaged in counter intelligence, counter insurgency and counter terrorism" [*Statesman*, 20th May, 1998]. All prevailing terrorists activities tell upon the infrastructure framework of the country. For example, "in December 1996, the Brahmaputra Railway mail, which provide a vital link with the rest of India was damaged by the terrorists. A few years back the terrorists had destroyed oil pipelines, a highly essential component of the infrastructural framework of the region. As Bandyopadhyay and Chakraborty (1998) pointed out "the problem of security resulting from the migration to the region may be viewed from different angles. Firstly, there is the problem of a feeling of insecurity both among the local people as well as among the migrants. The local people feared that the migrants would overwhelm them because the migrants are better off now and give the local youth tuff competition in almost every sphere of life. The migrants, on the other hand, feel insecure in the region as they face an agitation against "foreigners". These pose a grave threat to their lives and livelihoods. Besides, their settlement in the region is itself uncertain, as there are differences between the Centre and the State governments regarding the cut-off date for the determination of the "foreigner" status. The migrants are, therefore, leading a risky life and faced different types of obstacles. It is also difficult for them to return to their native places to start their economic activities afresh."

Secondly, there is a problem of security for the country as a whole. The turbulent North Eastern region, an area bordering Myanmar, Bangladesh and Bhutan, is weakening the security of the country, which is loosing its valuable resources. Also, development works are being delayed because of the tension in the region. Further, it is alleged that the militants are taking shelter in the neighbouring countries to avoid the law of the country and also getting financial help from those countries. Also it was alleged that some foreign agencies are promoting illegal influx of Bangladesis to upset the demographic balance and thereby to disturb the stability of the region. As a result, India is facing strains in her relationship with neighbouring countries.

As it is commonly known that without peace and stability no region could move in proper path of development. The region is rich in valuable resources. But efficient utilisation of resources assumes prime importance in the context of development and accumulation of material wealth of the society or region. The region with its present situation has not enough successful in attracting investments as both domestic and foreign firms are reluctant to invest. "Added to this is the social opposition to development and the associated free flow of entrepreneurial talent and drive" [*Statesman*, 21st April, 1998].

The present situation in the region has hindered the people to enjoy the fruits of development. Unless the fruits of development percolate to the grassroots level no region can enjoy proper development. At present, most of the people still remains poor as Table 12.5 reveals that the proportion of the poor people in all most all states of the region except in the state of Mizoram is high in comparison to the all India average. Among the North Eastern states Assam has maximum and Mizoram has minimum proportion of people below the poverty line.

Table 12.5: Poverty Proportion of North Eastern States, 1999-2000

States	Poverty (Per cent)
Arunachal Pradesh	33.47
Assam	36.09
Manipur	28.54
Meghalaya	33.87
Mizoram	19.47
Nagaland	32.67
Tripura	34.44
All India	26.10

Source: Economic Survey 2001-2002.

The situation in the region that has arisen because of unrest in the region is very serious. It is popularly believed that a more developed infrastructure and industrialisation for the region wiping out militancy is going to be a Herculean task for the Central Government.

SECTION III

CONCLUSIONS

The situation in the region needs special attention. On January 22nd, 2000 the Prime Minister Mr. A.B. Vajpayee announced a Rs. 10.271 crore "Agenda for the Economic Development" for the North East and Sikkim, implying that two earlier packages of Rs. 6,100 crores and Rs. 7,000 crores—announced by two former Prime Ministers, Mr. H.D. Deve Gowda and Mr. I.K. Gujral, have been given the go-by . . . . Mr. Vajpayee also said that some projects in the new scheme were time-bound while others were not but efforts would be made to complete them in the shortest possible time. He said the North East Council (NEC) would be the nodal agency for implementing the schemes. However, monitoring the progress of work on different projects will be done by the Prime Minister's office (PMO) as the Prime Minister himself will oversee development and anti-insurgency exercises in the North East. On security-related expenditure (SRE), the Prime Minister assured that the Centre would further expand the list of items of expenditure incurred by the Police eligible for reimbursement. It would include 50 per cent cost of petrol, oil and lubricants. He also added that village guards, village defence committees and homeguards would be extended to Meghalaya and Arunachal Pradesh. Mr. Vajpayee also said the government would also sanction three Indian Reserve Battalions (IRBs), one each for Tripura, Mizoram and Manipur. With an estimated annual expense of Rs. 15 crores for three years, setting up of these battalions would cost Rs. 45 crores. Also he said it has been decided to fence the remaining portion of the Indo-Bangladesh border and construct border roads with a total outlay of Rs. 1,335 crores. He has promised to make the North East "as par if not ahead of other states".

Apparently, the problem of the region cannot be solved within a short period. Not only economic but also political solution is need of the hour. Because only economic packages cannot help to ease the situation. It is necessary to involve more and more local people in the peace-process as well as in development process. People's participation would accelerate both. Let the solution come from them. The confidence of the people should be winning back by reducing the severe unemployment to lift them above poverty line. Also Government should attempt to prevent further influx to the region. It should discuss with her neighbouring countries so that they also can cooperate in this regard.

REFERENCES

Agarwal, A.K. (1988), *North Eastern Economy Problems and Prospects*, Mittal Publication, Delhi.

Bandyopadhyay, S. and Chakraborty, D. (1995), "Inter District Migration in West Bengal 1971-81 Pattern and Causes: An Exploratory Study", *Demography India*, Vol. 24, No. 1, pp. 133-46.

Bandyopadhyay, S. and Chakraborty, D. (1998), "Migration to the North Eastern Region and the Problem of security", in Sanjukta Banerjee Bhattacharya and Rochana Das eds., *Perspective on India's Northeast BIBHASA*, Kolkata, pp. 94-116.

Barpujari, H.K. (1980), *Assam in the Days of Company (1826-1858)*, Gauhati.

Baruah, S. (1986), "Immigration Problem and Population Trend in Assam", in Dr. B. Datta Ray (ed.), *Pattern and Problems of Population in North East India*, Uppal Publishing House, New Delhi, pp. 201-07.

Bhattacharya, B. (1996), "Inter-districts Migration in Response to Disparities in Human Development—A Case Study of West Bengal", in Debjani Sarkar and Ajitava Roychoudhury (eds.), *Economy of West Bengal: Problems and Prospects*, Allied Publishers, pp. 281-99.

Bose, A. (1967), *Indian's Urbanisation, 1901-2001*, Institute of Economic Growth.

Census of India of different years.

Chakraborty, D. (1968), "Migration and Population Growth in West Bengal, 1951-1961", *Indian Demographic Bulletin*, 1(1).

Chakraborty, D. and Khasnobis, H. (1984), "Migration and Population Growth in Tamil Nadu during 1951-61", *Demography India*, Vol. 13, Nos. 1 and 2, pp. 133-40.

Chakraborty, D., Gupta, G., Bandyopadhyay, S. (1997), "Migration from Bangladesh to India during 1971-91: Its Magnitude and Causes", in Barun De and Ranabir Samaddar, (eds.), *State, Development and Political Culture: Bangladesh and India*, Har-Anand Publication, Delhi, pp. 266-79.

Choudhury, T.K. (1982), *Demographic Trend in Assam in 1921-71*, B.R. Publishing Corporation, Delhi.

Connell, J., Dasgupta, B., Laishley, R., Lipton, M. (1976), *Migration from Rural Areas: The Evidence from Village Studies*, Oxford University Press, Delhi, India.

Dasgupta, B. (1984), *Issues of Migration and Employment with Reference to Calcutta*, paper presented in the Conference in Problems of Development of Metropolitan Areas with Special reference to Calcutta, Organised by Centre for Urban Economic Studies, Dept. of Economics, Calcutta University.

Dass, S.K. (1980), "Immigration and Demographic Transformation of Assam, 1891-1981", *Economic and Political Weekly*, Vol. XV, No. 19, 1980, pp. 850-59.

Dey, C. and Chakroborty, D. (1994), "Migration in the Andaman and Nicobar Islands during 1901-1981: Trend and Pattern", *Demography India*, Vol. 23, No. 1 and 2, pp. 167-82.

Economic Survey 2001-2002, Government of India.

Goswami, A. and Gogoi, T.K. (1984), "Immigration and Demographic Transformation of Assam 1901-71", in Abbi, B.L., (ed.), *North East Region: Problem and Prospects of Development*, CRRID, Chandigarh.

Goswami, P.C. (1984), "Foreign Immigration into Assam", in Abbi, B.L., (ed.), *North East Region: Problem and Prospects of Development*, CRRID, Chandigarh.

Greenwood, M.J. and McDowell, J.M. (1991), "Differential Economic Opportunity, Transferability of Skills and Immigration to the United States and Canada", *The Review of Economic and Statistics*, Vol. LXXII, No. 4, pp. 612-23.

Guha, A. (1977), *Planter Raj to Swaraj: Freedom Struggle and Electoral Politics in Assam 1926-1947*, ICHR, New Delhi.

Guha, A. (1991), *Medieval and Early Colonial Assam: Society Polity Economy*, K.P. Bagchi and Co., Kolkata.

Guha Roy, S. and Dutta, P. (1995), "Nepali Migration to West Bengal", *Demography India*, Vol. 24, No. 2, pp. 211-23.

Gupta, A.K. and Arora, D.R., Agarwal, B.K. (1988), "Sociological Analysis of Migration of Agricultural Labourers from Eastern to North Eastern Region of India", *Indian Journal of Industrial Relations*, Vol. 23, No. 4, pp. 429-45.

Mahalingam, N. (1964), "India's Population Problem and Internal Migration", *Population Review*, July.

Mitra, A. (1967), *Internal Migration and Urbanisation in India*, Report submitted to the meeting of expert group of problem on internal migration and urbanisation in Bangkok, ECAFE.

Nair, P.S. (1985), *Inter State Period Migration in India 1971-81: Levels and Flows* (Mimeo), IASP.

Narayana, M.R. (1990), "Market Equilibrium in a Two Region Federal Economy: Alternative Theoretical Formulation and Empirical Implication", *Journal of Quantitative Economics*, pp. 93-114.

Narayana, M.R. (1994), "Continuity of Inter-regional Migration of Workers in India: A Spatio Temporal Analysis", *Demography India*, Vol. 23, Nos. 1 and 2, pp. 183-202.

Oberai, A.S. and Singh, H.K.M. (1982), "Migration, Production and Technology in Agriculture: A Case Study in the Indian Punjab", *International Labour Review*, 121(3).

Pathak, L.P. (1986), "East Bengal Immigration in Assam Valley—An Analysis of Census Data", in Dr. B. Dutta Ray (ed.), *Pattern and Problems of Population in North East India*, Uppal Publishing House, New Delhi, pp. 89-126.

Piplai, T. and Majumdar, N. (1969), "Some Socio-Economic Implications", *Sankhya Service Series*, B 31.

Pravakar, N.R. (1986), *Internal Migration and Population Redistribution in India: Some Reflection*, Concept Publishing Company, New Delhi.

Premi, M.K. (1980), "Aspects of Female Migration in India", *Economic and Political Weekly*, 15(15).

Premi, M.K. (1989), "Pattern of Internal Migration in India" in Singh, Premi, Bhatia and Bose (eds.), *Population Transition in India*, B.R. Publishing Corporation.

Rele, J.R. (1969), "Trends and Significance of Internal Migration in India", *Sankhya*, B-31 (3-4).

Rustomji, N. (1983), *Imperiled Frontiers (India's North East Border Land)*, Oxford University Press, Oxford.

Saikia, P.D. (1986), "Immigration into the Tribal Areas of North East Region of India" in Dr. B. Duttaroy (ed.), *Pattern and Problems of Population in North East India*, Uppal Publishing House, New Delhi, pp. 239-49.

Sarin, V.I.K. (1980), *India's North East in Flames*, Vikas Publishing House, New Delhi.

Sarkar, P. (1989), "Determinants of Rural-Urban Migration in West Bengal" in B. Dasgupta (ed.), *Urbanisation, Migration and Rural Change—A Study of West Bengal.*

Saxena, D.P. (1977), *Rural Urban Migration in India: Causes and Consequences*, Popular Prakasan, Mumbai.

Sebestian, A. (1986), "Migrants in North Eastern Region of India", in Dr. B. Duttaroy (ed.), *Pattern and Problems of Population in North East India*, Uppal Publishing House, New Delhi, pp. 63-88.

Sekhar, T.V. (1993), "Migration Selectivity from Rural Areas Evidence from Kerala", *Demography India*, Vol. 22, No. 2, pp. 191-202.

Selvaraj, K.G. and Rao, P.S.S. (1993), "Household Migration—Urbanisation and Consequences", *Demography India*, Vol. 22, No. 2, pp. 203-10.

Sharma, K.M. (1980), "The Assam Question: A Historical Perspective", *Economic and Political Weekly*, Vol. XV, No. 31.

Singh, D.P. (1998), "Internal Migration in India: 1961-1991", *Demography India*, Vol. 27, No. 1, pp. 245-61.

Sivamurthy, M. and Kadi, A.S. (1983), "Inter-State Migration in India: 1961-71", *Demography India*, Vol. 12, No. 2, pp. 239-58.

The Hindustan Times, 28th December 1995, New Delhi

The Hindustan Times, 22nd March 1999, New Delhi.

The Statesman, 21st January 1999, Kolkata.

The Statesman, 26st October 1999, Kolkata.

The Statesman, 28th December 1995, Kolkata.

The Statesman, 9th February 1996, Kolkata.

The Statesman, 21st April 1998, Kolkata.

The Statesman, 20th May 1998, Kolkata.

The Telegraph, 21st November 2000, Kolkata.

Weirner, M. (1978), *Sons of the Soil, Migration and Ethnic Conflict in India*, Princeton University Press.

Xexa, V. (1983), *Tribal Migration to Plantation Estates in North East India: Determines and Consequences* (Mimeo), IASP.

13

DEVELOPMENT ISSUES AND SECURITY CONCERNS
The Search Within

GORKY CHAKRABORTY

Introduction

Security and development are mutually supportive where a lack of either 'one' accentuates the problem for the 'other'. However, in the present era of neo-liberal globalisation it seems that both these concepts stand in antagonistic juxtaposition.[1] Development has become synonymous for well-being of selected global elites whereas security is nothing but securing the right of these elites and their 'brands' in the global market. It is, therefore, but obvious that both these concepts in the present context seems to have a *Janus* face—one reflecting the interpretation of the state which today more or less acts as a protector of global capital and is, therefore, dominant on all accounts, and another the undercurrent of passive poignant perception of the people. In these circumstances both security and development falls far short of their respective ideals leading to added schism and contradiction between the state and its collaborators on one hand and the masses on the other. This lack of (re)conciliation among the two points of view provides ample space for 'others' to eploit for their own purpose ultimately balkanizing the situation for worse. The development and security scenario of India's North East is no different from the above mentioned formulation.

Security as the term goes in multi-dimensional and multi-disciplinary in nature and therefore, open to various interpretations. But the 'sense of security' is not very easy to define due to its normative connotation. However, it may be safely said that the process and character of distribution of the 'fruits' of development among various groups influences the 'sense of security' to a great extent. This is more so in a country of hundred million with nearly 50 per cent illiterate, roughly 1/3rd of the population living below the state determined poverty line, out of 20 core children in the age group of 6 to 14 years, 5 crore 90 lakhs never visit any school, where at least 1 lakh human settlements have no educational institution within a radius of 1 km—at this backdrop when one attempts to understand the security scenario in the country as a whole or any specific region like the North East the investigator has ample reason to growingly become convinced that the perceived security for the state and for various population groups having differential access to the 'fruits' of development need not always be one and the same. When the politico-legal structure of the state is perceived to have failed to ensure the desired level of reward and protection, the concerned people's security perception may need not necessarily tally with that of the state for which security is basically uninterrupted continuation of its structure. Similar is the case with development, where the conflicting interest of the agencies of development and that of the perceived beneficiaries are manifested in various so-called development projects around the world, e.g., building of dams, power stations, allowing the use of genetically modified seeds, access to forest and its produce etc.

Schism generated due to divergence of views among the people and the state concerning security and development[2] has another dimension, namely internal and external contradictions. In case of security of the state the external contradiction is given more importance *vis-a-vis* the internal one.[3] The internal contradictions emanating from various sources, e.g., faulty distributive justice, lack of proper opportunity and representation of particular population groups(s) for accommodation and assimilation in the mainstream, change in character of the state etc. are often dealt at the level of law and order problem. The state and its functionaries often deal internal contradictions in a historical space without understanding the socio-economic realities and historical continuities. This faulty understanding process often marks certain population groups either linguistic, religious or ethnic with doubtful integrity who often are further labelled as unpatriotic and anti-national. Thus overemphasising upon the external threats and contradictions (without of course denying that these are serious threats) and equally neglecting the internal contradictions (which of course enumerates from the malfunctioning of the state apparatus) leads to a hiatus in security perception among the state and its people. Movements for assertion of identity and space of several population groups are often labelled as handiworks of agents of external powers unfriendly to the state, often aggravates the situation in the long run. The existential reality of India's North East is no different from the above mentioned framework.

The *Char* Issue

In any discourse whether public or private in India's north east, terms like non-indigenous, immigrant, migrant, outsiders and foreigners are commonly used and frequently misused. It often leads to mistrust and misconception among various population groups in this region resulting in loss of life, livelihood and property. However viewed from the macro perspective each population group in North East is a minority and only a handful of them can wear the badge of indigenous identity.[4] Without entrapping oneself in the 'indigenous-foreigner' debate it can be safely concluded that until all the population groups spread over different geographical locations of this region are included in the development process neither will there be security nor will there be development which is sustainable in nature. Exclusion either intentional or accidental of any population group from the development process will enhance the internal contradictions which when pampered by external agencies will generate security concerns for the region. Reconciliation and resolution of these contradiction are, therefore, essential for security and development of the nation state as a whole.

Much has been investigated by various scholars about the story of various struggling groups of North East and how their frustration out of their perceived sense of insecurity has been utilised by unfriendly external forces to cause security threat for the state. However one of the largest population groups of North East, who were encouraged to leave their motherland and to migrate to the Assam valley in order to convert the barren lands into a granary ensuring food and related items of life to the growing population of Assam in the initial phase of British consolidation, somehow missed the attention of the scholars so far. Their sacrifice, their contribution, their occasional frustration have of course been noticed yet the real depth of their frustration and this frustration to infuse in them a real sense of insecurity under the present state arrangement and its potentiality to cause security threat to the state in turn has not yet been noticed at the level that should have shouldered the responsibilities. An attempt is being made in this paper to understand the *char* dwellers of Assam in their historical continuity, their contribution towards the economy, their schisms and contradictions over a period of 100 years in the state. The paper deals with their existential reality by analysing their socio-economic conditions. The internal contradictions which arises due to the failure of policies and unaccommodative nature of the state may force the *char* dwellers towards an assertive movement which considering the vacillating secular character of the state and the geo-political situation can easily be labelled as anti-national by the state and its dominant partners. An insight is, therefore, necessary to understand and analyse the ground realities meaningfully.

The *Char* Dwellers

This section deals with various issues concerning the *char* dwellers in its historical continuity—their advent, their contribution towards the state's economy, the socio-politico-cultural schisms due to their migration, the debate over their linguistic identity etc.

Detailed exposition of the *char* dwellers are scanty and scattered in various secondary sources (mainly in vernacular languages) and therefore, a judicious attempt is made in this section to place and analyse them within a particular framework.

The Advent of the *Char* Dwellers

The Britishers consolidated their grip over India's north east in seven eventful decades starting from 1826 to the first decade of the 20th century. With the Treaty of Yandaboo in 1826, Assam Plains came under British administration and thereafter Cachar in 1830, Khasi Hills in 1833, Jayantia Plains in 1835, Karbi Anglong in 1838, North Cachar Hills in 1854, Naga Hills in 1866-1905, Garo Hills in 1872-73, NEFA in 1875 and Lushai Hills during 1890.[5] This pattern of political consolidation necessitated revenue consolidation and various attempts were made to implement the process. During the initial phase revenue consolidation was attempted by means of geographical reorganisation which when failed to generate desired results was then attempted through migration. Various areas in north east including Assam has been a part of this British experimentation.

The colonial administrators have experimented with the geographical boundaries of Assam since February 6th, 1874 when Assam was separated from Bengal and turned into Chief Commissioner's Province along with Cachar, Goalpara, Garo Hills and other Hill districts. But the new province was vast in terms of geographical area but small in terms of population (2,443 thousand) and meagre in terms of revenue potential. In order to rectify it Sylhet was incorporated into Assam in September 1874.[6] There were several other attempts[7] of this sort in the name of revenue consolidation.

When the above mentioned attempt of geographical reorganisation failed to generate desired revenue potential the colonial administrators stressed upon the option of human habitation through migration into those particular sectors which had enough potential for revenue generation. This process started with tea plantation when during 1858-59, the first batch of 400 labourers were brought to Cachar from Banaras, Ghazipore, Chota Nagpur and Bihar to serve the emerging plantation sector.[8] When this process of encouraging migration to the plantation sector met with success, the Britishers attempted the same in the agricultural sector where hard working skilled peasants and farm labourers from the erstwhile districts of East Bengal were encouraged to migrate into Assam and turn it into a granary to serve the food requirements of the state and its emerging sectors. The issue of revenue generation was, of course, an inseparable part of the entire process.

Preliminary evidence regarding British encouragement for settlement of farm labourers in Assam has been evident from various colonial reports. Starting from Mr. Francis Jenkins, Mr. Jonson, Col. Hopkins, Mr. Northbrook, Mr. E.A. Gait and various colonial administrators put forward number of plans and proposals for encouraging the migration of farm labourers from East Bengal into Assam.[9] These attempts were equally supported by the emerging elites of the Assam middle class.[10] Nevertheless till 1901, there were no instances of large scale migration of farm labourers from East Bengal to Assam. Out of the 7,66,000 number of foreigners in the province nearly 83 per cent (6,45,000) were in ten gardens and of the remaining 17 per cent, the number of farm settlers were insignificant.[11]

The situation changed after the Partition of Bengal (1903-05) due to which Assam and East Bengal became one single entity thereby making transfer of population easy and also natural. The Census Report of 1911[12] for the first time mentioned the movement of migrants from East Bengal to wastelands of Assam. These settlers came from the districts of Mymensingh, Bogra, Rangpur, Pabna to uninhabited areas, wastelands including *char* areas of Goalpara district. During 1904 to 1911, there were 54,000 migrants from East Bengal to Assam out of which 51,000 settled in Goalpara alone. The population of Goalpara which increased by 2 per cent during 1891-1901, increased by 30 per cent during 1901-1911 due to migration of these labourers from East Bengal.[13] After 1911, these people along with new batches of migrants moved beyond Goalpara to other parts of the Brahmaputra region as well. In 1921, peasants from East Bengal numbered around 3 lakhs which increased to 5 lakh 75 thousand in 1931[14] and now their presence was fell in the districts of Nowgaon, Kamrup, Darrang, Sibsagar and Lakhimpur also.

About 85 to 90 per cent of these migrants from East Bengal comprised of Muslims. Although there has been a substantial Muslim population[15] in Assam prior to this referred wave of migration yet the demographic pattern changed in the state particularly due to the latest wave. So what Prof. Guha[16] describes as a demographic change due to a (i) shift in ethnic composition of the population and (ii) change in its spatial dimension over the districts was added by another trait, namely religious diversification. The human habitation of the *char* areas started during this process when the cultivators settled in these uninhabited and inhospitable areas leaving their motherland for good.

Contribution of the *Char* Dwellers

Due to the existence of several factors[17] agriculture in Assam remained backward. Whatever agricultural production was there proved to be insufficient (mainly in terms of food grains) and the state had to depend on import from various sources. The agricultural sector and the rural economy during pre and early colonial era was such that it did not encourage cultivators to produce more by reclaiming uncultivated land. So Assam remained a food grain deficit state unable to feed its local population. This deficit increased further when there was large scale migration of labour in emerging sectors, namely tea, oil, coal, railways, inland waterways etc. The annual import of food grains into the valley increased from 0.3 million *maunds* around 1872 to 0.7 million *maunds* during the last five years of the 19th century.[18] The colonial administrators, therefore, desperately wanted to increase the local food grain production to a particular level which could meet the requirements of the local population and of those engaged in the emerging sectors.

The traditionally skilled and hard working peasants from several districts of erstwhile East Bengal[19] happened to be the harbinger of hope and prosperity for the food deficit state of Assam. Their migration and settlement as has been stated in the earlier section brought about unprecedented change in agriculture in the state. These migrants cleared jungles and opted for cultivation and habitation in far-flung inhospitable areas which were beyond the thought of local farmers. They revolutionised agriculture by giving it a commercial character and introduced new crops, increased crop intensity and enhanced yield several times by introducing superior techniques of production. During 1921-31, these migrants brought 5,42,000 acre of uncultivated land and added another 2,51,000 acre during 1931-41.[20] Along with jute various crops such as buck wheat, *moong*, sesame, linseed, mustard, wheat, tobacco, chilli, ginger, turmeric, potato, sweet potato, cabbage, cauliflower, radish, tomato, onion, garlic, brinjal, corriander and various spices and condiment were cultivated in a commercial scale for the first time in Assam.[21] Even today those districts which has large number of settlement of migrant peasants from East Bengal produces the above commodities in huge quantities. Moreover, these farmers could mix various crop varieties in a season for maximum yield and diversify production, e.g., mustard and *masur* is mixed with *dhania, tishi* is mixed with *dhania* and/or *masur*, wheat is mixed with *masur*[22] etc. They also introduced the cultivation of *son khetl*[23] which when cultivated in between two seasons enhances the productivity of land (nitrogenous fertilizer) and the bush is used for feeding the livestocks.

The single largest contribution of these peasants towards revenue generation has been the large scale production of jute cultivation in the Brahmaputra valley. Jute cultivation was almost unknown in Assam and it was in the later half of the 19th century that they introduced jute cultivation in Goalpara district. During 1902-03, jute was cultivated in 25,850 acres out of which 25,000 acres were in Goalpara district alone.[24] It got spread to different areas of Assam particularly Nowgaon with the settlement of these migrant population. With the rise in Muslim population in Nowgaon from 4 per cent to 40 per cent during 1901-51, jute cultivation increased from 879 hactares to 86,245 hactares[25] accordingly. It was similar for the entire Brahmaputra region. Indian Jute happened to be the major revenue earner[26] for Assam during the late colonial phase and early independent period and till today the state is one of the leading producers of Jute in India.

Thus these migrant peasants brought about the much needed relief to the agricultural sector of Assam. They not only brought large tracts of uncultivated land under plough but also introduced new varieties of crops and techniques of production thereby increasing food grain production and revenue generation for the state and its various organisations.

The Schism

The Assamese elites pleaded for migration of farm labourers from East Bengal and supported the colonial scheme to a great extent. The migrants with due encouragement from the Britishers started cultivation in uncultivated, forest, marshy and *char* areas. Their settlements were uninhabited areas and so the local population remained either apathetic or indifferent towards them. Gradually things started to change as ever increasing waves of migrants started pushing for extra cultivable land in *kayam* or mainland areas and settled either near or in those areas where the local population resided. The sudden demographic change, settlement patterns and ever increasing craze for new cultivable land on the part of the migrants disturbed the then existing socio-cultural and economic dynamics of the state which was skilfully exploited by the colonial administrators and local political gentry for serving their respective purposes. The local population feared about the loss of their identity in their own state and asserted for various rights which included curtailment of rights for the migrants whereas the migrants wanted more land for cultivation. This resulted in schism and strife at various levels of the civil society and got reflected in the political arena.

The Britishers had to serve both the population groups for maintaining their colonial power. They encouraged migration in order to enhance the process of revenue generation in the state and on the other hand posed themselves as the custodian and saviour of the identity of the local population. The Line System introduced in Nowgaon and then implemented in other parts of the state camouflaged both the purposes skilfully. According to this plan there were three lines of habitation. The first known as 'Immigrant's Line' where only the immigrants (read migrants) could settle; secondly, the 'Assamese Line' where only the indigenous Assamese could settle; and thirdly, the 'Mixed Line' where both the groups could co-habit together. In reality, however, the line system did not restrict the flow of farm labourers from East Bengal but only demarcated their areas of livelihood and habitation. It created an artificial distance between the migrants and the locals and the later population groups was assured of protection and identify from the ever increasing migrant population.

In the oft quoted Census Report of 1931[27] Mr. Mullan serves the above mentioned proposition by speaking in two different voices at the same point of time. On the one hand he raises the alarm bells for the local Assamese speaking Hindu population regarding the threat to their identity due to large scale migration from East Bengal. . . "where there is waste land thither flock the Mymensinghias. In fact the way in which they have seized upon the vacant area in Assam Valley seems almost uncanny. Without fuss, without tumult, without undue trouble to the district revenue staff, a population which must amount to over half a million has transplanted itself from Bengal to the Assam Valley during the last twenty-five years". He continued in a war tone that they have. . ."Almost completed the conquest of Nowgaon. The Bapeta sub-division of Kamrup has also fallen to their attack and Darrang is being invaded. Sibsagar has so far escaped completely, the few thousand Mymensinghias in North Lakhimpur are an outpost which may, during the next decade, prove to be vulnerable basis of operation." On the other hand in the same report he was full of praise for the skilful and industrious farm labourers of East Bengal. . . . "These people have brought in their wake wealth, industry and general prosperity to the whole district. Their industry as agriculturalist have become almost proverbial. Their love and care of cattle is also an object lesson to others. Government revenue has increased. The local Assamese at first did not like the advent of these people in their midst but gradually as they came to see their better sides, their industry, their knowledge of agriculture, their contribution to general prosperity of the district—their prejudice and dislikes are beginning to disappear." All the above utterances of Mr. Mullan were read, re-read and misread by various organisations and political parties according to their foresight, necessity and above all their respective constituencies.

The entire political scene revolved around two particular issues[28]—the perceived loss of identity, culture and religion of the Assamese speaking Hindu population and the movement for withdrawal of line system and release of more land for cultivation on the part of migrant Muslim cultivators. Ambikagiri Roy Choudhury represented the former perception and related movement while Maulana Abdul Hamid Khan Bhasani represented and led the later issues and people concerned with it. The question of more land for cultivation by an ever-swelling and over-enthusiastic migrant cultivators was the real issue where the perceived threat of loss of identity got tagged with and the entire movement got sharply divided into two camps in terms of religion. Congress Party vaccilated between these two extremes or camps according to its political requirements but often took up the 'identity crisis' notion on the part of those groups representing the agenda of threat perception during the course of 1940s. With the enactment of Foreigner's Act, 1946, the situation became worse. Repression on the part of the state machinery increased and the brunt of that repression had to be borne by the migrated peasants from East Bengal in the name of identifying foreigners. Simultaneously, during 1941, the demand for Pakistan gained momentum and Bhasani led lakhs of migrant peasants in his support for the withdrawal of line system under the banner of Muslim League. It was basically an agrarian protest for more land in the guise of certain religious paraphrases. Due to linguistic and religious affinity of the peasants with that of Muslim League and failure on the part of Congress to provide these migrant peasants with a genuine platform and plan for their welfare, they rallied with Muslim League who took up their cause along with the demand for creation of Pakistan.

The situation became worse during the *Bongal Kheda* agitation during 1945-46 when the *Jatiyo Mahasabha* led agitation with the tacit support of the government unleashed a reign of terror in all the migrant settlement areas of Barpeta, Mongoldoi, Gauhati, Goalpara and various other places in the state resulting in extensive damage both to life and property of the migrant settlers. Independence in 1947 ended that particular form of repression with large scale migration on both sides of the border resulting bifurcation and creation of two new nations. Nevertheless this bifurcated freedom could not settle the issues concerning the *char* dwellers of Assam and till date they live with several derogatory tags attached to their heads resulting in schism, strife and discord.

The Language Question

Language certainly is one of the major element determining both nationality and ethnicity of various population groups around the world. It is an inseparable part of the entire construct and overall identity formation. This becomes more apparent when we consider the case of mother tongue. Through mother tongue people not only honour themselves and fellow speakers but also rally around for various assertive movements. "... In its mother tongue every people honours itself, in the treasury of its speech is contained the charter of its cultural history. For the peoples without history, history and language were two sides of the same coin. The vernacular was not merely the highboard to history, it was itself the voice of years that are gone. ..."[29] Mother tongue is, therefore, always sacred and a mysterious vehicle of all endeavours concerning its speakers. It is thus an inseparable part of the soul.

Linguists and scholars of language has undoubtedly placed an overwhelming emphasis on mother tongue as a symbol of identity but this particular issue of mother tongue has always been a bone of contention for the *char* dwellers of Assam. Their language or mother tongue has been Bengali (in its various dialects depending upon the district and habitation from where they migrated). They migrated, and settled here using the same language. However, with changing political scenario they decided to change their mother tongue in the census declaration as Assamese to prove their loyalty to the state. It was undoubtly a farsighted decision considering the changed realities of the subcontinent and also the easiest way out for proving their assimilation with Assam where the pivot quizically revolved around the Assam-Assamese-Assimilation axis.[30]

The changed census declaration in favour of Assamese as their mother tongue on the part of the *char* dwellers enabled Assamese to be the state language of Assam. The number of Assamese speaking people increased from 31.4 per cent in 1931 to 56.7 per cent during 1951 while there has been a striking decrease in the percentage of Bengali speaking people during the same period.[31] Without getting entrapped in the 'coercion-spontaneous' debate regarding language declaration on the part of the *char* dwellers it can be easily termed as a significant decision with a clear perview of the emerging future of Assam. This has been termed as revolutionary by Prof. Guha who nevertheless also cited that during partition as Muslim League offices changed into Congress offices overnight so did Bengali medium schools change into Assamese medium institutions. He poignantly pointed that minority at both fronts—namely religion and language, would have been unwise and, therefore, they might have opted to change their language in the census declarations.

All the educational institutions in the *char* areas impart education in Assamese language till date. Interestingly those who thought, fought and rebelled against the *char* dwellers since they had perceived threat perception regarding loss of their culture, language and identity have shown an uncanny knack and craze for English medium (instead of Assamese medium), the language of Mr. Mullan. The *Char* dwellers or at least their representatives stood for the Official Language Bill in 1960 and for Assamese as a medium of instruction during the movements of 1970s. However, in spite of undue loyalty to the state and its official language time and again, their status has been once again questioned during the Assam Agitation or Anti-Foreigners Agitation (1979-85) and the same spectre of fear, agony, uncertainty, disrespect and conspiracy haunt them today as they used to during the pre-partition days.

The Existential Reality

The preceding section has dealt with extensively about the advent, contribution, schism and socio-political realities concerning the life of the *char* dwellers in its historical continuity. It is certainly an exposition of displacement, toil, suffering as well as contribution, innovation and ultimate triumph of human spirit, grit and determination against several odds. Somehow the moot question which needs to be dealt now is regarding their current socio-economic status. How has the development process benefited them? Where do they stand today *vis-a-vis* other population groups in mainland? A look into various statistics will highlight the reality of the *char* dwellers.

Table 13.1: Number of *Chars* in Different Districts of Assam

Sl.No.	Districts	Char Villages	Districtwise Population of these Char Villages
1.	Darrang	121	1,35,876
2.	Barpeta	351	2,75,525
3.	Kamrup	148	1,05,687
4.	Nalbari	58	62,892
5.	Bongaigaon	150	1,10,215
6.	Goalpara	187	1,30,007
7.	Dhubri	313	2,33,206
8.	Morigaon	41	55,581
9.	Nowgaon	29	45,161
10.	Dhemaji	95	68,998
11.	Lakhimpur	182	1,10,200
12.	Sonitpur	118	92,061
13.	Tinsukia	86	33,034
14.	Jorhat	210	1,41,901
	Total	2,089	16,00,244

Source: *Socio-Economic Survey Report*, Directorate of Char Areas Development, Assam, 1992-93.

The *chars* with their unique geo-morphology are spread over 14 districts of Assam, starting from Sadiya and stretching up to

Dhubri. According to the Char Area Development Authority there are 2,089 *char* villages in Assam with a total population of 25 lakhs[32] or about 10 per cent of the total population of the state. More than 85 per cent of these *chars* are inhabited by migrant peasants from the earstwhile districts of East Bengal. In terms of population *chars* of Barpeta district has the highest numbers while in terms of land area Dhubri district has the maximum area. Total *char* area in Assam is estimated as 2.39 lakh hectares out of which 1.69 lakh hectares is suitable for agriculture. In other words although the *char* areas hold 9.37 per cent of its agricultural land yet has 4.30 per cent of its agricultural land. This gives an estimate about the pressure of population on agriculture in these areas.

Pressure on land and habitation is also high in *char* areas. Density of population for the state happens to be 3 persons per hectare whereas in the *char* areas it is as high as 9 persons per hectare. Land ownership in the *char* areas are extremely skewed and 10 per cent of the population own about 80 per cent of land. About 30 per cent of the population are landless and the rest are small and marginal farmers. The skewed pattern of land ownership is reflected in social terms too and a rampant feudal relation prevails where a few rule the roost and hold the sway over the impoverished landless masses.

The *char* dwellers undoubtedly revolutionised agricultural practices in Assam. By dint of their traditional skill and hard work they cultivated in those areas which were not only inhospitable and uncultivable but inacessable too. This process of practising advanced agriculture is continuing till today and a visit to any *char* will bear its testimony. However due to number of social, economic, political and institutional factors (despite they being the actual producers) half of the *char* dwellers are below the official poverty line. Table 13.2, depicts this tragic feature of our development model.

Literacy status of a particular region or population group is one of the glaring indication of the level of human development of the concerned group. It is also a reflection of its socio-cultural reality. Unfortunately the *char* areas of Assam presents with despicable literacy figures. The overall rate of literacy is 15.45

per cent where Nalbari, Goalpara, Morigaon and Nowgaon has a literacy rate which is even below the double digit mark.

Table 13.2: Population below the Poverty Line in Char Areas

Sl.No.	District	Population Below Poverty Line	% of Population Below Poverty Line
1.	Darrang	74,732	55.0
2.	Barpeta	1,51,538	55.0
3.	Bongaigaon	59,516	54.0
4.	Dhubri	1,26,398	54.2
5.	Kamrup	56,014	53.0
6.	Nalbari	34,087	54.2
7.	Jorhat	35,475	25.0
8.	Morigaon	29,110	52.5
9.	Nowgaon	71,503	55.0
10.	Goalpara	24,993	53.2
11.	Dhemaji	32,244	46.8
12.	Sonitpur	39,586	43.0
13.	Lakhimpur	53,998	49.0
14.	Dibrugarh	11,397	34.5

Source: Socio-Economic Survey Report, Directorate of Char Areas Development, Assam, 1992-93.

Table 13.3: Literary Status of the *Char* Areas in Assam

Sl.No.	Districts	Char Villages	Literacy (%)
1.	Darrang	121	10.12
2.	Barpeta	351	12.90
3.	Kamrup	148	16.85
4.	Nalbari	58	7.90
5.	Bongaigaon	150	12.85
6.	Goalpara	187	8.38
7.	Dhubri	313	19.06
8.	Morigaon	41	8.02
9.	Nowgaon	29	9.44
10.	Dhemaji	95	14.44
11.	Lakhimpur	182	14.01
12.	Sonitpur	118	12.63
13.	Tinsukia	86	14.20
14.	Jorhat	210	31.90
	Total	2,089	15.45

Source: Socio-Economic Survey Report, Directorate of Char Areas Development, Assam, 1992-93.

The existential reality of the *char* dwellers, therefore, raises several doubts and question marks regarding our development process. Is this development model worth continuing where the actual producers are relegated to filthy surroundings and poverty stricken status whereas the brokers of development enjoy the fruits of lopsided growth without contributing meaningfully to the production process.

The Search Within

Today when we look at the internal scenario concerning the population groups of North East we essentially come to a point of no return, involving a sense of deprivation spreading like bon-fire, engulfing the population groups in the hills and the plains, in the valleys and in the not so permanent sandbars which we generally call *chars*. This observation is true for Mizoram, Manipur, Tripura, Nagaland, Arunachal, Meghalaya and Assam too. The immediate reason cited by various groups may vary but inherently they reflect a sense of insecurity for the present and the emerging future under the present state structure and the arrangements made by the same.

The socio-economic status, the cultural dilemma, the issue over language and identity as presented in the earlier sections of this paper amply suggest that this population group—the *char* dwellers, suffer from the same sense of insecurity like other population groups in the region. Their existential reality may, therefore, compel them to organise themselves and asset for their identity and rights in the emerging future. Such movements for political 'space', 'identity' and 'assertion' may easily be misrepresented (or deliberately misquoted) by state and its agencies as anti-national, fundamentalist and secessionist since the *char* dwellers represent a religious faith (Islam) which is different from the religious majority (Hindus) in India, the geo-political situation in the South East Asia (particularly in Bangladesh) and the recent rightward shift and questionable secular (?) character of the state.

Under these circumstances the internal contradictions emanating from the structure of the Indian state will be deliberately kept aside and the external contradictions highlighted upon. But for any serious observer, internal contradiction happens to be the principal contradiction which can either be accentuated or resolved[33] by the external forces. Overemphasis on external forces (of course, without ignoring the external threat perception) may make us blind towards the root cause, i.e., the internal schisms and contradiction which may ultimately balkanize the region.

From the analysis in the paper it seems that the goodness and loyalty of the *char* dwellers has been stretched to its maximum limits. They left their motherland for good and even sacrificed their mother tongue in their census declaration to prove their loyalty to the state and to the concept of integration and to the enrichment of their adopted society—the Assamese. But the negligence, the deprivation and the darkness thrust on them may one day ignite the latent force of protest and change the entire course of history in Assam and jeopardise both security and development of India's North East. The sooner we are ready to acknowledge the reality and act accordingly—the better.

NOTES

1. What is said about security and development in the paper is also reflected by David Washbrook while explaining the linkage between democracy and development. "Democracy and development, which ought to be mutually supportive, stand today in sharp and antagonistic juxtaposition". . . . For details see Washbrook, David, "The Rhetoric of Democracy and Development in the Late Colonial India", in Bose, Sugata and Jalal, Ayesha, (eds.), *Nationalism, Democracy and Development: State and Politics in India* (New Delhi: Oxford University Press, 1999).
2. There are number of works by various eminent scholars and activists challenging the present development model enacted by several developed and developing countries either in tandem with Fund-Bank institutions or independently on their own. However for a lucid analysis and exposition of the Indian development model since independence see Roy, Arundhati, *The Greater Common Good* (Mumbai: Indian Book Distributors, 1999).
3. As internal and external contradictions and threats are both equally important from the security point of view yet it is usually the external threats which is always overemphasised and highlighted by the state

authorities while turning a blind eye to internal contradictions. Even the *Group of Ministers Report* titled "Reforming the Security System" submitted to the Central Government in February 2001 deals internal security as a law and order problem, wherein all problems are reduced to their physical manifestations in militancy or even terrorism and where almost all recommendations are oriented towards reforming and improving the performance of the police and para-military organisations or towards arming the state with draconian legislation. The problem with J&K, the North East and others are all dealt with as chiefly externally-inspired and supported militant or terrorist insurgencies. Other than military solutions to these internal strifes it argues for strengthening various constitutional provisions, namely Articles 256, 257, 352, 355 and 359 to say the least. . . . The Report is completely silent about the inherent weakness of the Indian States which enhances internal contradictions leading to strife, discord and insurgency.

4. Prof. Roy Burman has considered the question of foreigner and indigenous keeping in view several parameters, namely "(i) time frame of migration and settlement, (ii) time frame of recognition of citizen with reference to state institution, (iii) historical context of migration or settlement, (iv) demographic structure of the population of the host area and of migrants, (v) role of migrants or settlers in the politico-economic and socio-cultural processes of the host area, (vi) nature of development activities, (vii) nature of link that the migrants or the settlers are having with the area of origin, (viii) geo-cultural area with deeper structural mutuality cutting across state political boundaries, (ix) wider geo-political context and short, medium and long term processes." Similarly the term indigenous has also been discussed by Prof. Roy Burman, "Broadly, I use the term indigenous people in the phenomenological sense of being close to earth, being non-alienated from (rather being in harmony with) the surroundings, its constituents being bound together primarily by ontologically as well as historically crystallised moral binding (rather than the coercive power of the state), absence or minimal presence of a crystallised elite sector usurping the role of community as a whole in the matter of perception, interpretation, elaboration, reformulation, legitimisation of essential elements of its culture. These features according to me represent the ideal type of indigenous people." For further details see 'Interview with Professor B.K. Roy Burman' in Datta, P.S., *North East As I See It* (New Delhi: Omsons Publications, 1994).
5. Datta, P.S., "Karbi-Dimasa Autonomy Movements", in Datta, P.S. (ed.), *Ethnic Movements in Poly-Cultural Assam* (New Delhi: Vikas Publishing House, 1990).
6. Guha, Amalendu, *Planter-Raj to Swaraj: Freedom Struggle and Electoral Politics in Assam, 1826-1947* (New Delhi: ICHR, 1977).
7. There were several other plans of the colonial administrators, e.g., in 1892 Chittagong due to its accessability to port was sought to be

transferred to Assam. Again in 1896 it was thought to be prudent that Dacca and Mymensingh districts of East Bengal should be transferred to Assam. For further details see Baruah, Sanjib, *India Against Itself: Assam and the Politics of Nationality* (New Delhi: Oxfrod University Press, 1999).

8. Goswami, P.C., *The Economic Development of Assam* (Ludhiana: Kalyani Publishers, 1994).
9. Francis Jenkins was of the view that three communication corridors could link Assam with the areas of East Bengal. One through Rongpur in North, the other through Mymensingh in South and another from Khasi hills to Sylhet. Besides enhancing trade and commerce it could help in the process of transfer of population from East Bengal to Assam. He also pleaded for inland water communication from Gauhati to Dibrugarh. Similarly Mr. Jhonson forwarded several proposals regarding revenue-free grants, subsidised rate of travel in rail and steamer popularly known as Rs. 5 family ticket and information campaign through newspapers about abundant land in Assam. For further details see Seikh, Ahizuddin, "Brahmaputror Char Anchalot Jonoprobrojon: Songhat Aru Samanay", in Hussain, Ismail (Sr.) and Hussain, Anowar (eds.), *Char-Chaporir Jiban Charyya* (Guwahati: Natun Sahitya Parishad, 2000) in Assamese.
10. Choudhury, Medini, "Lohit, Barak Aru Islam" as cited by Karim, Rezaul, *Char-Chaporir Samaj Aru Asomor Musalman* (Guwahati: Lokayat Prakasharr, 2000) in Assamese.
11. (Goswami: 1994).
12. *Census of India*, 1951, Vol. XII, Part IA.
13. *Ibid.*
14. *Census of India*, 1931, Vol. III, Part I.
15. According to the first population census of Assam undertaken during 1871, there were only three population groups which had population above 2 lakhs. They were Koch-Rajbongshi's (2,99,346), Kachari's (2,58,810) and Muslims (2,50,470). In Goalpara alone there were 89,916 number of Muslims during 1871. This proves that there were substantial Muslim population in Assam during the later half of the 19th century.
16. (Guha: 1977).
17. The earthquake of 1897 had a devastating effect on Assam and large tracts of land became unsuitable for agriculture. Moreover due to outbreak of *Kala-azar*, cholera, malaria etc. thousands of people perished in Assam which also severely affected agricultural practices in the state.
18. (Guha: 1977).
19. Although the peasants came from several districts of erstwhile East Bengal, namely Pabna, Rongpur and Bogra yet the overwhelming majority came from Mymensingh alone.
20. Seikh, Ahizuddin, "Asomor Jatiyo Jibon Aru Char—Chaporir Krishi Arthaniti", in Hussain, Ismail (ed.), *Char-Chaporir Samaj—Sameeksha* (Jorhat: Assam Sahitya Sabha, 2001) in Assamese.

21. Hussain, Ismail, *Asomor Jatiyo Jibon Aru Abhibashi Asomiya Musalman* (Nalbari: Anamika Granthaloy, 1998) in Assamese.
22. Karim, Rezaul, *Char-Chaporir Samaj Aru Asomor Musalman* (Guwahati: Lokayat Prakashan, 2000) in Assamese.
23. *Ibid.*
24. Seikh, Ahizuddin in (Hussian, Ismail: 2001).
25. *Ibid.*
26. For further details see Medhi, S.B., *Transport System and Economic Development in Assam* (Gauhati: Publication Board, 1978).
27. *Census of India*, 1931, Vol. III, Part I.
28. For a detailed analysis see (Guha: 1977), Seikh, Ahizuddin in [Hussain (Sr.) Ismail & Hussain, Anowar: 2000] and (Hussain, Ismail: 1998).
29. Fishman, Joshua, "Language and Nationalism" as cited by Karna, M.N., "Language, Religion and National Identity", in Sharma, S.L. and Oommen, T.K., *Nation and National Identity in South Asia* (New Delhi: Orient Longman, 2000).
30. For an alternative analysis to the Assam-Assamese-Assimilation axis, see Chakraborty, Gorky and Chattopadhyay, Sriparna, "Asomer Char Anchal: Samannayer Chora Balite Chor Basir Antardohon", *Ninth Column*, Vol. I, No. 2, August, 2001, in Bengali.
31. For further details see Datta, P.S., *Autonomy Movements in Assam* (New Delhi: Omsons Publications, 1993) and the editorial note in [Hussain, Ismail (Sr.) & Hussain, Anowar: 2000].
32. This population figure has been cited by Mr. Wazid Choudhury, Minister for Char Areas Development, Government of Assam, While addressing a public rally at Dr. Zakir Hussain Higher Secondary School, Alopoti *Char*, Barpeta district on 29th October, 2002. He also stated that his ministry has been functioning with an annual budget of Rs. 110 crores out of which Rs. 78 crores is being spent for payment of salaries to the staff of his department and the rest is spent for various development programmes in the *Char* areas.
33. An example where external forces accentuates the internal contradiction, the role of ISI (Pakistan) in helping various insurgent groups in North East (as has been mentioned in various government reports and press releases) can be cited. Whereas on the other, the role of external forces in resolving the internal contradictions, the role played by Norway and Norwegian Minister's in resolving the ethnic crisis in Sri Lanka by acting as mediator between LTTE and Sri Lanka Government for the ongoing talks in Thailand, can be cited.

14

SECESSIONISM, EXTREMISM AND FUNDAMENTALISM A Comparative Study [With Special Reference to Assam]

SANJIB KUMAR BORKAKOTI

Secessionism and extremism in North East India are such problems which have defied solutions for a long time. The reason for that is the lack of in-depth study of these problems. The treatment of the problems has been symptomatic so far rather than based on search for their root causes. This author has highlighted many facets of these problems in the media for about a decade now. While there has been interest from the side of extremists in these discussions, the ruling governments have almost always preferred to go by the use of force only. This has estranged the extremists time and again.[1]

The mass base developed by the extremist outfit 'United Liberation Front of Assam' (ULFA) was due to several factors. First, they took up the issue of Assamese nationalism, which was at stake following unabated immigration of Bangladeshi infiltrators over the decades and which brought the Asom Gana Parishad into power in the mid-eighties. Secondly, ULFA spoke the language of the downtrodden and was inspired by leftist ideology.[2] Thirdly, they gave word to the general disenchantment of the Assamese people with inclusion of Assam in India. It may be mentioned that Assam and for that matter the North East was never part of any Indian empire. All emperors had failed to subjugate the

Assamese people. But the incorporation of Assam in British India in 1826 AD led eventually to its inclusion in independent India in 1947 AD. So the secessionist movement led by ULFA was a historical corrolary.

However, the first and the second causes were contradictory to each other. A narrow nationalism could not go with leftist ideology. Moreover, ULFA had to take refuge in Bangladesh following eviction of their camps in Myanmar by the military junta there in the late eighties. This ran counter to Assamese nationalism. So ULFA began to lose popular support in Assam since early nineties. Then the spate of surrender started and it was discovered that the leftist sermons mouthed by the ULFA activists were only a pretension.[3] Thus both the first and the second causes generating mass base for ULFA disappeared before long. The third cause disappeared by itself as the people of Assam gradually got round to the concept of Indianisation. They became pragmatic by witnessing the futile struggle by ULFA. They realised that being Indian was a better option. It was an irony that formation of ULFA made the Assamese people get out of their disenchantment with the rest of India. Thus, ULFA fulfilled a historical necessity and helped the people of Assam to go through a transition period. This facilitated the government efforts to weed out the outfit. But there still remain many loyal members in this outfit as well as topological advantage for their present camps in Bhutan, which has kept the movement alive.

Moreover, the excesses by the state machinery like custodial deaths of arrested youths and killings of disarmed militants willing to surrender have created a backlash and prevented a complete withering of the outfit. Raju Barua, a girl in early twenties was gang-raped and then killed by army personnel. Basanti Majhi of Golaghat, Labanya Barua and Numali Bania of North Lakhimpur, Unibala Das of Bongaigaon, and Dijumoni Nath of Barpeta became victims of lusts of army personnel. Nitu Rajbongshi, a budding industrialist of Dhekiajuli was killed by the security force in cold blood. These acts of human rights violation by the state is a very serious thing. The Human Rights Commission has repeatedly pulled up the government of Assam for gross violation of human rights in different parts of the state. So ULFA continues and will continue to be a force to be reckoned with, but without any strong mass base in Assam. However, things have come to such a state that the doves in the outfit have started appealing for public sympathy.[4]

North East India's dissatisfaction with the power that be in New Delhi is alleged to be a cause of the growth of extremism in this region. In case of ULFA, it has been repeatedly said that colonial attitude of the Central Government have pushed them to take up the cudgel on behalf of the Assamese people. However, that is not the whole story, the real and more important cause lies elsewhere. It has been proved by the government auditors that as much as Rs. 22,000 crores were misappropriated by the bureaucrats and legislators of Assam during the last one and a half decades from 1985-86 to 2001-02 AD. The Comptroller & Auditor General of India has also taken note of this fact. The instruction by the Public Accounts Committee for legal action has been ignored by the Government of Assam.[5] Had this amount been utilised well in creation of rural infrastructure, economic activities would have picked up and the massive unemployment problem faced by the state would have not arisen in the very first place. The recruitment base of the extremist outfits also would not have been there. Thus the real culprit of this unwarranted development is the corrupt practices resorted to by the senior bureaucrats and legislators of Assam. The State Government Employees Union in Assam has made it the main issue in their recent agitations.

The situation was not different in earlier decades too. For instance, the money earmarked for predominantly tribal areas in lower Assam under the tribal sub-plan were almost wholly siphoned away by the civil servants and engineers, leaving the region in a pristine state even in the twenty-first century. Thus the creation of Bodoland movement and the supporting extremism by Bodo Security Force, Bodo Liberation Tiger, National Democratic Front of Bodoland (NDFB) etc. can be ascribed eventually to the exploitation of the Bodo people by the non-Bodo non-tribal people within the state. The grabbing of land meant for the tribal people in the tribal belt areas by non-tribal migrants from outside the state in connivance with political leaders intensified the dissatisfaction further. Yet another reason of the militancy by the tribal outfits in Assam is the superiority complex of a section of non-tribal intellectuals in the state, whose pro-Aryan attitude has offended the tribal intelligentsia and then the tribal mass.[6] This factor has gradually become the main factor as seen in the statements issued by the tribal leaders in recent times where they refer to this factor only. The intensity of hatred felt by the Bodo extremists towards other communities can be seen in their reprehensible acts of ethnic cleansing.

So, ultimately we have the engineers, legislators, senior bureaucrats and the pro-Aryan intellectuals to blame for the malaise in Assam. Of course, the intermittent acts of indifference by Central Government, for example, in the case of delayed establishment of oil refineries and delayed construction of bridges on Brahmaputra, acted as catalysts in this process. The Government of India have always considered Assam and for that matter the entire North East as a risky border region for high level investment. But these facts acted only as a catalyst, not as the real cause in the growth of secessionism. It will be pertinent to note here that most of the victims of ULFA happens to be indigenous people, not outsiders.

An important point to be noted here is that there are two separate characters in secessionism and extremism in Assam. While ULFA has been outright secessionist from the very beginning, BLT or NDFB fall under the category of extremists only; they are not secessionists. BLT or NDFB wanted separate state for the Bodo people, not a separate country. Moreover these Bodo outfits did not have links with China, Pakistan, Myanmar etc. like ULFA to start with. They also steered clear of religious fundamentalists, it appears from the intelligence elements leaked to the media. But in recent times, ULFA and NDFB have come together for strategic reasons, which may have far-reaching implication for the region. The secessionist movement may now get a new fillip in the changed circumstance unless the Central Government respond favourably to the proposal put up by the government of Assam for unconditional dialogue with ULFA.

But things may improve for better also as NDFB may have a sobering influence on ULFA in their secessionist goal and ULFA also may have a sobering influence on NDFB in their hatred towards non-tribals. In fact these two sobering influences are already visible.

Regarding the connection of ULFA with Inter-Services Intelligence (ISI) of Pakistan, it has appeared from the confessions of many ULFA activists apprehended by the security forces that ISI in fact gave shelter and other helps to them. But the subsequent developments have shown that ULFA refuged to do the biddings of ISI. For instance, they did not blast the oil refineries or the bridges over Brahmaputra in Assam as wanted by ISI, one such arrested activist disclosed some time ago. But the most glaring difference came out in December 1992, when ULFA activists went all out to maintain communal harmony in the strife torn town of Nawgaon after the demolition of the disputed structure in Ayodhya. In fact the law and order of the district was managed by the ULFA in those fatal days, not the state police force. Not only that, a section of the police force itself had been involved in rioting and one of their officer consequently suspended. We think that the sudden growth of Islamic fundamentalist groups in Assam since mid-nineties can be ascribed to disillusionment of ISI with ULFA. There are sixteen such outfits in Assam now, which pose a greater danger to the security of the state [*See Appendix*]. Even Al-Qaeda members are reported to have sneaked into this state following the fall of Taliban regime in Afghanistan. As for ULFA, it has already been marginalised to a great extent even according to army. However, it can be expected to remain engaged in a low-key struggle for secessionism in the coming days, in close co-operation with NDFB. But that should not become a security hazard like the Islamic fundamentalists. Of course, we are talking in relative terms only here.

The strength of the Islamic fundamentalists seem to be very strong in districts like Nowgaon, Morigaon, Bongaigaon, Darrang, Karimganj etc. The state police have unearthed a racket of fake currency in Nowgaon district. Some people in this district are suspected to be involved in subversive activities and of maintaining close connection with the middle-East. These people have made a strong base among a section of the local populace belonging to minority faith. The subversive elements are so well-entrenched that they even assaulted a raiding party of magistrate and police officials in Nowgaon district in 2001. The main suspect of the infamous Godhra carnage, Nanhe Mian hails from Nowgaon district. On the other hand, the flag of Pakistan was reportedly hoisted in Garajan of Nowgaon and in Moriabari of the adjacent Morigaon district. Boats hoisted with the Pakistan flag seem to be plying along Brahmaputra. These are the real dangers faced by the state and the country. But the power that be seem to have misjudged about the real enemy. The entire attention of the government is concentrated on the secessionists like ULFA, NDFB etc., while the fundamentalists are having a field day. But ULFA, NDFB etc. can be won over, not the Islamic fundamentalists. Yet the major operations of army and police forces are engaged against the former only. In our opinion, a well meaning effort to bestow greater autonomy to the North Eastern states can bring secessionism to an end. Most of the revenue earning sources like corporate earnings are presently with the centre, while the states have to do with less revenue yielding sources like income from agricultural land. A thorough re-organisation of the Centre-State relationship in economic and political terms may help remove economic disparity as well as problems like secessionism in the peripheral states. It is significant that only such states have suffered from the problem of secessionism.[7] The current government policy of using force to deal with secessionism may prove counter-productive in the long-run.

The Islamic fundamentalists on the other hand have done a great harm to the socio-cultural milieu in Assam. This state was earlier renowned for communal harmony. Messages of saint Srimanta Sankaradeva (1449-1568 AD) and Ajan Phakir had kept the entire society glued together for centuries. But unfortunately that unity is no more there. Assam has seen several communal holocausts in last two decades. The elements of Hindu fundamentalism slowly creeped into the society as a reaction to the selective settlement of religious minority in sensitive areas by the erstwhile Congress regime with a view to creation of vote banks. The communal feelings reached the height in eighties as seen in the infamous Nellie massacre in 1983. Thereafter the Islamic fundamentalists also took a more violent turn, as seen in the communal conflagration of 1992 at Hojai in Nowgaon district. The ISI tried their best to align this force with secessionism, but failed in their mission. The secessionist ULFA seems to have chosen its target always on political line, not on communal line. So secessionism and fundamentalism remain two disjoint phenomena in Assam, unlike in Jammu & Kashmir. Therefore, it is a better condition in Assam to work in for a solution.[8] Unfortunately, the Government of India have not given sufficient attention to Assam and for that matter to North East, compared to Jammu & Kashmir. We hope it will not be too late when they finally wake up to the situation. At present, the North East policy of Central Government seems to be centred around NDCN(IM); the former are expecting other outfits also to fall in line as NSCN(IM) did, but that may not necessarily happen as each outfit has emerged from different socio-cultural background.

The security problems created by secessionism and fundamentalism have affected the development process in this region. The impact is more pronounced in the case of areas dominated by secessionist groups. This has happened in several ways. First, the level of investment have gone down in these places following a sense of insecurity among the investors. Flight of capital has taken place from districts like Dibrugarh, Tinsukia and Kamrup.[9] Second, the development funds already earmarked by the government for these places have been siphoned by the corrupt bureaucrats in the name of being expropriated by the extremists. This has specially happened in the Karbi Anglong district of Assam. Of course, the extremists have actually shared the loot in some cases. The most popular target of the extremists happen to be DRDA. The Nalbari district has faced this problem acutely. Third, the existing infrastructure have been destroyed by the extremists in a desperate attempt to draw attention and with a view to bring down the communication network. The burning and blasting of bridges all over the state have been going on since last two decades. In fact this trend was started by the AASU activists. On that count, AASU can be said to be the mother of all extremist activities in Assam. Fourth, the development of human resource has taken a severe beating in this state. Values have been distorted, youths have started running after easy money and quality of education has fallen.

However, all the above causes affecting the development process have either disappeared or these have been minimised to a great extent in the recent past following the marginalisation of ULFA. We suspect the statements issued by the governments to the contrary is actually an attempt to hide their own inaction or failure to take the development process ahead. It is now well known that the successive governments in Dispur and New Delhi have used the shield of secessionism to cover their own failures at different times.[10]

The economic impact of fundamentalism is, however, yet to crystallise in a pronounced manner in the state. We fear this will happen in another two or three years, but in a miniscule manner. However, if the war cloud gets darker in the Middle East, we can expect a fallout here much earlier than that. Assam is no more insulated from the political developments outside the North East as seen from the fall-out of Ayodhya demolition in 1992. A third world war starting in the Middle East will bring many productive capacities in Assam to close as these are situated in communally sensitive areas.[11] Moreover, the fugitive Al-Qaeda activists are reportedly trying to build a movement for formation of a greater Islamic country, comprising of Bangladesh, North East India and parts of Myanmar. They are reportedly lodged in two *Masjids* at Sherpur and Jamalpur of Bangladesh. Nine training camps have been set up in Bangladesh by the ISI to train Islamic fundamentalist groups from North East. These camps are situated in Cox Bazar, Jessore, Sylhet, Dhaka, Maulavi Bajar, Sherpur, Jamalpur, Rangpur and Dinajpur. If their effort succeeds even half way, there will be great instability in this region and all development efforts will come to a naught. The Muslim Liberation Tigers of Assam is reported to have contact with Osama Bin Laden, whose destructive potential is well known.[12]

In conclusion, it can be said that secessionism is a political problem, which may have political solution. Extremism by the tribal outfits also can be tackled by endowment of political and economic powers to the underdeveloped regions. But fundamentalism is a psychological problem and an aberration of the thinking process, which cannot be uprooted so easily. It remains ingrained in one's culture and one cannot generally be decultured. Thus fundamentalism pose a serious challenge before all of us. It is a crime against humanity and has no justification whatsoever. It is heartening to note that Hindu fundamentalism is nearly absent in Assam and for that matter in the entire North East in the virulent form one gets to see in Maharashtra and Gujarat. But that situation also may change for worse, if Islamic fundamentalism is not arrested immediately. If things are left as they are, we might have to face a civil war situation in another decade's time.[13]

NOTES

1. This author received hints from some sources that the ULFA followed the intellectual discourses very keenly. Their mouthpiece 'Freedom' reportedly contain excerpts from different articles by the political analysts. Not only that, they welcome critical views aimed at solution. This author has never received any threat from any extremist group in Assam in spite of being a vociferous critic of their activities since last one decade. This author was the first academician in Assam to challenge ULFA leaders in open public meetings as well as question their status in the society [*ULFA Samparke Duwasar*, Dr. Sanjib Kumar Borkakoti, in *Dainik Agradoot,* edited by K.S. Deka, Guwahati, June 26, 1996AD, reprinted in *Santras Aru Santras,* Dr. Sanjib Kumar Borkakoti, Abhiyatri, Guwahati, 1st edition, 1999 AD, pp. 136-41]. The attitude of the current regime in Dispur seems to be a bit matured, compared to the previous regimes, in dealing with ULFA. The former governments had gone the whole hog for an untenable military solution. The present government have approached the Central Government for unconditional dialogue with ULFA and other outfits. However, the response of the Central Government cannot be said to be satisfactory. The ULFA has declared its readiness for peaceful democratic solution, if the Government of India withdraw armed forces from the state [News-report, *The Sentinel,* edited by D.N. Bezboruah, Guwahati, November 28, 2002 AD]. It was

an opportune time to declare unilateral ceasefire and put the ball in ULFA's court. But the Government of India instead snubbed the statement by saying that ULFA would have to lay down arms first for any dialogue.

2. In fact most of the extremist outfits in North East India have followed the leftist ideology. ["Perspective of Development", in *Development Priorities in North East India,* edited by Bimal J. Deb, ist edition, New Delhi, 2002 AD, pp.116-22.]
3. *Ibid.*; "Santrasbadar Bibhisika", Dr. Sanjib Kumar Borkakoti, in *Ajir Batori,* edited by D.N. Chakravarty, Guwahati, August 4, 1993 AD, reprinted in *Santras Aru Santras,* Dr. Sanjib Kumar Borkakoti, Abhiyatri, Guwahati, Ist edition, 1999 AD, pp. 123-32.
4. "Yuddha ne Shanti?", Dr. Sanjib Kumar Borkakoti, in *Asomiya Pratidin*, edited by H. Hussain, Guwahati, October 12, 2002 AD. Here the author has questioned the right of ULFA to represent the Assamese people. It has been seen in several cases that ULFA activists have been assaulted and handed over to police by the public in recent times, when the former were on extortion drive. Some have been lynched too. [News-report, *The Asian Age,* Guwahati, edited by M.J. Akbar, Guwahati edition, November 9, 2002 AD.] But all these have not stopped fresh recruitment in the outfit. Massive unemployment in the state has pushed the youth to ULFA. The current figure of unemployment is suspected to be 20-22 lakhs according to an unofficial estimate, 70 per cent of them being educated. [News-report, *Asomiya Pratidin,* edited by H. Hussain, Guwahati, October 9, 2002 AD.] Regarding the custodial deaths, Justice Safiqul Haque Commission has held ten Assam Police personnel directly guilty in one incident occurring on February 17, 1995 in Darrang district, where two students Ripunjoy Acharya and Hem Chandra Sarma were killed in cold blood. Earlier, the state officials had hushed up the report of enquiry by the then Commissioner of North Assam Division. [News-report, *The Sentinel,* edited by D.N. Bezboruah, Guwahati, October 17, 2002 AD.] The cold-blooded murder of one ULFA activist Mitu Barua on October 30, 2002 in Dispur is on the other hand an instance of killing of disarmed militant willing to surrender. [News-report, *Asomiya Pratidin,* edited by H. Hussain, Guwahati, October 31, 2002 AD.]
5. News-reports, *Asomiya Pratidin,* edited by H. Hussain, Guwahati, November 25, 2002 AD.
6. "Banikantar Alokat Bhaben Baruar Itihas Charcha", Dr. Sanjib Kumar Borkakoti, in *Asomiya Pratidin,* edited by H. Hussain, Guwahati, September 17 & 19, 2002 AD. A prominent Assamese intellectual of yesteryears, Dr. Banikanata Kakoti termed the tribal influence in Assamese language as a 'contamination'. [*Assamese: Its Formation and Development,* Dr. Banikanta Kakoti, Ist edition, Guwahati, 1941 AD, p. 18.] A leading poet and writer of present time, Bhaben Barua is emulating

Dr. Banikanta Kakoti in this matter, as pointed out in the above article. These arrogant attitudes have proved costly for the state. The Bodoland movement was actually a reaction to this attitude. It took a huge proportion consequent upon the humiliation of their leaders by the then high-caste leaders of All Assam Students Union. Late Upendra Nath Brahma was even assaulted by some AASU activists at Jalukbari. The leaders of the Bodo Sahitya Sabha have time and again accused the mainstream Assamese intellectuals of bias against the tribals.

7. "Autonomy: A Political Solution for Secessionism", Dr. Sanjib Kumar Borkakoti, in *The Assam Tribune,* edited by P.G. Barua, Guwahati, March 5, 2002 AD.
8. The chairman of ULFA once had a dialogue with the then Prime Minister of India. This proves that ULFA was never totally opposed to dialogue. In a recent interview to *Asomiya Pratidin,* their political adviser has announced that ULFA may reconsider their preconditions for dialogue if the Government of India were sincere for dialogue. However, the latter seem to be eager for a military solution only. The NDFB also has expressed willingness for dialogue, provided it covers their "historical rights and right to self-determination." [News-report, *The Sentinel,* edited by D.N. Bezboruah, Guwahati, November 6, 2002 AD.]
9. Assam has witnessed a massive flight of merchant capital to the nearby state West Bengal, to be precise to Siliguri and Alipur in the last two decades. West Bengal now earns Rs. 59.84 crores as sales tax revenue from the Siliguri sub-division alone as per the 2001-02 report of the West Bengal Commercial Tax Department. And almost all these have been at the cost of Assam. Capital have also gone to Rajasthan, Maharashtra and New Delhi. ["Autonomy: The Need of the Hour", Dr. Sanjib Kumar Borkakoti, in *The Sentinel,* edited by D.N. Bezboruah, Guwahati, August 10, 2002.]
10. Several ministers and even chief ministers of Assam have been accused of misappropriating public money to the tune of hundreds of crores of rupees. The Central Bureau of Intelligence has been enquiring into the matter for more than a decade. Some of the accuseds could not be brought to justice as the governor of the state refused permission for prosecution. While some petty employees were suspended, the IAS officers involved in the scam were not punished in any manner in spite of recommendation by CBI. [News-report, *The Asian Age,* Guwahati, edited by M.J. Akbar, Guwahati edition, October 20, 2002 AD.] The political set-up is so corrupt in Assam that severe anomalies in the state public service commission did not invite any punishment at all, whereas similar anomalies in Punjab and Maharashtra led to the ouster of their respective chairpersons.
11. This author has shown that third world war is now a distinct possibility. ["Tritiya Viswayuddhar Sambhavana", Dr. Sanjib Kumar Borkakoti, in

Asomiya Pratidin, edited by H. Hussain, Guwahati, September 9, 2002 AD.] As the U.S.A. gets ready for assault on Iraq, the dooms-day also comes nearer. The third world war is going to be fought along communal line, according to this author. So the presence of so many Islamic fundamentalists in Assam will pose a real matter of concern.

12. New-reports, *Asomiya Pratidin,* edited by H. Hussain, Guwahati, October 21, 25 & 27, 2002 AD.
13. The psyche of young generation is increasingly coming under the influence of communalism. This author observed in this year's elections (held on November 26, 2002 AD) of the students union body in his college that the student voters cast their votes completely on communal lines. It was surmised from the fact that there were en-block voting for either Hindu or Muslim candidates. Only 5 per cent of the voters did cross-voting. Thus secularism is fast disappearing from the society.

APPENDIX

ISLAMIC FUNDAMENTALIST GROUPS ACTIVE IN ASSAM AND WORKING UNDER SPONSORSHIP OF ISI

1. Muslim Liberation Tigers of Assam
2. Muslim Liberation Front of Assam
3. Muslim Volunteers Force
4. Student Islamic Movement of India
5. Asom Minority Liberation Army
6. United Special Reform Army of Assam
7. Minority Liberation Tigers of Assam
8. Tiger Liberation Front of Assam
9. Islamic Revolutionary Army
10. Islamic Sewak Sangha
11. Saddam Bahini
12. Islamic United Reformation Protest of Assam
13. Liberation of Islamic Tiger Force
14. Muslim Security Force
15. Harkat-Ul-Zehad

Source: Asomiya Pratidin, edited by H. Hussain, Guwahati, October 25, 2002 A.D.

15

SECURITY AND DEVELOPMENT PERSPECTIVE IN ARUNACHAL PRADESH

R.P. BHATTACHARJEE

Introduction

Arunachal Pradesh is the largest State in the North Eastern Region with an area of 83,743 sq. km. which lies between latitudes 26°28′ N and 29°30′ N and longitudes 91°30′ E and 97°30′ E. The State is surrounded by Bhutan on the West, Tibet (China) on the North, Mayanmar on the East and Assam and Nagaland on the south. The geo-strategic importance of the State becomes evident from the fact that it has 1,628 km of international border of which 1,030 km is with Tibet, 441 km with Myanmar and 157 km with Bhutan (Bhattacharjee, 2000/Census, 2001). However, the border is disputed particularly the one with Tibet (China). The dispute led to Chinese invasion of India in 1962, which is a turning point not only in the history of India, but also in the development of the region under study. The border with Assam too, is not free from dispute.

The State is the eastern stretch of the Himalayas. The forest cover of the State is 82 per cent. The forested Siwalik hills rise abruptly to 800 m above the Brahmaputra valley. Most of the ranges of the lesser Himalayas are clothed with temperate forests. The elevation of the hills ranges from 150 to over 7,300 metres. The hill ridges in Arunachal Pradesh are situated in a haphazard manner. As soon as one ridge ends, the other starts either in opposite or in a parallel manner. At the intervals, the wide and narrow valleys come into existence. Because of these ridges the surface of Arunachal Pradesh is found varied almost everywhere which also results in numerous geographical isolations. The State is bisected into two halves, East and West by the river Siang which is known as Brahmaputra when it comes to plains and meets Dibang and Lohit rivers. The topography is also bisected by a number of prominent rivers flowing from north to south. All these rivers are separated from each other by steep ridges.

The geographical isolation makes the State vulnerable for any security perspective. Owing to lack of communications mobility is very limited. This has made some regions of the State most sensitive specially neighbouring districts of Nagaland and these areas are reported to be infested by NSCN groups. In recent months one state civil service officer was killed by these groups in Changlang district and this was echoed in State Assembly.

Security in Arunachal Pradesh

Arunachal Pradesh has a population of 10,96,702 as per 2001 census with a density of 13 person per sq.km. (Census, 2001). The State has 15 districts now and these are Tawang, West Kameng, East Kameng, Upper Subansiri, Kurung Kumey, Lower Subansiri, Papumpare, West Siang, East Siang, Upper Siang, Dibang Valley, Lower Dibang Valley, Lohit, Changlang and Tirap. The districts of Tawang, West Kameng, East Kameng, Lower Subansiri, Upper Subansiri, Kurung Kumey, West Siang, Upper Siang, Dibang Valley, Lower Dibang Valley, Lohit, Changlang and Tirap face international border and presently Tirap and Changlang districts are infested by insurgent groups.

The incidence of crimes in Arunachal Pradesh during the year 2001 was murder 68, dacoity 47, burglary 269, theft 432, robbery 100, kidnapping 58, riot 20, culpable homicide 7, counterfeiting 3, miscellaneous 1363, and total cognizable crimes under IPC was 2367 (DES: 2001). There are incidence of juvenile delinquency too in the State. Thus the state is no more a land of peace. The state had 5.0 per cent of annual outlay for police department during 2001-2002 (DES, 2001-

2002) which is about 3.8 per cent of GSDP (DES, 2000-2001). Thus a large amount is spent for police department of the state and people expects a peaceful situation. The reported infiltration of NSCN(K) into border area of Changlang and Tirap Districts is a major security problem for the state and this would not have been if the machinery of Inner Line (Regulation 1873) checking were strict and police forces are modernised and strong and capable to check it. In fact Inner Line Regulation Acts as shield of security for the autochthons. This system has prevented the indigenous people from being swamped by the outsiders. But this system could not stop the NSCN groups in the districts of Changlang and Tirap districts which are in hostile terrain and porus.

It is common adage that extreme economic destitution breeds conflict and ultimately the ground is set for the rise of militancy in a particular area, depending on the level of government neglect and irresponsibility (Dai, 2001). It is easy to allure youth who are unemployed, school and college drop-outs with no source of income to join in unlawful activities. I do not have any source to state that local youths have joined in organised crimes but it has a tacit support either due to fear or favour. There is another economic reason. The Hon'ble Supreme Court's order banning timber operations on 12th December, 1996, has reduced State's revenue. The thriving timber trade has stopped and this has helped indirectly in the virulent symptoms of insurgency in those two districts. It is no secret that the benefits of the timber trade was accrued by a very select, miniscule strata of local society and fringe benefits of the trade was dispensed as largesse to quell a potentially vociferous and demanding public. With the ban order this method of keeping a lid on things was suddenly removed (Dai, *ibid.*). According to Mamang Dai, "The Naga truce has put the North East in the limelight again, but even so Arunachal is barely there. In actual fact, the Naga underground has been working mainly in Arunachal territory during the period of the earlier ceasefire. The two districts of Tirap and Changlang have become a battleground for Naga insurgents of the Khaplang and Isaac-Muivah group where simple and innocent villagers are being brainwashed and terrorized. We share many historical and cultural ties." In the past villagers on the Myanmarese side of the border paid obeisance to the Chieftains of Tirap. Hornbill feathers were presented as a mark of respect. There was inter-marriage and trade with both Myanmarese and Naga villagers of Mon district.

In recent time, when NSCN(IM) made its presence felt early 2000, some sections of the people thought it was a god send. Let them fight it out, was what they say. This was a reaction against a powerless civil administration and a police force that failed to make a single conviction despite the numbers of deaths, disappearances and blatant cases of extortion and intimidation.

If we see the security scenario in India, we can count the attack of the Parliament House on 13th December, 2001, the recent Akshardham Mandir attack in Ahmedabad and Raghunath Temple episode in Jammu. We have to admit that our security system has failed in India and other parts of the North East in general and Arunachal Pradesh in particular specially on its eastern border. The terrorism is continuing in our country since last 2 decades and on 28th September, 2001 the U.N. Security Council passed Resolution No. 1373 which is a Resolution binding on all members of the Security Council. In which the Security Council told all its members recognizing the need for states to complement international cooperation by taking additional measures to prevent and suppress in their territories through all lawful means the financing and preparation of any act of terrorism. The United Nations Security Council decides also that all states shall deny safe haven to those who finance, plan, support or commit terrorist act or provide safe havens. And due to this, POTA has been enacted in India which is different from TADA. In the case of TADA as the conviction rate was so abysmally low and people were not punished as expected. In 1995 TADA was allowed to lapse principally because of the complaint that it had been misused.

And due to this, Maharashtra Control of Organised Crime Act, 1999 (MOCA) was enacted whose percentage has been claimed over 76. India is geographically situated between the countries of Golden Triangle and Golden Crescent and is a transit point for narcotic drugs produced in these regions to the West (Upadhyay,1980). India is a signatory to the South Asia Association for Regional Co-operation (SAARC) convention for suppression of Terrorism. But we find that Pakistan is the hub of all terrorism and Al-Qaida centre. Nepal is burning due to Maoist Rebellion and peace talk is going on in Sri Lanka. Recently India has complaint against Bangladesh about existence of over 130 training centres on its land which is a major cause of security concern for all the North Eastern States. The on-going peace talks with NSCN(IM) may lead to peace in Nagaland and neighbouring areas specially after the recent lifting of ban on NSCN.

Prevention of Terrorist Act (POTA), 2002 has been ushered to contain international terrorism specially after attack on our Parliament on 13th December, 2001. Indian Government makes its national security perspective appear as the presentation of an inescapable truth. In this internal conflicts acquire external dimension which is understood to mean seeing "ISI" behind every rebellion if not every phenomenon (Navlakha, 2002). But time will speak how POTA will contain terrorism and secured the people specially in North Eastern Region. The example of Tamil Nadu Government's decision to charge the MDMK leader Vaiko under Section 21(2) and (3) of POTA for supporting LTTE shows the twisted logic behind POTA. The logic is that once an organisation is banned under POTA then it becomes a crime to support them.

In Arunachal Pradesh, "The Arunachal Pradesh Control of Organised Crime Act, 2002 (Act No. 5 of 2002) has been passed by the State Assembly and received the assent of the Governor on 3rd October, 2002. It has 30 sections and enacted to make special provisions for prevention and control of and for coping with criminal activities by organised crime syndicates or gangs and matters connected therewith or incidental thereto. Section 3(1) states about punishment for organised crime which varies from imprisonment for three years to death sentence and fine from one lakh to five lakhs. The Hon'able Chief Minister of Arunachal Pradesh while making statement in the Assembly that during last few years, on the one hand the NSCN has been trying to spread its area of operation beyond Tirap and Changlang districts, in which they have succeeded to some extent. On the other hand, during last one decade or so, a number of unlawful organised underground groups such as Liberation Tigers of Arunachal (LTA), National Liberation Army of Arunachal (NLAA), United Liberation Tigers of Arunachal (ULTA) and Revolution Army of Arunachal Pradesh (RAAP) have sprung up in the State. Their main agenda is to obtain pecuniary benefits by resorting to intimidation and kidnapping. In the process, they have established a nexus with the well-established insurgents and separatist forces. It is really a matter of grave concern for the State and all of us (Assembly, 2002). All other political parties and student organisations including AAPSU—the leading student organisations has opposed the enactment of APCOCA which is a deduction of MOCA. It is clarified that APCOCA is enacted instead of accepting POTA is that POTA has element of discretion while APCOCA is applicable to all. But as my knowledge goes till date no one has booked under APCOCA.

Security lapse retards any developmental efforts either of the government or NGOs or any other private party. We find that the developmental activities in these districts has been slowed down mainly due to lack of security of the workers in particular. Let us have a glimpse of the developmental perspective of the State next.

Developmental Perspective

Traditionally Arunachal Pradesh is a peaceful state and its society. The traditional local bodies like Kebang, Mele, Nogongthun, Jung-blue, Buliang, Wancho-Wangas, Kava, Keba, Tso-Tsorgan etc. has been found answer to social and economic crimes and punish through the traditional institutions of village councils. The recent happenings specially in Changlang and Tirap districts have slowed down the economic development in the region. The dissentment caused by economic deprivation, ignorance and inaction on the part of the decision makers and consequent unemployment, drop-outs etc. fuelled the insurgency activity in this region. The State's revenue receipt from tax is 4.3 per cent and from non-tax is 6.6 per cent during 1999-2000 whereas grants-in-aid was 89.1 per cent (DES, 2001-2002, *ibid.*). It is stated that over 80 per cent of budget is spent on salaries. In this scenario today it has become evident that poor planning *vis-à-vis* the economic structure and the long years of political and bureaucratic negligence and lack of accountability has set the tone for a very hazy future. During 1999, the State Government announced an economic revival package for Tirap and Changlang districts through tea cultivation. But the people there want peace. This will have a perspective effect in economic development of the area. Poverty is everywhere. The rural development department has estimated Below Poverty Line (BPL) through household survey during 1997-98 (9th Plan). The poverty level is estimated as 54 per cent in the State. But this is not correct as the number of households taken into care is during 1991 and due to this the estimate has not reflected the correct position. We find that the BPL estimate made by NSSO during 1999-2000 is 33.47 per cent only which is more or less correct. Ignoring this fact, if we consider the estimate of R.D. Department, we find the highest level of BPL is in Upper Subansiri district (84%) while lowest in Changlang district (25%) and second highest in Tirap (74%). But if we compare the per capita income in Table 15.1 we find that the per capita income was third lowest in Changlang district (Rs. 7,000) after Lower Subansiri and East Kameng. Thus the BPL estimate by the Department is not free from doubt and error. The fact is that the economic conditions of these two affected districts are not so backward if we consider all these socio-economic indicators.

If security is not there no entrepreneur will invest in any project and even the governmental plans and programmes will fail to implement its schemes. For that we must have a glimpse of the basic socio-economic conditions of the people. Here a brief

Table 15.1: Developmental Indicators of Districts of Arunachal Pradesh

	Districts	PCI, 1998-99 at Constant Price (Rs.)	Urban Population (%) (2001)	Main-Workers (%) (2001)	Density (2001)	Sex Ratio (2001)	Literacy (2001)	Female Literacy (2001)	Population per Hospital Beds*	Population per Doctors*	BPL (%) (1997-98)	Length of Roads per 100 sq. km.
(1)	(2)	(3)	(4)	(5)	(6)	(7)	(8)	(9)	(10)	(11)	(12)	(13)
1.	Tawang	10,716 (5)	12.84 (9)	46.83 (1)	16 (5)	963 (4)	41.14 (12)	30.87 (11)	727 (12)	2,308 (7)	66 (8)	48.25 (2)
2.	West Kameng	14,364 (1)	8.96 (12)	38.73 (6)	10 (9)	749 (13)	61.67 (2)	48.56 (5)	521 (8)	3,105 (12)	49 (7)	23.23 (5)
3.	East Kameng	6,690 (12)	26.22 (3)	41.15 (4)	14 (6)	985 (1)	40.89 (13)	28.86 (13)	408 (3)	3,003 (10)	69 (10)	19.83 (7)
4.	Papum Pare	9,343 (6)	50.83 (1)	31.55 (13)	35 (2)	899 (9)	70.89 (1)	61.72 (1)	336 (1)	2,174 (4)	46 (5)	35.48 (3)
5.	Lower Subansiri	5,950 (13)	12.59 (10)	37.73 (9)	10 (9)	985 (1)	45.01 (10)	36.19 (9)	603 (11)	2,273 (5)	67 (9)	12.82 (10)
6.	Upper Subansiri	7,485 (10)	28.13 (2)	37.76 (8)	8 (11)	973 (3)	50.89 (7)	42.74 (7)	486 (7)	2,307 (6)	84 (13)	14.32 (9)
7.	West Siang	8,505 (8)	19.95 (5)	35.27 (11)	13 (7)	913 (6)	60.31 (3)	53.24 (2)	438 (5)	2,076 (3)	48 (6)	17.51 (8)
8.	East Siang	11,641 (3)	25.16 (4)	33.32 (12)	22 (4)	937 (5)	61.22 (4)	52.24 (3)	395 (2)	1,648 (2)	44 (3)	30.15 (4)

(Contd.)

Table 15.1: (*Contd.*)

(1)	(2)	(3)	(4)	(5)	(6)	(7)	(8)	(9)	(10)	(11)	(12)	(13)
9.	Upper Siang	10,916 (4)	Nil (13)	46.17 (2)	5 (12)	858 (10)	49.80 (9)	30.09 (10)	428 (4)	1,390 (1)	45 (4)	10.07 (11)
10.	Dibang Valley	13,160 (2)	17.56 (7)	37.96 (7)	4 (13)	840 (12)	59.45 (5)	48.96 (4)	443 (6)	3,385 (13)	38 (2)	6.32 (13)
11.	Lohit	8,575 (7)	18.54 (6)	35.51 (10)	13 (7)	857 (11)	56.05 (6)	44.59 (6)	563 (10)	2,609 (9)	53 (11)	9.63 (12)
12.	Changlang	7,000 (11)	9.85 (11)	39.15 (5)	27 (3)	905 (8)	51.98 (8)	39.85 (8)	928 (13)	3,057 (11)	25 (1)	21.99 (6)
13	Tirap	8,401 (9)	15.25 (8)	43.56 (3)	42 (1)	911 (7)	42.01 (11)	29.00 (12)	536 (9)	2,445 (8)	74 (12)	54.83 (1)
	Arunachal Pradesh	8,979	20.34	37.71	13	894	54.74	44.24	494	2,364	54	17.36

Note: Rank of districts shown in parentheses.

* Calculated by the author.

Sources: (1) Directorate of Economics & Statistics, Government of A.P. ,"Estimates of District Domestic Product, Arunachal Pradesh", (1993-94 to 1998-99), Itanagar, p. 28.

(2) *Census of India , 2001*, Arunachal Pradesh, Series 13, Paper 2, pp. 61-62.

(3) *Census of India*, Series 13, Arunachal Pradesh, Paper 3 of 2001, Statements 3.

(4) *Census of India, 2001*, Series 13, Arunachal Pradesh, Paper 1 of 2001, pp. 15-87.

(5) Directorate of Economics & Statistics, Govt. of A.P., "Statistical Abstract, 2001", pp. 41-73.

study of a few socio-economic indicators is depicted in Table 15.1.

Here in Table 15.1, we find that per capita District Income (DDP) during 1998-99 is lower in the districts of Lower Subansiri, East Kameng, Changlang, Upper Subansiri and Tirap districts. And if urbanisation is an indicator for economic development, the districts of Upper Siang, West Kameng, Changlang, Lower Subansiri and Tirap Districts are at a lower rank. The percentage of main workers are more in those districts where literacy is poor. The low density is a warning to state planning body as it would increase social and economic overhead cost in those districts specially in decentralisation of planning and consequently the benefit of economic development will reach to a few. Sex ratio can be an indicator of women's empowerment along with female literacy and we find that the districts of Western regions and Eastern regions of the State are at receiving end and poor. For health indicator, I could manage data on bed and doctor. The population per bed and population per doctor as the indicators of health in absence life expectancy and infant mortality. It is observed that Changlang district with 928 population per bed and 727 population per bed in Tawang district is in worse (rank) while population per doctor in Dibang Valley (3,385). Tawang (3,105) and Changlang (3,057) are in poor position. In respect of communication, road length per 100 sq. km. is worse in Dibang Valley with 6.32 km compared to Lohit with 9.63 km. It may be noted that the population in Dibang Valley is also low. The highest road length is in Tirap district but it must be noted that density is also highest in the district and next is Papum Pare. Therefore, for any plans and programme of the backward districts specially in the districts of Changlang and Tirap Security is a major issue for any venture of entrepreneurs. If internal investment is a far cry—we cannot expect any FDI. Now, the State has a per capita income of Rs. 14,587 during 2000-2001 compared to national average of Rs. 16,487 (DES, 2001). Thus if per capita income is an indicator of development, the state is far behind and it is poor in central and eastern most districts of the state. The literacy rate in the state is 54.74 (2001) while it was lowest in

East Kameng district (40.89), and other low percentage of literacy are in Tawang (41.14) and Tirap (42.01) similar to female literacy. The Human Development Index in the state was 0.37 during 1996 (Bhattacharjee *et al.*, 2002). In a recent estimate by Antony and others (2001: 2977), the HDI of Arunachal Pradesh was estimated as 0.623 compared to Assam (0.546), Mizoram (0.839), Meghalaya (0.585), Tripura (0.582) and all-India (0.640). This shows a better position of the State in this N.E. Region. To have higher Human Development and poverty alleviation in the State, congenial atmosphere is to be created first. Security nay social security is an important index for any development.

Conclusion

The 10th Five Year Plan (2002-2007) has been finalised by NDC and Planning Commission. Hon'ble Prime Minister has mooted 8-point agenda for 8 per cent growth in 10th Plan. These are:

(1) Implementation of policies and programmes.
(2) Speed up economic reforms with government withdrawing from production barring a few clearly specified strategic sectors.
(3) Government to shoulder dominant though not exclusive responsibility for physical and social infrastructure.
(4) Speed up employment-oriented growth.
(5) Remove imperfections plaguing financial markets.
(6) Reduction and retargeting of subsidies to reduce over all fiscal deficit. Barring few who deserve subsidy, make others pay for what they use.
(7) Government to launch initiative for accelerated completion of railway projects that are critical and remunerative.
(8) Align long term growth strategy to population, encourage demographic transition.

Now the first year is at its 3rd Quarter and the Hon'ble Finance Minister Shri Jaswant Singh has submitted mid-year Economic Survey in Parliament on 3rd December, 2002. The economic growth is projected for the 10th Plan is 8 per cent but as per mid-year survey, the growth in this inaugural year will be 5 per cent to 5.5 per cent. To achieve 8 per cent growth rate during 10th Plan fiscal situation facing the Centre and States has to improve. A peaceful environment is necessary to make a congenial environment for investment both by inside and outside investors. It is necessary for industrial and economic development of Arunachal Pradesh to have a peaceful atmosphere and security to its citizen. The investment from inside and FDI can be materialised only by proper security environment and relaxation of ILP, RAP and land policy for a longer lease period with better communication and marketing facility. Industry starved Arunachal Pradesh has relaxed land lease policy to encourage outside entrepreneurs to set up ventures in the State through New Industrial Policy. Agriculture and Tourism policies have also been announced to lure the investors. But all efforts for development of the State must be with human face and empowerment of the women. The State's immense power potentiality must be tapped and tourism industry must be given a face lift to mobilise resources for economic development of the State. Marketing is another problem area which must be solved through better communication facility. Research and Development is another area lacking in North East and almost absent in Arunachal Pradesh. This needs special attention for development of the State. We must ensured our own accountability which will reduce the parallel black economy and corruption in our society. Above all social security is a must. We have assured the security of our citizen specially in the eastern most districts of Changlang and Tirap as these are hot spots of militancy and the lifting of the ban on the NSCN(IM) might add to the problem and rise in militancy. It is reported that the outfit has about 300 cadre under its Hevuto battalion under the charge of self-styled major Rockwang. But the ongoing peace talks might be blessings in disguise to future peace in the regions and socio-economic development of the people. We should pray for peaceful settlement of the Naga problem without disturbing the territorial integrity of other States and its people.

REFERENCES

Antony, Grace Maria; Rao, K. Viswawara and Balakrishna, N. (2001): "Suitability of HDI for Assessing Health and Nutritional Status" in *EPW*, Vol. 35, No. 31, August 4-10, 2001.

Assembly statement made on *Arunachal Pradesh Control of Organised Crime Bill, 2002*, by Hon'ble Chief Minister, Shri Mukut Mithi, Arunachal Pradesh in the Assembly, para 6.

Bhattacharjee, R.P. (2000), *Economic Development of Arunachal Pradesh*, Himalayan Publishers, Delhi, Itanagar, pp. 1, 12, 17.

Bhattacharjee, R.P. and Upadhaya, N "Human Development in North East India" in *Development Priorities in North East India*, (ed.) By Bimal J. Deb (2002), Concept Publishing Company, New Delhi-59, p. 140.

Census of India 2001, Series 13, A.P., Paper 1 year 2001 According to this report the Arunachal Pradesh has international border with Bhutan to the West (160 km) China to North and North East (440 km).

Census of India, 2001, Series 13, A.P., Paper 3 of 2001.

Dai, Mamang, "Arunachal Pradesh Conflict & the Economic Factor-I, II, III" in *The Arunachal Times*, Dated 28, 29, 30 August 2001.

Directorate of Economics & Statistics, *Statistical Abstract of Arunachal Pradesh 2001*, Govt. of A.P., Itanagar p. 71.

Directorate of Economic & Statistics, *Budget-in-Brief, 2001-2002*, Government of A.P., Itanagar, p. 15.

Directorate of Economics & Statistics, *Quick Estimates, S.D.P. of Arunachal Pradesh 2000-2001*, Govt. of A.P., Itanagar, pp. 13, 15.

Novlakha, Gautam, "Security Policy: Enemy of Democracy" in *EPW*, Vol. 37, No. 33, pp. 3423-27.

The Arunachal Pradesh Control of Organised Crime Act, 2002 (Act No. 5 of 2002).

The Arunachal Times, dt. 14 July, 2002.

The Maharashtra Control of Organised Crime Act, 1999, (Maharashtra Act No. 30 of 1999).

The Prevention of Terrorism Act, 2002 (No.15 of 2002).

The Telegraph, 10-12-2002.

Upadhyay, Sanjiv Kumar, *Crime in India*, Jt. Director, Anti-corruption Headquarter, CBI, India, Paper presented in Resource Material Series No. 58, at 116th International Training Course (Participant's papers) pp. 197-207.

16

NEED FOR A SECULAR OUTLOOK
A Case Study of Meghalaya

R.K. PURKAYASTHA

The genesis of the hill state movement leading to the creation of Meghalaya can be found in the words of Mr. J.J.M. Nichols Roy, one of the architect of the Sixth Schedule to the Constitution, when participating in the debates of the Constituent Assembly he said, "Finally, Sir, I support the amendments moved by Dr. Ambedkar. At the same time I must say before I sit down that these hill people feel that even the Sixth Schedule has controlled them too much and they have not got enough what they would like to have. I think many of us realise that. Even Mr. Bordoloi the Honourable Premier of Assam realises that. But under the circumstances we have agreed in order to have a compromise and in order to bring peace between all parties. Therefore, do not think that the hill areas have been given too much. They have not been given enough according to their ideas".[1] Even on June 27, 1952, the day the United Khasi-Jaintia District Council was inaugurated, there was a big student and youth demonstration led by Hoover Hynniewta, a Khasi graduate.[2] When Pandit Nehru visited Shillong on October 19, 1952, a memorandum was submitted by hill leaders demanding unification of all hill areas of Assam under one administrative unit. The appointment of State Reorganisation Commission gave impetus to regional aspirations. A conference of the Chief Executive Members of all District Councils was held in Shillong on June 16-17, 1954 and it was decided to urge for creation of separate Hill state and send a set of suggestions to Members of Parliament to amend Sixth Schedule to the Constitution. This was followed by Assam Hills Tribal Leaders Conference held in Tura, in Garo Hills, on October 6-8, 1954. It reiterated the demands for creation of Hill state. The rejection of demands of Hill State by State Reorganisation Commission led to the formation of Eastern India Tribal Union in October 1955.[3] The separate state movement led by Eastern India Tribal Union reached its peak during the general elections of 1957 and experienced a lull when a coalition ministry was formed between it and the Congress in 1958. It took just a single government bill envisaging to introduce Assamese as the official language in Assam to break the fragile relationship of the coalition. 1960s saw the emergence of new political platform of hill leaders of Assam known as All Party Hill Leaders Conference (APHLC).[4] It was under the banner of APHLC a non-violent movement was undertaken which culminated in the formation of Meghalaya in January 1972. APHLC was rather a platform to demand for a hill state then a political party, it enjoyed the goodwill and confidence of all sections of people residing in the hill state. Conscious of the presence of large non-tribal population, particularly in and around Shillong, the tribal leaders spearheading the movement for a separate state gave a solemn assurance to the non-tribals of their safety and security in all spheres.[5] This can be also inferred from the fact that in the third APHLC Conference held a Halflong North Cachar Hills of Assam from November 16-18, 1960, in the plan for creation of "the Eastern Frontier state" which had fifteen chapters, interestingly two chapters contained the legitimate interests of the non-tribal residents of the state, including their representation in the Legislative Assembly.[6] The fact of non-violent movement enjoying the support of all sections was appreciated much by central leadership, the then Prime Minister Late Mrs. Indira Gandhi while speaking on the introduction of Meghalaya State Bill on November 10, 1970 said in the Parliament, "Meghalaya came into existence with the goodwill of all sections of the House. I hope that the decision to raise it to Statehood will be welcomed by the whole House".[7] Thus Meghalaya emerged as a State with much hopes and expectations. The common man thought all his problems will come to an end and his basic wants fulfilled.

In less than a decade of formation of the State social tensions started emerging often breaking into social conflict threatening the stability of the society and often resulting in severe or widespread violence requiring the intervention of the administration.[8] This regular and persistent social instability coupled with growth of armed insurrections in recent years makes it necessary for us to comprehend this phenomenon existing in our cosmopolitan milieu eroding our image as multi-cultural and secular state. The root of this problem lies probably in our model of development undertaken since the creation of the State. Meghalaya today, represents a case of poverty in midst of plenty. The state is rich in mineral resources, the coal reserve of the State is estimated to be 460 million tonnes,[9] the highest among the North Eastern States, there are as many as 15 main coalfields. The coal is characterised by high sulphur and low ash content, and a small quantity of it is exported to Bangladesh, but due unscientific mining much of this resources cannot be used and has resulted in degradation of environment. The limestone deposit of the state are estimated to be 2100 million tonnes, most of the limestone is of high grade with Calcium content of 98.5 per cent.[10] The Sillimanite-Corundum deposits of Sonaphar in the Khasi Hills are of the best quality found in the world. It is an interesting fact that Sonaphar area accounts for nearly 90 per cent of the total production of Silimanite in our country. There are altogether 27 deposits in the area and the reserves are estimated at 25,000 tonnes.[11] Besides these minerals the other minerals in the state includes white clay, copper, glass, sand etc. The State is blessed with immense capacity for production of Hydro-power, as on March 31, 1999 the production of hydel power capacity stood at 185.20 MW, the highest among the North Eastern States,[12] but if we look into the number of villages electrified till March 1999, we find out of 5,485 inhabited villages according to 1991 census only 2,510 villages were electrified which constitutes merely 46 per cent of villages, the lowest among the North Eastern States.[13] The State has immense potential of development of dairy, poultry, horticulture and floriculture activities due to predominant agrarian economy and suitable climate. Meghalaya has the highest number of high yielding crossbred cattle in India.[14] The economy of the rural population can be improved if scientific method of dairy farming is adopted. As far as agriculture is concerned only 8 per cent of total geographical area is available for cultivation and only 13 per cent of cultivated land produces more than one crop.[15] According to the report of Task force on Shifting cultivation constituted by Ministry of Agriculture and submitted in 1983 it was estimated that a total of 530 sq.km was under shifting cultivation with a total number of 52,290 families practicing it,[16] though in the recent years the number of families practicing shifting cultivation has decreased. The total production of food grains during 1998-99 was 1,87,000 tonnes, the lowest among the North Eastern States.[17] Rice constitutes the most important crop of the State, the other crops grown includes maize, pulses, millet and commercial crops like cotton, sugarcane, rubber etc. The State is rich in horticultural crops like bananas, oranges, pineapple etc. But due to lack of preservation and marketing facilities the people in the rural areas have not been able to benefit from horticultural crops. As far as industries are concerned Meghalaya though rich in minerals, forest and agricultural resources is industrially backward. The only large industry is Mawmluh Cherra Cement Factory established in Cherrapunjee in 1962 by the then Assam government. It has the capacity to produce 250 tons of cement per day.[18] Some saw mills were established in the State but after ban on the felling of timber by Supreme Court their number has decreased adding to the problem of unemployment especially in the rural areas. In recent years some industries have been established in Byrnihat area of Ri-Bhoi District but these industries have not become an avenue of employment but basically established to benefit from various subsidies and tax concessions announced by the Government from time to time. The lack of industrialisation can be gauged from the fact that the number of factories as in 1997-98 in the state was merely 43 employing 7,000 persons.[19] The State is blessed with some of the most scenic and beautiful places in the country, there are as many as 69 Tourist Spots identified but tourism has not developed into any major industry and during the year 1998-99 the State attracted only 1,59,730 domestic tourists and 1,971 foreign tourits.[20] During the period from the Fourth Plan (1969-74) till the Eighth Plan the State Government had received a total Central assistance of Rs. 2,254.27 crores. The backwardness of the State can well be comprehended when we compare the economic indicators of the State with that of India.

Thus after 30 years of the creation of the State if we examine how far the benefits of development has reached to the people living at the grassroots level it is far less than what was expected by the people, the persons living below the poverty line in the state in 1993-94 was 37.92 per cent compared to National average of 35.97 per cent.[21] It will be equally untrue to conclude that no development has taken place, but the strategy of development adopted so far has created a small enclave of neo-rich among the tribals located in the urban centre and this small class has been able to appropriate the benefits of development with active collaboration of politicians and bureaucrats. In order to remain themselves in power the ruling elites have been raising the issue of threat to cultural identity instead of addressing the real issue of food, clothing, shelter, education and health care for all. This issue of preservation of identity has often lead to conflicts among different groups residing in the state which has in turn has distracted investments in the State and also resulted in flight of capital from State to elsewhere in the country. Due to lack of industries and reduction in Governmental employment the number of educated unemployed in the State is sharply increasing who becomes easy prey for recruitments to various armed groups operating in the region. The increase in activities of the armed groups leads to further diversion of funds, which could be fruitfully utilised for developmental works to maintenance of law and order. The ruling elites who feels threatened by the activities of various groups try to also strengthen the coercive arms of the State while the majority of people are caught between the terror of the state and of the groups indulging in violence. The solution to the problems can be found only if the ruling is sincere and make an effort to redress the secular grievances of the people through secular means and not divert the issues to preservation of identity which in other parts of the country is done in the name of caste and religion which is no doubt important but not as much as question of survival, the issues that affects the common man in the State both tribal and non-tribal is no different from any other part of the country.

NOTES

1. Kyndiah, P.R., *Meghalaya Yesterday and Today*, Vikas Publishing House, New Delhi, 1990, p. 19.
2. Chaube Shibanikinkar, *Hill Politics in North East India*, Orient Longman, New Delhi, 1973, p. 108.
3. *Ibid.*, pp. 107-23.
4. Kyndiah, P.R., *op. cit.*, p. 22.
5. Sarma Commission of Enquiry of the Disturbance at Shillong in 1992, Inquiry Report, Directorate of Printing and Stationery of Meghalaya, Shillong, 1995, p. 5.
6. Kyndiah, P.R., *op. cit.*, p. 23.
7. *Ibid.*, p. 25.
8. Purkayastha, R.K., "Social Instability in Shillong, 1980-90", NEICSSR Seminar, Shillong, 1993.
9. Where Do We Stand in 2000, "Meghalaya in North East and India and the World", Govt. of Meghalaya, Directorate of Economics & Statistics, Shillong, 2001, p. 32.
10. Bhakta, G.P., *Geography of North East India*, Akashi Book Depot, Shillong, 1992, p. 172.
11. *Ibid.*, pp. 172-73.
12. *Basic Statistics of North Estern Region 2000*, North Eastern Council, Shillong, 2000, p.102.
13. *Ibid.*, p. 97.
14. Bhakta, G.P., *op. cit.*, p. 178.
15. *Ibid.*, p. 173.
16. "Basic Statistics of North Eastern Region 2000", *op. cit.*, p. 29.
17. "Where Do We Stand in 2000", *op. cit.*, p. 19.
18. Bhakta, G.P., *op. cit.*, p. 179.
19. "Where Do We Stand in 2000", *op. cit.*, p.37.
20. *Ibid.*, p. 74.
21. *Ibid.*, p. 10.

17

SECULARISM UNDER STRAIN IN NORTH EAST INDIA

J.B. GANGULY

Characteristics of Tribal Religion

Excepting for the Buddhist and Hinduaised or Islamised Tribal communities the tribals were generally considered animists by the Colonial rulers and even some scholars. It is, however, wrong to think that tribal peoples are animists. They have their own respective religious systems having five basic characteristics as explained by Verrier Elwin. There is a general belief in a 'Supreme God' (such as, Doini-Pollo, the Sun-Moon god of all the Adi groups) who is just, benevolent and good and also 'upholder of truth'. Secondly, there is a awareness of the spiritual realities behind the material realities of everyday life. Thirdly, tribal mythology linked with their religion in fact represents, according to an American writer, 'metaphorically a world picture and insight into life generally and may, therefore, be considered as primitive philosophy or metaphysical thought'. Fourthly, tribal religion upholds a social ethic 'that unities the tribe in its discipline and undoubtedly makes for a certain nobility of conduct. The great tribal virtues are discipline, devotion to work, genorisity, truth, kindness'. "Finally, tribal religion gives the people the power to reconcile themselves to the eternal emergencies of life".[1]

Proselytisation of Tribals

But during the colonial rule, considering the tribal people as animists or even not civilised. Christian Missionaries of different denominations were involved in proselytising many tribal communities. Such missionary activities were directly or indirectly patronised by the colonial government. The missionaries have done very good work in respect of providing medical services and opportunities for education for tribal peoples, particularly, the baptised ones. Yet spread of Christianity among the tribal people has also caused certain losses of traditional tribal values, customs and celebrations of ceremonies. J.P. Mills strongly the fact that in the Naga villages, the American Baptist Mission has abolished some of the traditional ceremonies interpreting them as un-Christian. About "such ceremonies as the great Feasts of Merit, at which the whole village, rich and poor alike, is entertained, and of which the religious aspect is far less important than the social, have not been remodelled on Christian lines, but have been utterly abolished among converts. . . . To abolish these feasts is to do away with the very occasions on which the awful monotony of village life is broken. They are, too, the natural Naga and Kuki way of distributing wealth. . . .

> ". . . It is part of the tendency to abolish old things just because they are old, and substitute for the strong communal feeling which has enabled the tribes to survive for so long an individualism which is foreign to them.
>
> ". . . An Animist puts his village before himself. A Baptist puts himself before the village. No Semas are as prone to disobey their chief as Christian Semas, and Christian Aos have often refused to take part in village government to which their years and experience called them. A "civilised" Naga is apt to call customary discipline restraint, and many of them are eager to leave their villages and live free of all control."[2]

About the consequences of Christian Missionary activities among the Lushais, C.G. Helme, I.C.S., observes: ". . . Domestic life, methods of cultivation, village habits and customs, food and drink, amusements—all with a few exceptions . . . remain as they were half a century ago. It is only in the relations between village and village and between the Lushai Hills and the outside world, in religion and in education that any marked difference can be observed.

> "The first Missionaries arrived in the Lushai Hills in January 1894, and the spread of Christianity has been extraordinarily rapid. I estimate the number of professed Christians at about one-half of the population of the district. Conversion to Christianity operates as a powerful solvent of ancient customs which are gradually falling into neglect and disrepute. The new religion—adopted mainly in the form of Calvinistic Methodism—is effective chiefly in the field of ritual observance. The standard of morality which was never low, remains the same."[3]

Helme further mentions that "education has been left entirely to the Mission' and most Lushais, Christians or non-Christians are now able to 'read and write'. Lushais have adopted in a few suitable localities the system of wet rice cultivation. They adopt clothes of European style and cut the hair short. Helme also notes that there has been 'a slight rise in the standard of comfort. They drink tea, milk and fruits which they also grow with avidity. The use of milk, according to him, has been effecting a considerable reduction in the rate of infant mortality."[4]

Proselytising of tribals by the Christian missionaries has resulted in the spread of literacy and education, health care facilities and adoption of modern (mainly Western) ways of living. But Christian Missionary activities has been in some places encouraged the converted tribals to consider themselves separate from the other indigenous people. Verrier Elwin has underlined this consequence of the proselytising process in order to sound a word of caution that in the frontier areas, it would not be "wise to disturb the people with new forms of religion which may puzzle them and which may even compete with one another for their allegiance." He has also noted that "the effect of some of the foreign missions on the tribes of eastern India has been to create a separatist mentality, both towards India and among the people themselves." Elwin further observes: "The political effect on the covert is to diminish his enthusiasm for India and its culture, the social effect is to isolate him from his non-Christian brethren in the villages. In Manipur separate Christian hamlets have been established resulting in disputes and litigation about land. In return the non-Christians sometimes insist on the Christians living separately, in view of the fact that the latter refuse to observe the traditional taboos, at which the others, believing that this brings bad luck to the village, are naturally resentful."[5]

Similarly, Hindu missionaries in their enthusiasm for reforming the tribal habits, propagate vegetarianism and teetotalism, besides other taboos and customs unknown to the tribal society destroy village unity.[6]

Religious Aims in NEFA

Verrier Elwin effectively formulated the different aspects of Government's aims in administering North East Frontier Agency including the religious aims. And he asserts that the "NEFA Administration observes a policy of strict religious neutrality and would not impose even tribal religion on those who do not want it. It takes exactly the same attitude to Hindu, Buddhist or Muslim missionaries as it does to Christian Missionaries."[7] This policy clearly reflected the constitutional provision for secularism as the state policy and it has been strikingly different from that of the colonial Government which directly or indirectly patronised Christian Missionary activities in North East India.

The ultimate religious aim of the NEFA Administration was to provide a favourable climate in which the tribal religions can grow and 'reform themselves from within' so that in NEFA religious concepts will be truly in character, yet having a wider view and a purer conception of God and man.'[8]

Jairamdas Doulatram made almost a prophetic statement about religious attitudes and aspirations of the tribal peoples. It is worth quoting: "Just as Hindu society in Assam recoiled against the approach of the Christian proselytising programme, so also will one day the tribal people recoil against our approach to them, if we fail to understand their life and culture in their true light and miss the spirit of their belief simply because its forms and terms seem to be different from what we are familiar with. We must shed our subtle sense of superiority which makes us picture ourselves as "reformers", commissioned to work for the uplift of the backward tribes. . . . The people of the hills to the north and south of the Brahmaputra are no more animists than the Hindus of the Assam Valley."[9]

In the spirit of Elwin's thoughts on the future course of development and modernisation processes under way in North East India it may be noted that rapid progress in material prosperity needs to be matched by 'a parallel spiritual and ethical revival'.[10] But there must not be any propagation of such values by the organised religious 'gurus' or missionaries as it will violate the basic principle of secularism.

Constitutional Provisions for Secularism

Secularism, as envisaged in the Objective Resolution adopted by the Constituent Assembly on 22 January, 1947, stands for securing to all the people of India freedom of thought, expression, belief, faith, worship, etc. subject to law and morality. Accordingly, the Constitution of India enjoins the state to protect all religions equally but it itself shall not uphold any religion as state religion. The individual citizen's 'liberty of belief, faith and worship' is ensured by incorporating fundamental rights which guarantee to each citizen freedom to profess and practise any religion of his choice. The state and all its institutions are required to maintain strict impartiality towards all religions.

Jawaharlal Nehru, the chief architect of building Independent India as a secular state, rightly thought that in India's pluralistic religio-cultural and social structure secularism should be the basic philosophy of the Indian State. He was, of course, aware that it would be very difficult to follow the path of secularism as he conceived it as an individual's liberty of faith. For, secular behaviour was 'not wholly reflected in our mass living and thinking'. Even as politicisation of religion, religious conversions by allurements, religious fundamentalism, etc. have been vitiating the climate of secularism in India, the basic tenet of secular values still guide the conduct of many individuals belonging to different religious communities who affirm and practise religious tolerance. The independent judiciary, free press, neutral bureaucracy, at least at the higher ranks, etc. also ensure the pursuance of and preservation of secular values as enshrined in the Constitution.

Challenges to the Spirit of Secularism

In North East India, however, of late, some happenings have been posing a serious challenge to the philosophy of secularism as interpreted in an individual's context and also its practical bearing. Revivalism of indigenous faiths and tribal cultures in a number of areas in the region has been confronting competitive religious influences and conversions of the indigenous tribal peoples by organised religions by various means including politicisation of the methods of religious conversions. The spirit of revivalism has emerged in the wake of resurgence of assertions of ethnic indentities and indigenous cultures all over the world and upholding of indigenous peoples' rights and privileges under the auspices of the UNO sponsored international fora. This recent trend may also be a reaction of the people of their continued feelings of deprivations and loss of access to the productive resources as they had been enjoying traditionally. The ideology of "development" followed by the government has failed in a large measure to fulfil the felt needs and aspirations of the masses of people.

As a reaction to such disappointments, people and even the educated youths, have been turning to their traditional faiths, values and cultural indentities and opposing the attempts by the organised religious bodies to win them over into their folds. They are even, in a sense betraying the signs of fundamentalism in restricting the functioning of people of other faiths to interact with them in the religious, social and cultural planes.[11]

In the context of such developments in North East India the view of Asghar Ali Engineer about secularism is relevant. While upholding the Nehruvian model of secularism he opined that common people's religious sensibilities should be respected while taking measures 'to depoliticise religion (without any compromise on this).' He asserts: "Secularism can never succeed in India if western model is adopted. Our social ethos are very different. It would succeed only if an Indian model is evolved with creative application of the concept."[12]

At least in North East India, we think, secularism can strike deep roots if the ideology respects 'collective religious sensibilities of its people'.

NOTES

1. Verrier Elwin (1988), *A Philosophy for NEFA*, Directorate of Research, Government of Arunachal Pradesh, Itanagar, 1988, pp. 210-14. All the quotations in this paragraph are from this source.
2. J.P. Mills, I.C.S. (1932), "The Effect on the Tribes of the Naga Hills District of Contacts with Civilization", Appendix A, *The Census of India, 1931*, Volume III, Assam Part I, Report, pp. (ii)-(iv).
3. C.G. Helme, I.C.S. (1932), "The Effect on the Lushais of Contacts with Civilization, Appendix A, *The Census of India, 1931*, Volume III, Assam, Part I, Report, p. v.
4. *Ibid.*
5. Verrier Elwin (1988), *op. cit.*, p. 219.
6. *Ibid.*
7. *Ibid.*, p, 218.
8. *Ibid.*, p. 216.
9. Quoted in Elwin, *ibid.*, p. 218.
10. *Ibid.*, p. 222.
11. For detailed account of the religious and cultural fundamentalism that has been vitiating the climate of secularism in North East India, see Sanat K. Chakraborty (2002). 'Faith War!', published in *Grassroots Opions*, Monsoon-Autumn 2002, pp. 14-19.
12. Asghar Ali Engineer (1992), "Nehru, Secularism and Nation Building", published in C.D. Tripathi and B. Datta-Ray (ed.), *Jawaharlal Nehru and the Disadvantaged*, North East India Council for Social Science Research, Shillong. p. 25.

18

ASSAM RIFLES IN THE NORTH EAST SCENARIO
An Upgraded Security Role and Development Dimension

GAUTAM SEN

Management of security in North East cannot be thought of without the involvement of the Assam Rifles. This Force, a Paramilitary Force in the truest sense, though called a Central Police Organisation in the parlance of the Ministry of Home Affairs, has been intimately associated with direct internal security operations in Mizoram, Nagaland, Manipur and Tripura and in a supporting role to other security and state police forces in Arunachal Pradesh and Assam.

Historical Experience

The crucial role played by the First Battalion of Assam Rifles in holding on to Aizawl and ensuring the presence of the Indian State in Mizoram during the MNF uprising in 1966, is a part of history. It was the Assam Rifles which fought its way back to Dimapur and Kohima initially and then to the rest of Nagaland to restore order and control, when in the aftermath of the Bangladesh Campaign in 1971 and re-deployment of the Indian Army, the National Socialist Council of Nagaland (NSCN) ultras had seized *de facto* control of the State. Prior to these events, the Assam Rifles had functioned basically as a Force for frontier administration of the erstwhile North East Frontier Agency or NEFA with its financial resources budgeted under the Ministry of External Affairs.

Counter Insurgency Activities

The recent past has seen a more extended role for the Assam Rifles. This phenomenon has been observed in Tripura, Manipur and Nagaland. While the State Government of Tripura has a well-trained and motivated armed police force in the Tripura State Rifles, because of the deep-routed and extensively foreign-aided militancy and the inadequacy of the institutional resources of the Tripura Government, the Assam Rifles have come to play a major role in the containment of insurgency in the State. A Range HQs and at least four Battalions of Assam Rifles are presently engaged in anti-insurgency operations and concomitant aid to Civil Authorities.

The position of the Force in Manipur is unenviable. With two Range HQs at Ukhrul and Imphal respectively, and a number of battalions thereunder, the Assam Rifles is involved in anti-insurgency operations and supporting the State administration in controlling anti-civic and disruptive activities of a host of ultra organisations such as the United Liberation Front of Manipur (UNLF), Kanglei Yol Kanna Lup (KYKL), People's Liberation Army of Kangleipak (Prepak), etc. It has assisted various Manipur State Governments under different political dispensations, in the holding of a number of State Assembly and Parliamentary elections. It would not be a exaggeration to claim that had the Assam Rifles' well established presence has not been there, the hostilities between the different ethnic groups as well as between the Hill districts and the Imphal Valley districts would have become uncontrollable.

While the Army has played a major role in retaining the Central Government's control on Nagaland, it is the Assam Rifles' spread-out deployment in the most difficult terrain in the State which has contained the spread and ascendancy of the NSCN and its factions. The Assam Rifles has a presence in the entire State, structured in two Range HQs with a number of operational battalions below them. In nearly all significant towns of Nagaland such as Zunebhoto, Wokha, Dimapur, Kohima, Mokukchang and Phutsero, the Assam Rifles have a presence. With the institution of a Ceasefire Agreement between Government of India and the NSCN (Issac-Muivah) since August 1997, the role of the Assam Rifles have become more onerous towards ensuring a tactical balance and counterpoise at the ground level with the ultras to ensure that, while the Ceasefire and condition of non-hostilities prevail, the ultras do not take advantage to regroup, surreptitiously arm and spread their political influence. The very fact that the initial Ceasefire for a year since August 1997 has held and been extended year by year and continues till date, and also that there has been another Ceasefire Agreement involving the Government of India and the NSCN (Khaplang), is indicative of the successful security management by the Assam Rifles. Lt. Gen. R.V. Kulkarni (Retd.) a former Director General of Assam Rifles, is incidentally the Chairman of the Ceasefire Monitoring Committee in Nagaland.

The measure of confidence of some of the North East State Governors in the Assam Rifles is indicated by the fact that a Company of the Force has been protecting the Nagaland Governor House over the past few years and a similar demand has been raised in 2000 from the Meghalaya Governor for the Raj Bhavan at Shillong. The demand in regard to the latter was not implemented because of anticipated adverse consequences from some political quarters in the State and the consequential inhibitions of the Assam Rifles authorities.

Reassessed Role on Internal Security

It would be appropriate if we re-assess the role of the Assam Rifles in the pan-North East scene and give it more content in keeping with the overall policies of Government of India towards the region. The Force equivalent to more than an Army Corps manpower-wise, consisting primarily of hill tribes, deployed dedicatedly in the North East under the administrative control of the Ministry of Home Affairs and with an annual budget of more than Rs.1000 crores, is ideally suited to form the backbone of the security management structure in the region. However, some basic aspects have to be reckoned to give this Force its due role.

The operational control of Assam Rifles has to shift from the Army to the Ministry of Home Affairs. The Group of Ministers constituted in the aftermath of the Kargil Conflict, also have opined as such. This entails that GOC-in-C, Eastern Command would no longer exercise operational control over Director General of Assam Rifles. This situation should not be unacceptable in conditions of less-than-hot-war or full scale conflict with hostile neighbours or a state of uncontrollable insurrection in any part of the North East. The Assam Rifles with its present and expanding strength with new raisings of ten battalions already approved by Government of India in January 2001, should be able to handle the existing and prospective security situation.

Role Apropos State Governments

Law and order is the responsibility of State Governments as per the Constitution. There should, however, be no dilution of its Constitutional ambit or reneging from the State Governments' role and responsibility in this regard. Any trend or action to the contrary will disbalance our polity and adversely impinge on the political and functional autonomy of the States. As it is, the North East State Governments are already affected by numerous factors of instability such as, political demands of various ethnic groups and administrative pressures from the various district and tribal autonomous councils. Diluting their responsibility in the matter of law and order maintenance would certainly undermine their role in internal security management.

The role of the Assam Rifles in the overall security scene in the North East has to be supportive nature and complementary to those of the Regional State Governments. The aspects to be looked after by the Assam Rifles and its conditions of deployment have to be clearly delineated to avoid conflicting perspectives between the State Governments on the one hand and the Assam Rifles authorities as well as the Ministry of Home Affairs on the other. While the North East State Governments could continue to deal with law and order in normal conditions, and could also draw upon additional resources from their Indian Reserve Battalions (armed police battalions raised with Central assistance) or even Central Police Forces like the Central Reserve Police Force (CRPF) and also other sister State forces on requirement, the Assam Rifles could be involved in conditions of severe challenge to security from organised cadres like those from the present NSCN in Nagaland, National Liberation Front of Tripura, All India Tripura Tiger Force of Tripura, United Liberation Front of Assam and the Manipuri insurgent groups, etc. The scope of Assam Rifles' operational involvement could be decided by an Apex Board constituted by the Government of India with political participation at a high level from the Central and North East State Governments and including Director General Military Operations of Army and Director General Assam Rifles.

Beyond Narrow Security Confines

In disaster management and for ensuring back-up security cover to infrastructure like highways, power plants and air and river ports, etc., the Assam Rifles could be assigned an important role. Their past experience, present training, available and prospective operational resources as well as their familiarity and linkage with the local milieu, would certainly facilitate undertaking these responsibilities which impinge on development of the region.

A classic example is the Centrally funded North East Council (NEC) Power Project of 75 megawatt installed capacity at Doyang in Nagaland. The Project was completed in 2001 at an exhorbitat cost of Rs. 758 crores against the initial cost of less than Rs. 200 crores, with a substantial time overrun. The Project completion was possible only when an Assam Rifles battalion based at Wokha town in Nagaland, moved in and secured the Project complex after evicting the Naga militants who were not only extorting a substantial part of the Doyang Project construction payment funds on a regular basis, but were also using the Project resources of the North East Electric Power Corporation for rest and recuperation of their cadres despite the presence of the Central Industrial Security Force and CRPF at the site.

Security and Development Nexus

Security and development cannot be considered in isolation. They are interdependent phenomena and complementary to each other. Smt. Indira Gandhi as Prime Minister had a deep realisation and foresight in this regard when, while setting up an unique regional developmental organisation and planning body as the NEC in 1972 and having the NEC Act of 1972 enacted by Parliament, she institutionalised the role of Director General of Assam Rifles as the Security Adviser of NEC in the Statute.

There was no security apparatus created or appended to NEC and Director General Assam Rifles associated with it. There was no direct security based operational role envisaged for the Director General. The essence of the NEC institutional arrangements was that its Security Adviser would provide advisory opinion and guidance on security implications of development schemes and projects. It is worth reckoning that the then Prime Minister and Government of India had deemed it appropriate to entrust the responsibility of appraising the security dimensions of NEC Schemes and projects to Director General Assam Rifles. It was considered appropriate that the North East States' Governors and Chief Ministers who constitute the North Eastern Council proper, obtain the benefit of advice from the Head of the Assam Rifles on the macro dimensions of security in the regional context while formulating and executing the development plans, schemes and projects under the NEC mandate.

The Assam Rifles is an integral part of the security scenario in the North East. Its position can only be upgraded. The Central Government is conscious of the benefits which can be derived by institutionalising a more pivotal role for the Force for internal security and also border management. Its track record, Force characteristics and operational ability seems to justify an enhancement of its security role in the North East without detriment to the local State Governments. It is also a cost effective proposition because with incremental administrative and financial support, the Assam Rifles' capability would be measurably upgraded as against the enormous expenditure and logistical problems which would result from induction of other Central Police forces from across the country without attuning them to the local environment. The historical experience of the Assam Rifles in various activities tertiary to their security-oriented operations has also made it ideally suited for providing inputs on security dimensions of policies and programme for development of the region to the political executives and development planners. The Assam Rifles is thus uniquely placed to deal with the dualism of security and development with a harmonious outcome.

REFERENCES

Annual Reports of Ministry of Home Affairs, Government of India for the years 1997-2002.

NEC Act—Act No. 84 of 1971 of the Central Legislature.

Reports of the C&AG of India pertaining to the State Governments of the North East and Central Transactions covered by the Ministry of Home Affairs, Government of India.

19

SUB-REGIONAL MATRIX FOR DEVELOPMENT
Constraints and Framework

P.K. BANDYOPADHYAY

The paper seeks to examine the sub-regional concept of development—its framework and various constraints. The proposal basically consists of a sub-regional grouping within the SAARC involving India (primarily the North East India), Bangladesh, Nepal and Bhutan. This sub-regional cooperative arrangement may also be given a broader canvas keeping in mind the grouping of the Bay of Bengal rim states, which include Myanmar and Thailand. These are obvious benefits because of various factors like geographical proximity, natural resource endowment base and their potential economic possibilities.

The concept, though apparently attractive, has got some inherent bottlenecks in view of historical legacy and an unhelpful mindset among the peoples of the region. So it requires an understanding and delicate handling of the whole gamut of issues involved.

Recent reports about the increase of activities of the Inter-Services Intelligence outfit of Pakistan and the elements of Al-Qaeda in the territory of Bangladesh have far reaching security implications for the northeastern states of India. Both India and Bangladesh have, however, differing perceptions on the issue. The meeting of the Director General, Border Security Force (BSF) and the Director General Bangladesh Rifles (BDR) in October,

2002 in New Delhi, while focusing on border issues, infiltration of illegal migrants, smuggling and other related problems, and agreeing to work together to maintain peace, tranquility and security on the border, could not come to any agreed conclusion about the alleged training camps of the ISI backed elements.

The BSF raised the issue of the insurgents of the northeastern India finding shelter in Bangladesh and added that it would provide proof about the existence of training camps to its Bangladesh counterpart, Bangladesh agreed to look into the issue.

Even the assertions by the Deputy Prime Minister and Home Minister of India, Mr. L.K. Advani on the subject have been described the Bangladesh Foreign Ministry spokesman as 'baseless and motivated'. The Bangladesh Foreign Minister is reported to have stated that his government would soon send a list of criminals who have crossed over to India to save themselves from the current countrywide drive by Bangladesh Army and other law-enforcing agencies, for extradition.

In this climate of polemics the relations between the two countries need careful handling. The creation of the new country in 1971, which had been part of India before 1947 has 'led to a new set of problems' (Krishan: 2001). There are issues dealing with narcotic drugs, crimes across the border, law and order and insurgency, and the problem of enclaves, and adverse possession and the nagging problem of illegal migration. Yet it is also a fact that there is tremendous amount of interaction between the peoples of India and Bangladesh.

India shares an international border, which is as long as 4,096 km with Bangladesh, out of which the share of the North East India comes to about 1,956 km.

The position in respect of Myanmar, Bhutan and even China is no less complex. It may be recalled that the North East India shares 1,643 km border with Myanmar, about 1,000 km with China and about 650 km with Bhutan. The need of proper management of such a long international border cannot be over-estimated. That is essential for stability in the region. This has to be ensured through a mechanism of cooperative and consensual arrangement and continuous dialogue. In addition, there is the problem of the enclaves—51 *Bangladeshi* enclaves with a total area of 7,110 acres in India and 111 Indian enclaves with 17,158.1 acres in Bangladesh pose numerous security hazards. There are also several pieces of land in adverse possession of both the countries. Fifty-two pieces of land which actually belong to Bangladesh are in the adverse possession of India, while forty-nine pieces of land belonging to India are in the adverse possession of Bangladesh. A six and half kilometre stretch of the border is yet to be demarcated. The Indira-Mujib Accord of 1974 (Article 2) stipulates that all the areas in adverse possession of each country would be demarcated at the earliest. Bangladesh has ratified the agreement. The Indian viewpoint is that the Bangladesh ratification is 'conditional to the entire border being demarcated and India would ratify it once the process is completed'.

Security Considerations

A region with such a long international boundary and inherent border related peculiarities requires a suitable doctrine and security strategy. More so because it has a history of ethnic assertiveness, aggressiveness 'and a clamour of self-determination' (Medhi: 2002). In four of the seven states, namely Arunachal Pradesh, (69.82%), Meghalaya (80.58%), Nagaland (83.99%) and Mizoram (93.55%) the tribal people constitute the predominant segment. The percentages of the tribal people inhabiting Manipur, Tripura and Assam are 27.30, 28.44 and 12.84 respectively. Various movements for assertion, lack of communication and development have aggravated the problems of the north east. There are numerous constraints to the initiatives for tribal development. The economy being mostly subsistence economy there is heavy dependence on the primary sector. Moreover, there are chronic problems of land alienation, lack of entrepreneurship, generation of adequate savings and investment, which create a vicious cycle impeding the growth rate.

This led to unrest among the people and the consequent rise of numerous sub-nationalistic movements, insurgency situations and outbursts of aggressive identity. The Mizo revolt of 1966 has been sorted out with the Mizoram accord in the mid-eighties but then Naga problem, Manipur crisis are still to be resolved. In the Brahmaputra valley also there was the anti-foreigners movement launched by the All Assam Students Union in 1979-85. Though the Assam accord led to the suspension of the movement and gradual entry of the All Assam Students Union leaders into the electoral politics in the state, it heralded a number of ethnic movements like the ULFA movement, the Bodoland movement, the Karbi-Anglong movement, Rabha-Hajong movement and Ahom Tai movement. The insurgency among a section of the tribal people in Tripura is another example of the tribal unrest in the region.

As one of India's 'soft underbellies' the region is susceptible to various external powers and agencies which are out to exploit the ethnic, religious and linguistics diversities (Das: 2002). The narrow security approach has further accentuated the divisive situation calling for a new development model being factored into the country's overall strategy. Despite abundant natural, mineral and water resources and also wide biodiversity the region remains underdeveloped and underutilised. The lack of transportation facilities and market accessibility and other infrastructure remains a bottleneck and reduced the competitiveness of the local products emanating out of the primary sector of the economy.

The porous border—both land and maritime between India and Bangladesh has helped various insurgent groups of the north east take shelter and secure safe haven to carry out their activities and exploit disenchantment of the people to their advantage. As mentioned earlier, the prominent among such groups are United Liberation Front of Assam (ULFA), National Democratic Front of Bodoland (NDFB), National Liberation Front of Tripura (NLFT). and All Tripura Tiger Force (ATTF). Frequent border clashes generated associated problems of security and bilateral relations. According to an estimate, in 2001 alone 50 Indians and 41 Bangladeshis were killed in border disputes (Datta: 2002). Clashes between the border forces, namely Border Security Force (BSF) and Bangladesh Rifles (BDR), particularly in the disputed enclaves on the Assam-Meghalaya-Bangladesh borders portend ominous events. Added to this is the problem of the river borders complicated by the shifting river routes, soil erosion and frequent floods with formation of numerous islands and *chars*.

This vulnerable border situation is responsible for another serious problem—the illegal migration taking a much larger dimension of a socio-economic and cultural and, therefore, political issue. Even some observers describe it as 'a demographic invasion' (Biswas: 2002). In Tripura the migrants have outnumbered the tribal population. In fact the illegal migration has generated 'serious social tension in the entire northeastern region'. The rate of growth of population in Assam has been much higher than that of India's average (Monirul Hassein).

As the popular saying goes, one cannot change one's neighbours and hence one has to grapple with the problems and issues on a realistic basis and evolve a suitable framework. The problem, being quite grave, the appropriate authorities must look into the entire gamut of the question. E.N. Ram Mohan, former Director General of the Border Security Force suggested a three-point formula to address the issue:

(a) Sort out once and for all with Bangladesh the issues of territorial dispute pending since 1947, namely the enclaves in each other's countries, the issue of adverse possession, and the demarcation of the border along the 6.5 km unmarked stretch.
(b) Ensure that the BSF gets its full quota of battalions on the Bangladesh border so that each battalion has to cover only 30 kms of the border, as in Punjab.
(c) Quickly fence and light up the Bangladesh border as has been done on the western front.

The need for a structured programme to handle the security related issues cannot be brushed aside. But then there is the overriding requirement of growth and development with a long-term perspective to go beyond the immediate border management. Despite the occasional minor aberrations the logic of the ties between the two countries demands greater coordination at the field levels as well. Moreover, the geo-strategic reality and the economic compulsions have made Bangladesh the eighth largest 'formal' export market for the Indian goods. But if what is euphemistically called 'informal trade' is considered it is the third largest 'destination for Indian merchandise'. As a result the trade imbalance between the two countries is quite staggering. From about $150 million in 1990-91, the trade imbalance had gone up to one billion US Dollars in 2000-2001. It would be much higher, when the informal trade is considered. A Bangladeshi analyst went as far as to say that 'for India there are only two neighbours—Pakistan and China, the rest of us are mere geographic entities deserving very little attention and understanding. India really has no time for its smaller neighbours. Neither does the Indian media'. (Mahfuz Anam: 2001). Anam adds that 'we are a $3 billion market for Indian goods and services, the single biggest trading partner in the developing world'.

Sub-Regional Model

The regional economic cooperation is one of the major motivating factors for evolving cooperation among the countries of the South Asian region, namely, India, Bangladesh, Pakistan, Sri Lanka, Bhutan, Nepal and Maldives. The idea of a regional economic group got fillip during the visits of former Bangladesh President Zia-ur-Rehman to India, Nepal, Pakistan and Sri Lanka during 1977-78. The first meeting of the Foreign Secretaries of the seven countries was held in Colombo in April 1981 to formalise the idea of regional cooperation. The South Asian regional cooperation was officially launched in August 1983 in New Delhi at the first meeting of the seven Foreign Ministers. The first ever-regional summit of the heads of the governments of the seven SAARC countries was held in Dhaka on December 7-8, 1985 and a charter of SAARC was adopted. The charter, among other things advocated mutually beneficial, desirable and necessary regional cooperation to promote economic development of the one-fifth of the world population.

Among the SAARC countries India and Bangladesh occupy a dominant position in the intra-regional trade, though such trade among other SAARC countries is very small. So economic cooperation was given highest priority in the SAARC Summits. The seventh SAARC Summit held on April 10-11, 1993 in Dhaka 63 point Dhaka Declaration and signed a South Asian Preferential Trading Arrangement (SAPTA) with a view to reducing the trade barriers in the region. The eighth SAARC meeting in New Delhi in 1005 called for making SAPTA operational by December 1995 to coincide with the tenth anniversary of the SAARC. Under SAPTA several commodities were earmarked among the SAARC countries for tariff concessions. India offered tariff concessions for import of selected 106 items, Pakistan for 53 items, Sri Lanka for 31 items, Maldives for 17 items, Nepal for 14 items, Bangladesh for 12 items and Bhutan 7 items. During the eighth SAARC Summit a proposal was also mooted to initiate measures for setting up of a South Asian Free Trade Area (SAFTA) with the aim of heralding 'a new and significant process of regional cooperation'.

SAPTA is governed by the following principles:

(a) SAPTA shall be based and applied on the principles of overall reciprocity and mutuality of advantages in such a way as to benefit equitably all Contracting States taking into account their respective levels of economic and industrial development, the pattern of their external trade, trade and tariff policies and systems;
(b) SAPTA shall be negotiated step by step, improved and extended in successive stages with periodic reviews;
(c) The special needs of the Least Developed Contracting States shall be clearly recognised and concrete preferential measures in their favour should be agreed upon;
(d) SAPTA shall include all products, manufactures and commodities in their raw, semi-processed and processed forms.

The special treatment for the Least Developed Contracting States stipulates, among other things, duty-free access, exclusive tariff preferences or deeper tariff preferences for the export products, removal of non-tariff barriers, and removal of para-tariff barriers, where appropriate. It also includes a special consideration of exports from Least Developed Contracting States in the application of safeguard measures.

The SAARC Experiment with SAPTA and SAFTA has not met with much headway. With a history of mistrust, and a sense of alienation among the countries of the region and also Pakistan's attempts to raise bilateral issues the SAARC is now facing stalemate.

Growth Quadrangle

$$\text{Growth} = (PA + CI) \times SM$$

Against this background a new idea was mooted in 1997-98 for Sub-Regional cooperation involving Bhutan, Nepal, Bangladesh and the North East India. This would be some sort of 'growth quadrangle'. This sub-regional concept will be developed within the framework of the SAARC to harness the abundant natural, mineral and water resources of the northeastern region. The region has close trade ties including some border trade primarily because of close geographical proximity. According to a study by the Planning Commission there is greater need for rail link and enhancement of trade for development of the north east region. An estimate says that the informal trade between Bangladesh and the northeastern region is to the tune of rupees 300 crore annually and there is considerable potential to increase that level.

The northeastern region with an area of 2,54,983 sq.km. And a population of 36 million and Bangladesh with an area of 1,47,570 sq.km and a population of 120 million may work as the gateway to the burgeoning markets of South Asia and ASEAN countries. There is immense potential for joint ventures between the investors and entrepreneurs of the north-eastern region and Bangladesh. The Federation of Industries of Northeastern region (FINR) has identified specific industries for implementation under joint ventures keeping in view various natural resources. These are:

(a) Industries based on mineral resources, petro-chemical projects and downstream projects based on natural gas;

(b) Industries based on the agricultural and horticultural produce in the region, processed food products, canned vegetables bamboo based industries etc.;

(c) Projects for thermal and hydel power based on water, coal resources and gas reserves;

(d) Tourism-related industries in view of the natural scenic beauty in the northeastern region and Bangladesh.

Arrangements for avoidance of double taxation and a sub-regional mechanism for resolution of commercial disputes coupled with a strong private sector effort can go a long way to implement the growth quadrangle effectively. The Indian joint ventures in Bangladesh with buy-back arrangements in areas where India meets its requirements through imports and Bangladesh has adequate natural resources can further reduce the wide trade gap and would be mutually beneficial to both the countries.

At present track connections between Bangladesh Railway and Indian Railways exist. On the western side of Bangladesh there are two connections on broad gauge and one connection on metre gauge, which are operational. In the east there is one operational connection on metre gauge. These rail connections are used for movement of export-import cargo between the two countries. The proposed Trans-Asian Railway network covering a distance of about 14,000 kms would connect its southern corridors with Singapore and Indonesia, embrace the hinterland of Central Asia, the Indian subcontinent with Myanmar and Thailand in the southeastern region. The implementation of the network will require coordinated efforts involving structural adjustments and elimination of various inter-State bottlenecks.

It may be recalled that the proposed South Asian Growth Quadrangle (SAGQ), which is a sub-regional grouping comprising Nepal, Bangladesh, Bhutan and the northeastern India was mooted in its Kathmandu meeting in 1997 and its objectives and principles were enunciated. The railway network through the northeastern states of India is crucial for effective implementation of the Growth Quadrangle.

Mowdood-ur-Rashid, a Bangladeshi analyst has advocated railway connection with the north east India:

> 'As Myanmar has no viable road at present in the region bordering Bangladesh, there is no alternative to using both the highways and railways through the northeastern states to Myanmar. Furthermore, after the formation of BIMST-EC, a regional forum of economic cooperation comprising Bangladesh, India, Myanmar, Sri Lanka and Thailand the idea of competition needs to be substituted by the spirit of collaboration for the greater benefit of the member states and from that point of view a train journey through North East India will be a fruitful venture.'

The Trans Asian Railway (TAR) would be basically an inter-lock of national tracks of different countries. Linkages among Myanmar, Bangladesh and the northeastern states will facilitate transportation of goods for trade purposes. A proposed TAR route *via* Biral-Parbatipur-Ishurdi-jamtoil-Joydevpur-Dhaka-Akhaura-Kulaura-Shahbajpur-Mohishashan (Latu, India)-Myanmar will augment the transport infrastructure requirements of the Sub-regional grouping for economic cooperation. Moreover, a rail link between Agartala and Chittagong *via* Karimganj, upgradation of the rail network in Bangladesh to handle added traffic, expansion of port facilities and linkage by a new Highway from Agartala to Akhaura (Bangladesh), and Dudhnoi to Dala in Meghalaya are also necessary for realisation of the full growth potential of the region. The integration with the Trans Asian Railway Route connecting Thailand, Malaysia, Singapore, Bangladesh, India and Central Asia would open up immense possibilities for the North East India.

The issue of transhipment and transit of Indian goods through Bangladesh is a sore point in bilateral relations between India and Bangladesh. The idea of granting transit facilities to India was amended to the concept of transhipment. In short the transhipment means transfer of the Indian goods to a Bangladeshi carrier at the Indo-Bangladesh border and are re-transferred to an Indian carrier after the goods reach the Bangladesh-Northeast borders. This arrangement is economically beneficial to both the countries. If Tripura is allowed to use the Chittagong port, it can transport its goods to Chittagong which is about 75 kilometre away at a much cheaper transport cost as against the present practice of using a much longer route to Calcutta port through the Siliguri corridor. Transhipment of Indian goods offer economic advantages additional revenues and employment opportunities to Bangladesh. The issue needs resolution at a political and policy-makers' level primarily in Bangladesh.

The North East India is in the throes of turmoil for a variety of factors. Be it ethnic assertion, identity crisis for the smaller groups/tribal population, craving for preservation of their independent existence, problems of underdevelopment, demographic compulsions or socio-cultural and political necessities, the region has remained plagued with one eruption or the other. This necessitated occasional army intervention and counter-insurgency measures. Various states in the region including Assam were sometimes declared a 'disturbed area' and brought under the Armed Forces Special Powers Act. The security forces have to remain active while the operations are in progress to curb the violent ethnic movements 'degenerating into extremism and terrorism'. Even in the field of over-ground political activities the region sees cases of what may be described as 'politicisation of ethnicity'. Imbalance in economic development, lack of adequate people's participation, and political change and 'reassertion of ethnic affinities' coupled with 'mobilisation of popular sentiments to further group causes' (Medhi: 2002) can be cited as primary reasons for the volatile situation.

In this context a choice of strategy with a judicious mix of various initiatives is essentially called for. And herein is the need for a multi-pronged approach. The administrative and coercive policies are not adequate. Nor is the counter-insurgency measure sufficient. One has to find out a suitable model for all-round development. The problem is essentially a problem of the people, their aspirations, and felt needs. The idea of the sub-regional as enunciated in the paper assumes added relevance in the new millennium.

The Sub-regional matrix can function as a development multiplier. It may be expressed in a formula: Growth in the North East becomes a function of Political and Administrative initiatives and Counter-Insurgency measures coupled with the Sub-Regional Matrix.

$$\text{Growth} = (PA + CI) \times SM$$

As mentioned earlier. The Sub-Regional Matrix may further be dovetailed into the BIMST-EC concept. The countries within this grouping have resolved to :

(a) fully exploit the complimentarities within the region;
(b) exert combined political will for the success of the organisation;
(c) ensure that each of the countries individually is able to reap adequate benefits from BIMST-EC cooperation with special attention to those at lower stages of development;
(d) develop short, medium and long-term plans and strategies and to implement them in a systematic and coordinated manner;
(e) act as a bridge between the South Asian and South East Asian regions;
(f) strive to develop BIMST-EC into a free trade arrangement and to focus on activities that facilitate trade, increase investment and promote technical cooperation among member states;
(g) foster South-South cooperation and help in equitable and beneficial integration into the global economy;
(h) act as a vehicle for making the international economic and trading system more favourable to the developing countries;
(i) remove the constraints and facilitate trade in goods and services and in people to people contact;
(j) pursue sub-regional energy cooperation; and
(k) work towards transport and communication network and linkages.

The basic principles as enumerated above bring into sharp

focus the various constraints as well to realise the full potential of the Sub-Regional Matrix.

There is an element of asymmetry in the relationship among the smaller neighbours of India. There are contradictory pulls and pressures resulting out of the internal political dynamics in the countries within the proposed sub-regional grouping. And, therefore, a new approach is necessary leaving behind the junk of historical baggage.

REFERENCES

Ahmed, Mohiuddin, *Bangladesh Towards 21st Century*, Dhaka, 1999.

Anam, Mahfuz, "For India there are only Two Neighbours", an article in *Times of India*, New Delhi, April 29, 2001.

Barpujari, H.K., *North East India: Problems, Policies and Prospects*, Guwahati, 1998.

Biswas, Ashis K., "Slide Down the Crescent", *Outlook*, February 18, 2002.

Bordoloi, B.N., *Constraints of Tribal Development in North East India*, 1990.

Datta, Sreeradha, "Indo-Bangladesh Relations: An Overview of Limitations and Constraints", *Strategic Analysis*, Vol. 26, No. 3, IDSA, New Delhi.

Hazarika, Sanjoy, *Strangers of the Mist*, New Delhi, 1994.

Krishan, Kulbir, "Policing the Indo-Bangladesh Border", *Strategic Analysis*, Vol. 25, No. 5, IDSA, New Delhi.

Madan, Devinder Kumar, *Indo-Bangladesh Economic Relations and SAARC*, New Delhi, 1996.

Medhi, Kunja, "Intervention of Military in Civil Society: A Perspective of North East India", *Journal of NEICSSR*, April 2002.

Mowdood-ur-Rashid, "Trans Asian Railway for Regional Co-operation", An article in *Independent*, a daily published from Dhaka.

Ram Mohan, E.N., "The Government must Look Eastward and Quickly", An article, published in *Hindustan Times*, New Delhi, April 29, 2001.

Sarin, V.I.K., *India's North East in Flames*, Delhi, 1980.

Shukla, B.P., *What Ails India's North East*, New Delhi, 1980.

20

FRIENDSHIP BUT NOT CONFRONTATION

XAVIER P. MAO

The North East India comprising Meghalaya, Mizoram, Nagaland, Assam, Manipur, Tripura, Arunachal Pradesh and Sikkim is situated on international border, Myanmar, Bangladesh, China, Bhutan and Nepal are the countries with which these states have common border. But is most unfortunate that India does not have good relation with its neighbours. Further, Bangladesh which became a sovereign nation with the explicit support and help of India does not have also good relation with India. Perhaps, the adage that neighbours become worst enemies and strangers good friends has some truth in it. For some reason or other the relationship between India with its neighbouring countries is far from satisfactory. As a result, it has created problems not only for India but for those countries as well. Further, taking advantage of this embittered relations Pakistan which is far away from the North Eastern part of the country manages to operate in this region for engaging in subversive activities. After all, in international politics befriending an enemy's enemy is a much easier job than making a new friend. It is obvious that the North-eastern states are as sensitive as the state of Jammu and Kashmir which has border with Pakistan. But there is a difference between the problems faced by these two regions. They have to be discussed and understood with the help of two different and distinct parameters.

The North-eastern region except Sikkim and to some extent Assam is by and large a tribal area. The tribals inhabiting this part of the country are as diverse as anything. The Nagas, Mizos, Khasis, Garos and a host of other belong to various ethnic and linguistic groups. Even there are sub-groups among the Nagas and they speak different and distinct languages so much so that one group does not understand the language spoken by the other group. This type of diversity has posed insoluble problems. The Khasis and Garos inhabiting the same state of Meghalaya speak different languages and one group cannot easily understand the language of the other group. If the principle of formation of states in linguistic consideration is accepted nobody knows as to how many states the North-eastern region would be divided in future. Insurgency has been resorted to as a means by certain groups to solve their problems. The Naga insurgency is the oldest in the region followed by insurgency of other tribal groups. Scholars have tried to trace out various causes of insurgency in the North East. Some of the causes are real and certain others are imaginary, vague and sometimes exaggerated.

Though it is necessary to pin-point the exact causes of insurgency yet in human situation remedies could be prescribed and situations could be improved even though no exact cause of a problem is ascertained. As a matter of fact, there cannot be a single cause of a problem in the human world. In this context, the defence of the North East could be planned keeping in view two important points: (i) Insurgency prevailing in the region must be brought to an end immediately, and (ii) the neighbouring countries must be befriended. But these things are the most uphill tasks to achieve. No country in the world can be said to have achieved absolute and perfect equilibrium in these respects. In other words, every country in the world has some sort of internal problems and no country in the world has ever befriended all its neighbours. But this is no consolation that the Indian situation is no exception to that prevailing in the world and so these need not be cause for worry and anxiety on this count. But we must take our decision independently of what is happening around the world. While taking a decision on such issues the interest of the nation has to be kept uppermost in mind. Accordingly, we must take a decision in this regard without waiting for any other consideration. The first and foremost thing to be done in this respect is to create a sense of confidence among the indigenous people of the region. The suggestion may appear very vague and ambiguous but at the same time this is the first stage of establishing internal peace in the region. An attempt must be made both by the Government agencies and the Non-Governmental Organisation (NGOs) including the conscientious citizens of the region in this regard without further delay. There can be no cut and dry formula to guarantee confidence among the people. The contextual situation has to be taken into account while embarking upon such a proposal. Infrastructural facilities including minimum basic utilities like, all weather roads to all villages, clean drinking water, primary schools and health care units to all villages have to be extended so that the indigenous people get the feeling of being cared for by the government. Environment and eco-friendly small scale industries have to be set up to generate employment in the region. It is no more possible to give white colour jobs to the unemployed teeming millions in the country what to speak of absorbing the unemployed youths of the region in government offices. The country goes on mindlessly producing graduates and post-graduates in Arts, Science and Commerce at the expenses of primary and secondary education and the North East is no exception to it. What is needed in the North East today is establishment of good secondary and primary schools in the rural areas and not more universities with post-graduate departments that continue to spread half-baked ideas among the students. Education in the country in general and the North East in particular has to be need based and employment oriented. Otherwise production of unemployable graduates and post-graduates is likely to result in frustration and consequent emergence of insurgency, terrorism and extortion. Once the internal problems in the region are solved it becomes easier to befriend the neighbouring countries that have border with North East.

For ages people from the North East used to have trade and commerce with neighbouring countries like Myanmar, China, Nepal and Bhutan. The case of Bangladesh is very significant and crucial. Till the other day, it was a part of the subcontinent. In fact, India and Bangladesh share in common thousand years old history and civilisation. The Nagas in India have many things in common with the people of Myanmar. It is quite likely that most of the decorative pieces that the traditional Nagas put on their dresses meant for specific occasions have been brought from Myanmar through trade and commerce. Besides India has very ancient ties with Myanmar, China, Nepal and Bhutan. India must explore these ancient ties for mutual benefits. In a sense, mankind is one and attempt must be made by all nations to build good and friendly relations with one another. This is a moral maxim and noble political ideology and takes long time to cultivate it. But as a matter of fact historical connectivity and ancient socio-cultural ties are easy to explore and sustained relations could be re-established without much effort. This does not mean that national interest has to be sacrificed in order to befriend the neighbouring countries. In fact, national interest is not incompatible with friendship with neighbouring nations. It is true that in human history empire building and emergence of nation state had embittered relation among nations and gave rise to the phenomenon of subjugation of relatively weaker nations by stronger ones. The two World Wars in the last century were the result of such embittered relations among some nations. But the institution of emperor and empire-building have become things of the past like the colonialists and the colonies though superiority complex and feeling of supremacy among some nations are still very prominent even till today. There are nations in the world who try to overpower other nations someway or other. That is why tension and conflict still continue in the world.

On many important issues powerful European countries have come together under the leadership of the United States of America. As a result, a kind of Euro-Centric International relation obtains today in the world. Unfortunately, though the Asian countries like India and China are the inheritors of the most ancient civilisations in the world yet such a strong political and economic tie among the Asian nations is yet to emerge. Historically speaking, though Pakistan was a part of the Indian Subcontinent yet the relation between India and Pakistan has run into rough weather. The relation between India and China though not very bad at present is yet to improve perceptibly. Unless the relation of India with its neighbouring countries improves peace including defence of the North East will be in question: In the context of global economy it is in the interest of the Asian nations that they come together. First of all the border dispute including outstanding issues between India and its neighbouring nations must be resolved. This is a hercules task and requires political will on parts of both the countries. It is time that these are historical reasons for such conflict and dispute but political leaders must be sagacious and wise to resolve the dispute because war or cold-war like situation is not going to be in the interest of any nation. In this context India is required to play the most crucial role. To begin with border trades opened and encouraged. After all for countries trade and commerce used to be carried on by the people from both sides. Of course, opening the border for trade and commerce may create fresh difficulties, i.e., influx of population from one country to another. Such an influx has already created problems in the North-eastern states particularly in Tripura. The indigenous people of Tripura have been reduced to minority because of constant influx from Bangladesh. The Assam Ganaparishad in seventies started its agitation against such an influx from Bangladesh, while it is required that the border is to be opened for trade and commerce at the same time it is most important to see to it that it does not pave the way for influx. To do both, i.e., to open the border for trade and commerce and to check infiltration is a very difficult problem. The proposal can succeed only when border trade permit is issued on strict basis and it is checked from time to time. Besides, cultural exchange programme including visit of scholars, students and artists between North East, and the neighbouring countries should be encouraged so as to bring the people from both sides much closer than ever before. Once mutual trust and confidence is built outstanding disputes if any relating to border should be dissolved. The principle of live and let live should be the motto particularly for the Government of India. For whatever reasons for past many decades after independence successive political leadership in India did not do much to improve the relationship with its neigbouring countries bordering North

East. The slogan of *Hindi-Chini, Bhai Bhai* coined by late Prime Minister Nehru and echoed by Mao Tse-Tung did not bear expected fruit. India-China war in 1962 disillusioned people on both sides of the Himalayas. It is upto the political analyst to tell us whether the then Chinese leadership was on the wrong or the Indian leadership was on the wrong. But the fact remains that the 1962 war between India and China embittered the relation between the two countries for many many years. Now time has come for both the countries to work very hard to heal the wounds caused due to war in the past. In the interest of the South East Asia region China and India must come closer and all sorts of confrontations between the countries should be replaced by friendship. Friendship has to be cultivated by both the countries. For the simple reason that if one country cultivates it but the other country takes advantage of it. There is every likelihood that the attitude of the former may be interpreted as a sign of timidity. But any country can take initiative in this direction. In a sense it is imperative on the part of India to take initiative and cultivate friendship with its neighbours. Friendship is not a sign of weakness and timidity but is indicative of strength and stamina.

It is outdated idea that the defence of a country or a region depends solely on military strength. It may be pointed out in this connection that military superiority and militarisation of a country or a region simply creates further tension and conflict in the long run and does not solve any problem at all. Moreover, in human world all the problems are highly interconnected. That is to say to understand one problem is to understand all others and to solve one problem one has to solve all other problems in a way. Defence of North East, as has been argued out depends, to a large extent upon internal security and internal security in turn depends upon a just socio-economic order. Like any other part of the country, the North-eastern region suffers from internal subjugation and exploitation. That is to say, even if the colonialists, have left the country long since internal colonialism still persists and manifests in various forms. It is a fact that the North-eastern region by and large is a tribal society and it is widely said and believed that tribals by nature are egalitarian. But as a matter of fact, the so called equalitarianism is just a theme of the text books. It has no connection with what is known as the ground reality. The tribals in the North East are as good or as corrupt as their counterparts in other parts of the country corruption in public offices particularly relating to public funds is very high in the North East. This phenomena has thoroughly disillusioned the conscientious youth in the region. It is high time that the politicians and the bureaucrats working in the region reflect on this aspect of social evil. After all no country or region can survive purely on high sounding but empty slogans. The politicians and the bureaucrats must exhibit in their daily official activities that they are really honest and works for the people. Politics in majority of cases has proved to be a very lucrative job of all and North East is no exception to it. Central assistance comes pouring into the region but it has not made any visible impact on the common man. Thus unequal distribution of national assets has caused widespread resentment among the people and this is likely to affect internal security to a very great extent.

India has produced personalities like Buddha, Gandhi and many others but honesty and truthfulness are yet to be implemented in public life. Instances are not very rare in the country including the North East where even justice and the so called high level inquiry report could be purchased. Besides commodities, the so called big bosses and even in certain cases those who deal with dispensation of justice in this country too have a price tag on them. The common man gets bewildered at it. He starts suspecting and doubting everybody around him. It is not that the non-tribals exploit and subjugate the unfortunate tribals in the North East but the well placed tribals do not hesitate to exploit their fellow tribal brethren. This trend is very much in vogue in the North-eastern region. The so called openness in administration is absolutely absent. In fact, the high ranking tribal officers have been using the non-tribal officers have been using the non-tribal officers to exploit and subjugate the innocent tribals. It would not be outside of the mark to cite certain concrete instances in support of this nefarious trend prevalent in the region. His Excellency Dr. A.P.J. Abdul Kalam, the President of India and the visitor of North

Eastern Hill University visited Shillong in 2002. Two tribal research scholars from the region wanted to submit a memorandum to His Excellency in his capacity as the Visitor of NEHU bringing to his notice the fact of their harassment by the NEHU Vice-Chancellor in collaboration of some non-tribal teachers on submission of Ph.D. thesis. The scholars approached the State Government and completed all formalities two weeks before the arrival of the President in Shillong. But just on eleventh hour the highest official of the Government of Meghalaya in connivance with the Vice-Chancellor NEHU did not allow the research scholars to meet the President and submit their memorandum though there was no criminal record nor any Police report against the scholars. In this case, the Vice-Chancellor was a tribal the government official was a tribal and the two research scholars were also tribals. One wonders as to where has the proverbial egalitarianism among tribals gone! But the Vice-Chancellor in order to take revenge, collaborated with the State Government official and saw to it that the research scholars do not meet the President of India. This is one of innumerable cases where tribals are being exploited even by their fellow tribals. As a result, educated young men get alienated and at the earliest opportunity take to guns.

Secessionism has often raised its head in North East. Late A.Z. Phizo was the first to articulate it. As a matter of fact, the late Naga leader did not use the concept secession. According to him, the Indian Government had forcibly occupied Nagaland and they must vacate it. The Mizos under the leadership of late Laldenga also demanded secession but in due course the Mizo problem was solved. Today, there are stray groups in Assam, Manipur, Tripura as well as Meghalaya who demand secession. It is heartening to note that the peace talk held recently between the Prime Minister and the leaders of the NSCN(IM) groups in New Delhi is very significant and if the Naga problem is solved it will go a long way finding out solution to secessionist move in the entire North East. It may be noted here that the demand for secession by some groups in North East has disturbed internal security and in turn it has affected defence of the region.

Historically speaking, no national boundary is sacrosanct. As a matter of fact, such lines are being drawn and redrawn from time to time. The subcontinent was divided into India and Bangladesh too was carved out of Pakistan. The Soviet Union disintegrated to form separate units. These instances are not cited to justify further division of the country and side with the secessionist demand. Rather these instances are cited so that we including our leaders learn lesson from the historical past. It is true that India like many other countries of the word was never a political unit in the hoary past. In pre-Buddhist period India consisted of sixteen separate republics. The First King who tried to integrate different units, into one country in the past was Chandragupta Maurya. The Turko-Afghans and the Moghuls tried to integrate it for their own purposes but soon it disintegrated. The Britishers too tried to integrate though for their own gains. After the British left and India became a democracy the demand for secession and integration have to be viewed from a fresh angle. The ideas of conquest and conquer including Master and Servant are things of the past though unfortunately in certain literature relating to Government of India and its citizens, the expressions 'Master' and 'Servant' still occur. It is high time that such expressions that smack of colonialism and slavishness must be deleted forthwith from any rule book on Indian Government and its citizen. In a democracy there is a mutual need of the Wits. One cannot grow and develop without the other and all the units are equal partners in the same joint venture. Though ideally speaking every group even for that matter an individual should be left free to decide his/her own fate. Self-determination at ideal level is the natural right of the individual and the group and no other external agency should interfere with it. This view leads to an extreme form of individualism and if accepted and the groups in isolation are likely to be completely extinguished. The Aristotelian model which lays equal emphasis both on the individual and the society is well grounded. That is to say, individual and groups need each other for their growth and self-development. Now the question is which groups and which individuals are to be chosen and on what basis for the purpose of living together? The historical connectivity and enlightened self-interest possibly constitute the two criteria for exercise of such a choice. Seen in this light, the people of the North-eastern part of the country have had close links with India rather than with any other neighbouring country for thousands of years.

Moreover, after more than five decades of independence, the socio-cultural tie has been strengthened to a very great extent. In fact interaction and unity in economic, political and judicial front is being forged day by day. What is lacking is what is known as emotional integration and this is most important which cements and sustains people together as a nation even if they belong to diverse ethnic, linguistic and religious groups. There is not a single way of achieving what is known as emotional integration. In fact, there are ways. Further, it is the larger group who has to take initiative and create cordial atmosphere so that mutual suspicion and doubts removed. It is only through discussion and parleys and not through violence that problems could be solved. Violence breeds violence though the *Bhagvat Geeta* advocates use of violence as the last resort when all democratic methods and alternative conflict resolution institutions fail in protecting righteousness (*Dharma*). But in India we have not yet reached that stage of no return to use violence for resolution of conflict.

It is true that Indian states has become very oppressive, callous and apathetic towards its people corruption, nepotism and favouritism have reached all time high. The so called "Guardians" of society, i.e., the politicians, bureaucrats including even some fragments of judiciary have not been able to generate confidence among the people. A democratic polity cannot survive and hold people together if its three pillars, namely the Legislature, Executive and the Judiciary are not manned by upright the honest people. Not only the defence of the country including that of the North East will be in jeopardy but the polity is likely to disintegrate with increase of dishonesty and malpractice in public life. In the dim past, Plato the philosopher could visualise in clear and categorical terms the causes of degeneration of society. That is why he pleaded for high level of honesty, probity and integrity in public life.

It is an outdated idea that the defence of the country or a region solely depends upon its military strength. It may be pointed out in this connection that military superiority and militarisation of a country or a region simply creates further tension and conflict in the long run and does not solve any problem at all. Moreover, in human world all the problems are highly interconnected. That is to say, to understand one situation is to understand all others and to solve one problem is to solve all other problems. Defence of North East as has been argued out to a large extent depends upon internal security and internal security in turn depends upon a just socio-economic order. Like any other part of the country, the North-eastern region suffers from internal subjugation and exploitation. This is to say, even if the colonialists have left the country long since, internal colonialism still persists and manifests in various forms. To save the situation an all out effort should be made without further delay to improve the socio-economic conditions in the North East so that the ground of demand for secession is removed root and branch. Improvement in the internal situation will surely go a long way befriending the neighbouring countries of the North East. However, the motto should be "Friendship but not Confrontation".

21

PROBLEMS OF SOCIAL SECURITY AND DEVELOPMENT IN MANIPUR

H. SUDHIR

"Insecurity permeates the lives and families of individuals affected by HIV/AIDS. But AIDS also shatters the security of whole societies, communities and economies. Indeed, it is one of the biggest obstacles to development itself. It affects regional and global stability and risks solving democratic development. In this way, AIDS not only takes away the present. It takes away the future. That is the toll of AIDS."

Kofi A. Annan
Secretary-General United Nations
1 December 2001

Introduction

A paradigm shift in international thinking on development concept is the recognition to social objective in overall development framework. A dominant indicator of development perspective lies in building up the specified institutional base of society and to the dissemination of values and attitude of a secure society. Bearing the shift in mind, the paper intends to touch on the problem of social security in the state relating the drug addictive behaviour of the youth and to identify the social values and objectives that support the social development.

Golden Triangle proximity exacerbated by the perforated geo-political environment speedily fuels drug trafficking permeating inflow of drug substances and easier accessibility to it by the youth of both the sexes transcending class-cultural barriers finally infected with HIV/AIDS en-route intravenous drug usage, and its consequential transmissions *via* unsafe sex, mother to child transmission, commercial sexual network breaking the social security. Formerly, a transit route to the wider lucrative overseas drug markets, Manipur since early 80s throws a concern as a major threat to social security. Qualitative progress is restricted for a promising social section as a social factor of development is dragged into drug addictive behaviour generating a social breakdown for which a priority is ought to accord for a pragmatic-holistic modality.

I

CONCEPTUAL FRAMEWORK

Development has no monolithic definition. It is multifaceted in qualitative and quantitative dimensions. It is also noticed that there have been some previous contributions on security-development relation in the north east India but mostly on armed conflictual situation denominator.[1] The social angle of development seems to be paid little attention in the region which gained prominence in the international development thinking. Even the UN Human Development Report since 1990 is a recognition to the measurement of development by economic indicator that alone conceals more than it reveals and "takes account of more human factor. It is in line with the current theoretical development thinking in development paradigmatic change what may be assigned as social sector of development exhibiting social sector-development relation touching the specified Manipur context."[2] Sensing that "development is accelerated and deepened by the strong support of a developed social sector",[3] the paper is intended to delve into the relation of the problem of security and development question on a specific denomination perspective as a parcel of the overall holistic approach. By social security problem, herein, signifies the problem of repercussions in the society arising out of the social indicator-

HIV/AIDS endemic among the youth in the state and to examine the path restraining the development. By youth in the paper meant the most promising-productive community of population in the 15-35 age cohort.

What is drug abuse?

> "Self-administration of a drug for non-medical reasons, in quantities and frequencies which may impair an individual's ability to function effectively and which may result in social, physical or emotional harm. It also means that when anyone uses illegal drugs on their own (although they are not sick or ill) it may ultimately lead to destruction of their lives and society."[4]

On the relation between the drug abuse and socio-economic life of the people, it is furthermore written:

> "Drug abuse has had a negative impact on both social and economic life in the region. The problem arising out of drug abuse by many youth has affected several families in the state."[5]

However, the author falls apart from going into the investigation of the correlation which this paper intends a bumble attempt.

Drug abuse, historically, is not an off late phenomenon as there are age-long traditions of abuse of alcohol, opium and cannabis in the state, however, what is of severity to the society now is the youth's access to drug abuse particularly heroin, pharmaceuticals and psychotropic substances thereby shacking base of the state's future generation.

II

PROBLEM

While the relation of the epidemic and development question has gained wide prominence in Ethiopia and Sub-Saharan Africa, the area appears to be adequately paid little attention in the North

East India more precisely Manipur which has earned the credit of being one among the foremost prime centres of the endemic. Perceiving the importance, the paper would be a small attempt to touch upon the area. Despite initiatives which have been taken in different capacities, one area that seems to be kept aside towards a successful response to the epidemic is research orientation. Writing the paper senses the lack of literature and proper documentation. This paper is attempted based mostly on the secondary data gathered from the governmental and non-governmental resource centres. Even the available literature having accessed in writing the paper are mostly of general information types and devoid of specific points which the paper hunts for. For example, there is no encounter of data on mortality or life expectancy rate, explicitly, of the youth or the children caused by the epidemic. Population of the orphaned children infected by the epidemic or health cost are well unrecorded. Writing the paper strongly felt the necessity of in-depth field survey work and it would certainly deepen to the overall understanding of the problem, yet, the author is restricted from going into it by time constraint, still short preliminary interviews carried out during the endeavour help to the shaping of the paper. Amidst all of these, the paper is an attempt.

III

SITUATIONAL GLIMPSE

The designation of the 26th June, yearly, as the *International Day Against Drug Abuse and Illicit Trafficking* commemorating the *International Declaration Against Drug Abuse and Illicit Trafficking* on 26th June, 1987,[6] UN proclamation of the period 1991-2000 as *Decade against Drug Abuse*[7] and the observation of the theme of the year just ended 2002 as the *Substance Abuse and HIV/AIDS* looked into the serious implications of drug abuse and illicit trafficking interwoven and the exposure of the youth to drug that brought the epidemic.[8]

Manipur, a small landlocked state of the North East India with hardly 0.2 per cent of the country's population, by sharing a long stretch of 358 km with Myanmar on the east and the porous boundary intimately nestled on the *Golden Triangle* famous for 20 per cent World heroin contribution precisely for production of high pure heroin type in crystal white injectable powder locally known as *No. 4*.

Table 21.1: Manipur at Glance

Boundary	Nagaland (North) Mizoram (South) Assam (West) Myanmar (East)
Area	22,327 sq. km.
Population	23,88,634 12,07,338 (Male) 11,81,296 (Female)
Literacy Rate	68.87% (Total) 77.87 (Male) 59.70 (Female)
Sex Ratio	978
Density per sq. km	107
Decadal Growth Rate	30.02
Per Capita Income	12,198
District	9 (4 Valley and 5 Hills)
Community Development Blocks	33
Villages	2,182

Source: Statistical Abstract of Manipur 2001, Directorate of Economics and Statistics, Government of Manipur.

The trade activities in between and among the areas that had fallen within the present North East region and the adjoining countries dated back to the remote past.[9] Precisely, Manipur's trade with the neighbouring Burma (Myanmar), an age-long phenomenon, is well documented.[10] Sensing the potentiality beneath the unregulated trade network, the Indo-Myanmar Trade was officially opened with the inauguration by the then Commerce Minister P. Chidambaram at Moreh, a border point, Chandel district, Manipur, about 109 km south east of Imphal along the Indo-Myanmar road, National Highway No. 39, 12 April, 1995 aftermath of the Indo-Myanmar Border Trade Agreement between the two governments of India and Myanmar, 21 January, 1994 unlocking the Moreh (India)-Tamu (Myanmar) sector on some regulated product items.[11] However, contravening the development target of this opened border trade, what herein lies a serious issue that restricts the infrastructure of development is the immediate and underlying repercussions of illicit narco-trafficking which is made easier by the absence of vigilance on the porous boundary. Of the two springs of narcotics, the Golden Triangle in the South East Asia, a rugged mountainous terrain of about, 20,00,000 sq.km with a population of approximately one million in around 3,000 villages comprising the Kachin Hills and the Shan plateau of Myanmar, the mountainous northern Laos and the northern hilly terrain of Thailand[12] is one where heroin is manufactured in many laboratories controlled by various drug kings and trafficked to various destinations. Shan plateau and its neighbourhood (Myanmar); mountainous Chiang Mai, Chiang Rai, Mae Hongson and Nan province (Thailand); Hongsa and Louang Prabang province (Laos) are prominent poppy cultivation centres in the Golden Triangle. (The Golden Crescent on Afghan-Pak-Iran border is another one).

As per data available, the proximate corridors of drugs into the state are Tiddim and some other spots in the north west Myanmar en-route Behiang, a Manipur-Myanmar border point in the Churachandpur district, far south Manipur touching the north west Myanmar from where moved along the Imphal-Tiddim road connecting the capital town of Imphal and the Myanmar terminal point, Tiddim passing through Behiang and the proper Churachandpur town. Yet, the modus operandi on which the drugs reached Tiddim and other north west Myanmar centres from the Golden Triangle calls forth a study. Another well significant trafficking path since the early 80s into the state that reached the state capital, Imphal is *via* Moreh amidst a number of police, para-military customs-excise check posts that found its way for filthy profitable export to Indian cities, Europe and United States. From being a transit in the trafficking, Manipur turned to be transit-consumer state characterised by the youth's entrance to drug addictive behaviour at a large proportion by the 80s and its consequential endemic in the society—the HIV/AIDS.

Contrary to homosexual history of the epidemic in the United States, in Manipur, the genesis of the endemic is related to the high risk addictive behaviour among the IDUS spreaded later by its own inherent multiplied potentiality. Interestingly, a huge per cent of the HIV population is in the age range 15-35 years.

Table 21.2: Youth Population of HIV Positive Cases—Manipur

Age Group	Male	Female	Total	% of Total Positives
11—20	773	157	930	8.56
21—30	4,905	1,164	6,069	55.88
31—40	2,307	553	2,860	26.34

Source: Epidemiological Analysis of HIV/AIDS in Manipur upto January 2003, Manipur State AIDS Control Society, Manipur.

Since the detection of the first HIV positive case in February, 1990 from a cluster of IDUS blood samples collected in October, 1989, HIV/AIDS has occupied a prime concern in the state. Prevalence rate among the IDUS increased from 0 to 50 per cent within a short span of one year during 1990-91. Manipur has earned the fame of contributing about 8 per cent of the countries total HIV positive cases. Epidemiologically, Manipur ranks highest third in the HIV positive cases after Maharashtra (first) and Tamil Nadu (second), albeit, calculation per one million population, Manipur's sero-prevalence rate is 6 times mightier than Maharashtra and 20 times that of Tamil Nadu.

Table 21.3: HIV/AIDS Profile upto January 2003—Manipur

	Sero-Surveillance	Sentinal-Surveillance	Total
No. of blood samples screened	61,810	32,829	94,639
No. of positives	10,867	3,930	14,837
No. of Females	2,187	—	2,187
No. of AIDS cases	1,701	—	1,701
No. of deaths	272	—	272
Sero-positive rate	175.81	120.93	156.77

Source: Epidemiological Analysis of HIV/AIDs in Manipur upto January 2003, Manipur State AIDS Control Society, Manipur.

Despite a decline on sero-prevalence rate since 1998, rate is still higher in the IDUS world.

Table 21.4: District-wise Break-up of HIV Positive Cases—Manipur

District	No. of Samples Screened	HIV Positives	Sero-Prevalence %	District %
Imphal (East and West)	37,394	7,160	19.15	68.14
Thoubal	5,482	996	18.17	9.48
Bishnupur	2,812	524	18.63	4.99
Churachandpur	2,023	612	30.25	5.82
Ukhrul	966	381	39.44	3.63
Senapati	1,633	403	24.68	3.81
Tamenglong	282	27	9.57	0.26
Chandel	1,291	404	31.29	3.85

Source: Epidemiological Analysis of HIV/AIDS in Manipur upto January 2003, Manipur State AIDS Control Society, Manipur.

Table 21.5: Positivity and Percentage of the Intravenous Drug Users Out of Total HIV Positives—Manipur

No. of Blood Samples Screened (Sero-Surveillance)	No. of Positives	Sero-Positive Rate	% Out of Total HIV Positives
10,441	6,248	59.84	57.65

Source: Epidemiological Analysis of HIV/AIDS in Manipur upto January 2003, Manipur State Aids Control Society, Manipur.

IV

TRANSMISSION FACTOR ANALYSIS

The youth in their prime times are accessed to HIV/AIDS by a ray of transmission modes generally termed as 'immediate factor' that include unprotective-penetrative sex both heterosexual and homosexual, pre, during and post birth, mother to child transmission, transfusion transmission (blood products or blood sharing among the IDUS. Below, we may have a general table (Table 21.6) on sero-positivity among different high risk groups under surveillance.

Table 21.6: Sero-Surveillance

High Risk Groups	Number Screened	Positive Number	Sero-Positivity Rate
Heterosexual	10,290	1,461	14.20
Homosexual	23	2	8.69
Intravenous drug Users (IDUS)	10,441	6,248	59.84
Antenatal Mothers	2,692	84	3.12
Perinatal Transmission	216	75	34.72

Source: Epidemiological Analysis of HIV/AIDS in Manipur upto January 2003, Manipur State AIDS Control Society, Manipur.

One point pertinent to be borne in mind is that while there has been some gains to reduce the high risk addictive behaviour among the IDUS, importance now herein lies into the perception and attitude of sexual behaviour otherwise the rate of transmission is triple the actual rate. This is what actually happened in the state where reduced high risk addictive behaviour is irreciprocated in terms of sexual behaviour increasingly transmitting to female spouses and children. But, what is of more relevance to the understanding of this epidemic is what could be designated as the 'underlying factor' which is 'structural' and 'environmental' in specific cultural context that encompasses poverty, social and gender inequalities, population movements, human rights abuse societal denial and so on. The young people in the state are more prone to the endemic largely by the inappropriate education, dialogue on sex, sexuality and personal relations, lack of social support infrastructure embracing youth counselling and health services, fluid political stability, high unemployment, absence of recreational facilities and usual violence confrontation that made the youth to addictive behaviour. The vulnerability is more to the young women. It is further catalysed by the older and sexually experienced men's preferential sexual tendency to younger women partnership, easier accessibility to money from the parents, family members and kin-network, influence of the drug addict peer group, temptation to taste, broken familial background, inappropriate parental care, frustration, unemployment, devoid of recreational accessibility and idea of a murky future.[13] The situation is made a complex phenomenon by the easier availability of heroin, psychotropic substances and low cost locally brewing alcohol.

V

IMPLICATIONS

HIV/AIDS poses serious inter-knotted issues for social development. Like the twin transmission factors of the epidemic, there has, reciprocally, two implication types which constrained the development that may be distinguished for convenient analysis as 'immediate' and 'long term'. The immediate implication is squarely related to the effects brought about by the epidemic directly to the household and kin-line. Youth's utmost yearning to quench their addictive behaviour, extravagant treatment cost, on micro economic level drained a considerable chunk of long term aggregated household saving uninvested in productive purposes destabilising the material well-being including household income, land and asset ownership, income stability etc. Reduced aggregate saving and productive investment are natural outcome. The endemic caused slacked health status, absence of entrepreneurship enthusiasm and of household labour fastening familial impoverishment. HIV/AIDS is not just an individual concern, rather it is a social crisis by its character of potentiality to undermine the social fabric. Normality of growth is stressed by the epidemic. Within a short span of about one decade since its discovery in 1990, the epidemic dramatically metamorphosised the population profile in the state. Since its detection among the IDUS in 1990, HIV infection rate increases to 50 per cent within six months. As the epidemic precisely strikes the active youth, a heightened mortality rate of this community of population is accounted that diminishes out a potential working force population leaving elderly and children at poles. The severity of the concern is the transmission of HIV infection from the IDUS to their non-injecting wives recording an increased per cent from 6 per cent (1991) to 45 per cent (1997). While the increasing rate of pregnant mothers with HIV infection records from 1.3 (1994) to 2.7

(1999).[14] The premature death of a promising section of the overall youth population erodes the infrastructure of human development of the state. Aside, the epidemic infected a considerable chunk of children. It heightened, considerably, the children being groomed under the single parenthood or orphaned by the death of both the parents or one. The situation of the orphaned children is quite acute by their vulnerability which is much more complex by the inappropriate extended familial and social support systems. In the long run, the endemic brought a demographic metamorhosis affecting human potential primarily due to enhanced youth's mortality in the productive time. In term of inter-generational consequences are clearly manifested by the sacrifice of long term household security to meet the immediate needs finally in productivity-consumption slash. It, too, reduced the sectoral productivity.

The matter is more complex by its inherent dynamics of concealed build-up nature over time and costly intervention and programme implementation. Yet, effective time commitment is necessity of the hours to save the future generation suffering the serious brunt of the epidemic towards social development orientation and to take care of the 'future risk of societal destabilisation' by the formation of a 'poorly socialised and unskilled youth group.'

VI

INITIATIVES

Governmental Initiative

District De-addiction centres and hospitals with staff members of doctors and nurses.

Non-Governmental Organisation's Initiative

Non-governmental initiative taking seriously into the account of drug abuse commenced in 1987 when its (drug abuse) alarming signal was acknowledged. The concern was made deeper by the identification of drug abuse-HIV infection linkage in 1990. Services embraces residential rehabilitation, HIV/AIDS prevention and care, ambulant care on harm reduction involving experienced counsellers (ex-clients of the rehabilitation centres who are 'abstent'), outreach workers (mostly male recovering addicts) and peer educators (selected from among the drug users who relapsed many times.

Civil Society Initiative

Traditional and modern institutions of civil society in Manipur earned the fame of significant roles towards social peace. One such institutional social force is the Meira Paibis, Meitei womenfolks' association undertaking a wide range of voluntary tasks to protect their community against evils arising in every community, locality and village. Meira Paibis are forcefully taking action against social ills precisely against drug abuse and alcohol since the mid-80s as a part of the larger programme for restoration of social peace. Meira Paibis have generated a significant social capital and fulfilled one functioning of a civil society organisation.[15] Fighting against the problem beginning from around the same timing by the women's organisation. All Manipur Women's Social Reformation and Development Samaj is noteworthy to be paid an accord.

Self-Help Group Initiative

Community Improvement Action Organisation, group of recovering addicts that sought to support the recovering addicts and family members of drug users, MNP+, by the positive people of the state and infected widows' self-help groups[16] are some instances of this category of initiative.

VII

SUGGESTIONS

Since the last few decades, there have been initiatives taking care of the endemic, yet, there are gaps to the effective prevention strategies. This is an issue as such which is needed to be assigned a pragmatic-holistic response. Some of the primordial points that could perhaps be borne in mind towards social security:

- — Create conducive environment that could influence positive behaviour check. Social role to deliberate HIV/AIDS openly. Local, national and international actions to make enabling environment.
- — Monitoring and Re-evaluation of the Harm reduction approach which is already in operation.
- — Development of youth friendly appropriate media for increasing awareness.
- — Sexual health education in school and to increase the educational recreational centres for youths.
- — Development to effective communication strategies at different channels and levels for HIV/AIDS prevention.
- — Providing care and support to the infected and affected children and to identify and strengthen the traditional child support mechanism in the society.
- — Prioritisation of issues by the governmental, non-governmental and general public support.
- — Reviewing the existing National and State AIDS policies. Need for culturally specific policy.
- — Greater involvement of community towards sustenance for the effective intervention programme.
- — Acknowledging HIV/AIDS not as a health issue rather a social concern within the larger context of development. It must not be considered as an isolated aspect of development.

NOTES

1. An approach as such as mentioned in Ajai Sahni and George, "Security and Development in India's North East: An Alternative Perspective", in Gill and Sahni (ed.), *Terror and Containment: Perspective in India's Internal Security*, Gyan Publishing House, New Delhi, 2001, pp. 295-318.
2. For instance, Dreze and Sen, *India: Economic Development and Social Opportunity*, Oxford University Press, 1995.

3. Hirashima, "Social Sector of Economic Development: A Japanese Perspective", *Indian Social Science Review*, Vol. 4, No. 1, Jan.-June, 2002, p. 182.
4. *Tarapot, Drug Abuse and Illicit Trafficking in North Eastern India*, Vikas Publishing House, New Delhi, 1997, introduction, xxii.
5. *Ibid.*
6. *International Conferer.ce on Drug Abuse and Illicit Trafficking*, Vienna, 17-26, June, 1987.
7. *Political Declaration and Global Programme of Action*, UN Decade Against Drug Abuse, 1991-2000.
8. 15th International Day Against Drug Abuse and Illicit Trafficking (Joint publication, United Nations Drug Control Programme, Manipur State AIDS Control Society, Social Welfare Department, Manipur and NGOs).
9. Kumar, "The Border Trade in North East India: The Historical Perspective", in Das and Purkayastha (ed.), *Border Trade: North East India and Neighbouring Countries*, Akangsha Publishing House, New Delhi, pp. 3-11.
10. Phayre, *History of Burma*; Hall, *History of South East Asia*; Dun, *Gazetteer of Manipur* can be cited.
11. Thomas, "Indo-Myanmar Border Trade: An Assessment on the Moreh-Tamu Sector", in Das and Purkayastha (ed.), *op. cit*, pp. 153-54.
12. *Drug Situation and Demand Reduction Activities in Thailand*, National Council on Social Welfare, Thailand, 1994, p. 2.
13. Tarapot, *op. cit.*, p. 55.
14. *Revisiting the Hidden Epidemic—A Situation Assessment of Drug Use in Asia in the Context of HIV/AIDS: India Case*, Centre for Harm Reduction, Australia, January 2002, p. 5.
15. For an idea on the Meira Paibi Movement, see Rajendrakumar and Mangi, "The Meira Paibis: A Profile of the Women's Rights Activists of Manipur", Lal Dena (ed.), *History and Society*, Imphal, 2000, pp. 74-84.
16. I would like to thank MNP+ and those self-help groups for lending me cooperation.

22

INSURGENCY IN NORTH EAST INDIA AND THE MYANMAR CONNECTION

KONSAM IBO SINGH

Understanding of insurgency in North East India and its Myanmar connection calls for a brief discussion on Indo-Myanmar relations for an objective study of the aspect. After independence India maintained good relations with Myanmar especially during the U Nu era (1948-62). It was during this time that Prime Minister U Nu sought India's arms to counter the advancing anti-government forces led by the pro-Communists and the Karens and, later joined by the Kachins who won successive battles and even occupied parts of Yangon. Prime Minister Nehru delivered tanks, artillery, mortars and other military hardware that enabled the Myanmarese Government forces to hold out advancing anti-government forces.[1] However, relations between the two became strained after the military take over in Myanmar because of the Nationalisation Law of 1963 that forced the Indians to leave the country without compensation; and the Citizens Act of 1982, which discriminated the Indians. In the seventies insurgencies operating from the Indo-Myanmar border became an aspect of mutual concern. In 1977 the Naga insurgents under NSCN banner established their Headquarters at Sahpa under the leadership of Thuingaleng Muivah and Isac Chisi Swu with three sub-divisions—Ukamol, Langcheng and Takti in Northern Myanmar.[2] The Eastern Naga Revolutionary Council of Myanmar was merged in their federal set up in March 1979 thereby strengthening their movement.[3] During August 1979, the Myanmarese security forces had launched an intensive combing operation in and around upper and northern Myanmar that was followed by another large scale combing operation against the Karens at an unusual timing, i.e., during the rainy season in 1983. In 1984 Ne Win visited India and sought India's co-operation to combat insurgency on the border.[4] Following his visit General Sunderjee of India visited Myanmar in 1986. Though the two countries felt the need for consultations towards the solution of insurgency operating in both countries no formal agreement was ever signed.

Attempts were made by Prime Minister Indira Gandhi during last years of her rule to improve the bilateral relationship. However, the task could not be fulfilled. In December 1987 Rajiv Gandhi visited Myanmar at a time when India was close to the Soviet Union and Myanmar was to China which was a source of friction between the two. In January 1988 the two governments agreed to intensify cooperation in fighting against trans-border insurgencies as well as the control of drug trafficking among the trans-border tribes and communities.[5] Then, the movement for democracy broke out in Myanmar in 1987-88. Myanmar sought limited non-lethal military assistance in 1988. India declined the request.[6] India's chances of improving relations with Myanmar went to the background.

Drastic policy changes have taken place regarding India's relations with Myanmar in particular and ASEAN in general following the movement for democracy in 1988. These changes have far reaching consequences on the security and development process in India's North East. The changes became imperative in view of the improvement of relations between China and Myanmar apart from other factors after the popular uprising of 1988 in Myanmar.

The uprising of 1988 in Myanmar is historic and epoch-making in the sense that the movement demanded an end to one-party authoritarian rule and restoration of democracy. The response of the military government came down heavily specially on student demonstrators in which not less than 1000 of them were killed. The brutal suppression invited international condemnation. The industrialised democracies of the West and Japan imposed various forms of penalty: suspension of aid, economic sanction, arms embargo etc. thus resulting in the non-participation in the development process of Myanmar.

India supported the movement. Its diplomatic mission in Yangon even provided "pocket money" to student activists and "advised" them to cross over to the Indian side for shelter.[7] The All India Radio (AIR) coverage on Myanmar overtook that of the British Broadcasting Corporation (BBC) on the country.[8] Myanmar's military junta knew all these and also the support extended by the Indian diplomatic mission in Yangon, encouragement and the AIR coverage, which displeased military junta. India, at this time was quite critical of the military regime in Myanmar which was evident from the remark given by the President of India R. Venkataraman in February 1992 when the newly appointed Myanmar's ambassador to India Mr. Wynn Lwin met the former to hand over his credentials. The President expressed his serious concern at the "delay and uncertainty" in the restoration of democracy in Myanmar and also the dissatisfaction over the refusal to release Nobel Laureate Aung San Suu Kyi who was under house arrest.[9] In short India's relations with Myanmar from 1988 to early 1992 was a continuation of this pro-democracy movement stance marked by a distant relationship with the SLORC.

While these industrialised democracies and India distanced Myanmar, China stepped in. It became Myanmar's second largest trade partner, formalised cross border trade; and above all, it became the largest arms supplier, actively participated in the developmental process and upgradation of naval facilities at Hianggyl Island, Sittwe (Akyab), Mergul, surveillance station at Coco Islands etc. thereby inviting India's security concern.[10] In the meantime ASEAN followed a policy of "Constructive Engagement", a policy of non-interference in the internal affairs of Myanmar while actively participating in the economic activities of the country.[11] In substance Myanmar is closer to its neighbour while its relations with the industrialised democracies and India became distant.

Another important consequence of the uprising of 1988 is that student activists were hunted down by the military regime wherever they were. For fear of reprisal the student activists headed for border areas controlled by the Myanmar's underground especially along the Myanmar-Thai border. These fleeing student activists came into contact with the members of the National Democratic Front (NDF), a frontal ethnic based insurgent organisation formed on 10 May, 1976 by 11 ethnic based insurgent groups. A new organisation was formed known as the Democratic Alliance of Burma having 23 insurgent groups plus students and monks on 19 November, 1988 on the initiative of Karen National Union leader General Bo Mya who was also the Chairman of the NDF for two terms. The DAB had five main objectives: (i) to overthrow the military government, (ii) the establishment of democratic rule; (iii) the ending of the civil war; (iv) the restoration of internal peace; and (v) national reconciliation.[3] Interestingly, two years after the students uprising of 1988 was crushed with brutality. The Indian diplomatic mission in Bangkok was accused of funding the NCGUB, which has close links with DAB. No doubt, India denied the charge. However, Myanmar's military junta claimed that they had all the evidences in support of their contention. India even gave shelter to the Thai airways plane hijackers and one of them Soe Myint was allowed to run a news agency with a website—*Mizzima*.

India did not end its activities of displeasing the Myanmarese military junta by simply supporting the pro-democracy forces. It even established covert ties with the DAB. Research and Analysis Wing (RAW), one of India's well known intelligence organisations established close ties with the Kachin Independence Organisation/ Army (KIO/KIA), an important constituent of the NDF and, later of DAB and even supplied with arms and ammunitions from an Indian Army base located at Vijaynagar. The KIO was even allowed to open an office in Delhi and the KIO chief sent Maran Brengseng, a confidante to liaise with the RAW. Perhaps, India's purpose of maintaining a close liaison with the KIO was that the latter denied all forms of support extended to the insurgent groups of the North East and also the use of their territory for anti-India activities. Not only in the Kachin area the Government of India also cultivated the Chin National Front (CNF) and the National Unity Party of Arakan (NUPA) for the same objective. The CNF and NUPA were allowed by India to set up their bases in Mizoram, provided limited amount of weapons and training.[12]

The formation of the DAB was considered to be a threat to the military junta. Therefore, attempts were made to break-up the DAB. First method adopted by the military junta was to carry out an intensive military campaign along the Myanmar-Thai border to wipe out their bases. Second was to break up the alliance which was successful by reaching an understanding with the Was in July 1990 after the collapse of the Communist Party of Burma (White Flag) in 1989 caused by the revolt of the members of the hill tribes against the Maoists leadership. Earlier the SLORC also reached a ceasefire agreement with the Shan State Progressive Party in 1989, which was followed by securing similar ceasefire agreements with the Pa-O National Organisation in February 1991 and the Palaung State Liberation Organisation in April 1991.[13] However, the most important of all these was the ceasefire agreement between the SLORC and the Kachin Independence Organisation (KIO). Why it is significant is that the Kachins inherited a large quantity of a half a million light weapons left by different forces at the end of the Second World War, which fell into the hands of insurgents.[14] The KIA supplied a large part of the consignment to the various insurgent groups of North East India. It also holds a vast area adjoining with southern China through which the insurgents from India like the Nagas, Mizos used to pass through in the past. It is also significant that it is in their territory that many of the insurgent groups from North East India like PLA, UNLF, PREPAK, ULFA etc. are actively operating in North East India but declared as terrorist organisations by an Act of the Government of India[15] take shelter and receive training though with a lucrative fee. The area is almost inaccessible except during the dry season.

Negotiations for ceasefire were started on the Chinese and Thai pressure. China could have thought that the CPB cadres were made up of hill tribes who had deserted the CPB with all the arms and ammunitions supplied by China should not fall into anti-Chinese forces and be brought under a proper authority; and the improvement of relations with the SLORC was necessary. Ethnic rebels could be difficult to be prevailed upon by Maoism. Moreover, it wanted to establish better relationship with the governments rather the rebel communist parties since Deng Xiao Ping came to power.[16] Or, Perhaps the Chinese knew the Indian penetration into the KIO and the latter's covert ties with New Delhi. Further, its intensification of economic and strategic activities in Myanmar should have no impediments in northern Myanmar, which is well connected with southern China for growing trade and commercial activities.

Negotiations of ceasefire between the KIO and the SLORC shocked the DAB, which suspended KIO from it for negotiating alone instead with the frontal insurgents organisation i.e., the DAB. The KIO happened to be the third largest in terms of armed strength after the Was and the Shans.[17] Moreover, its area of control was strategically important. The ceasefire agreement of October 1993 gave a death-blow to the Myanmar's insurgents. In substance so far 20 ceasefire agreements have been signed between the SLORC and the ethnic based insurgents thought the SLORC/SPDC allowed them to retain their arms. However, no untoward incident has been reported so far. The only significant insurgent organisations, which have remained outside the scope of the ceasefire agreements, are the Karens, the Chins and the Arakanese. The Chins inhabit along the Indo Myanmar border while the Arakanese settle along the Myanmar-Bangladesh border the area used as a transit point many times for various activities like the transfer of sophisticated small arms coming from Southeast Asia from where they go to the Indo-Myanmar border reaching the hands of the insurgents[18] of the North East India. What is more significant is that both the Chins and the Arakanese were trained, aided and sheltered by India.

The above developments show two things. One growing Chinese influence in Myanmar maintaining close ties especially after 1988 when Myanmar was isolated by industrialised democracies including India. As a result China has inflitrated

Myanmar for trade and commerce even reaching India's North East. Second is China's suspicious role in building port facilities around Yangon and installation of monitoring centres near the Andamans.

Two factors prompted India to reassess its policy towards Myanmar (i) China factor; (ii) containment of insurgency in the North East India operating in both the countries for which joint efforts were needed. In this connection it would not be wrong to highlight some of the developments, which had taken place inside the Indian government. In between 1989-91, a number of officials from the foreign office, defence and intelligence establishment opposed the India Government's support extended to the pro-democracy movement and the "limited support" extended to the Myanmarese rebels. These officials strongly felt that transition from military rule to democracy in Myanmar was a distant dream; and it was necessary "to emulate the ASEAN's policy of 'Constructive Engagement' with the junta. This group included senior military officials like General Shankar Roychoudhuri, and the military intelligence chief Lt. General Ravi Sawhney, some Navy and Research and Analysis Wing (RAW) officials and a few in the Foreign Ministry. They argued that if India did not improve relations with the junta and since democratic transition was a far-cry Myanmar would become a Chinese satellite."[19] It was during this time that the Industrialised democracies wanted India to join their diplomatic missions in Yangon in 1992 to lodge a formal protest to the SLORC regime against its policy of dishonouring the results of the elections held in May 1990. India did not take part preparing the ground for improving relations with the SLORC in view of the security considerations.

Taking into consideration of the advantages for normalising relations the Government of India extended an invitation to U Ba Swe, Vice Foreign Minister, Government of Myanmar, to visit India. He visited India in August 1992. During his stay in India he conferred with Indian Officials and "identified concrete areas for bilateral cooperation including border trade, prevention of narcotics trafficking and contacts between the civilian and military authorities in the border regions of the two countries to prevent illegal activities".[20] Following his visit J.N. Dixit, India's Foreign Secretary visited Myanmar from 11-13 August, 1992 and again from 29 March to 1 April, 1993 to Myanmar. During the visits further discussions took place on the basis of the earlier meetings.

At the end of Dixit's first visit an agreement was signed to control drug trafficking which was followed by an exchange of draft agreements for economic and commercial cooperation.[21] India offered to build a road from Kalemyo to Tamu and from there to Mandalay, as the Chinese did in Yunan and Kachin area, and, also to increase communications and trade between the two countries. Taking the advantage of the exchange of visits, views also were exchanged with Lt. General Khin Nyunt, Secretary No. 1, U Ohn Gyaw, Foreign Minister and Brigadier General Win Tin, Minister for Home Affairs regarding the import of arms, alleged Chinese interest in the establishment of a naval base in the southern part of Myanmar quite close to the Indian territories of Andaman and Nicobar islands. Myanmarese authorities explained that Chinese arms were necessary for the maintenance of internal security and defence purposes. Regarding the establishment of a Chinese naval base they cleared India's doubts saying that they will never allow any permanent foreign military presence in Myanmar.[22]

While these positive steps were taken for close ties the Indian Army launched operation "Golden Duck" to trap the North East insurgents along the Indo-Myanmar border. The Myanmar army was approached for cooperation. The Myanmar army readily complied. However, when the joint operation was going on in full swing the Government of India awarded Nehru Peace Prize to Aung San Suu Kyi. India's award shocked and humiliated the Myanmarese military junta. They withdrew their army in protest and consternation. Later in an interview conducted on 6 May, 1995 by Subir Bhaumik, BBC's Eastern India's correspondent, Lieutenant General Ramesh Batra, GOC-in-C, Eastern Command with disappointment told, "The right hand should know what the left is doing. The award should have been given at least after we finished the operation successfully".[23] The operation "Golden Duck" is a glaring example to show of how a genuine cause of national importance was thrown into the winds just because of the existence of a gap between two important establishments of the Government.

The reason why India has security concerns along the Indo-Myanmar border is that it has many illegal activities though the are looks to be quiet, calm and peaceful. Drug trafficking, small arms trade and insurgency are the three important activities so intimately associated with one another and carried on vigorously in the area. Myanmar cultivates opium using 50 per cent of the world's total area of land used for the purpose. In terms of production it ranks second after Afghanistan ranging the contribution from 28 per cent to 40 per cent of the world total which is on the decline, no doubt, after 1999.[24] What is alarming is the nexus between drug trafficking and proliferation of small arms. One writer says, "The linkage between drug trafficking and small arms is well established. It may not be possible to control the spread of small arms unless there is corresponding control of drug trafficking. Myanmar offers a classical example of the linkage between the drug trade and the small arms proliferation".[25] Reports indicate that arms purchase is done in Southeast Asia brought through Myanmar and reaches India. In the later part of 1995 a huge consignment was seized by the Bangladesh army and navy near Cox Bazar, and again in 1996 in which 600 rifles were seized, in the third incident a consignment of the PLA was intercepted in May 1997 from the PLA insurgents and Myanmar's nationals by the Thai navy while smuggling arms in a motor boat. Another huge consignment consisting of rocket propelled grenades, AK-47 rifles, M-79, heavy machine guns and an assortment of pistols in all 145 weapons, 40,000 rounds of ammunition and four motor boats mounted with anti-aircraft guns were seized in the high seas near the Andaman and Nicobar islands in a combined operation named as "Operation Leech" conducted by Indian Army, Navy, Air Force and Coast Guards on 9 February, 1998 in which six people were killed and 72 were nabbed. Security forces suspected those militants nabbed could belong to PLA, ULFA and NSCN, or, the intercepted consignment meant for the North East insurgents.[26] However, later on it turned out to be a different story.

Investigations revealed that 34 of the arrested 73 turned out to Arakanese rebels who resorted to gun running but fighting the Myanmar's military junta. Defence Minister George Fernandes, who has been giving shelter to many student activists and a stern supporter of democracy movement in Myanmar appealed for their release for which in 1999, India's GOC-in-C Eastern Command Lt. General H.R.S. Kalkat, said, "Myanmar's policy better be left to the army. We are soldiers, and they (Myanmar's junta) are soldiers and our blood is thicker than the blood of the bureaucrats and politicians".[27] BBC concluded that the Indian army was resentful because of the inept handling of national security issues by the political leadership.

However, latest reports appeared in some newspapers like the *Hindustan Times* after four years of the incident has revealed a story, which goes against the interest of the armed forces. The report says that 34 of those Myanmarese are Arakanese rebels who are now on bail, two have escaped in July 2001, 37 of them turned out to be innocent fishermen, who were released after 15 months in prison. According to the version of one of the arrested rebels—Dynya Lin, is that they were promised by a Lt. Colonel of the India Army—V.J.S. Grewal of the Indian Military Intelligence for such facilities such as jetty, barracks and training and a base in the Landfall Islands in the Andamans to help to fight the junta. He further disclosed that they were told to take the weapons from Thailand to Landfall. From there an India agency was to take the consignment to their base at Paruba in Mizoram. The *Hindustan Times* further writes about the observations of the CBI on the case "damning indictment of the Ministry of Defence". The paper says that the authenticity and *bona fides* of the encounter are in doubt". The agency, they further write, finds the militants story that they were drafted by the Indian army—is "more plausible" and accuses the MOD of concealing facts.[28]

What can be concluded from the above circumstances is that first Government of India still had covert ties with the Arakan rebels and they wanted to use them. Second, the Indian army wanted to deter North East insurgents. Third, probably they wanted to impress upon the Myanmarese military junta that they could respond to serious matters of security aspects of emergency nature more vigorously than before for mutual interest though it proved otherwise. It also proved then that India's armed forces were acting in favour of the Military junta; or, they wanted to snub George Fernandes, the Defence Minister. What is also important is that the area is a sensitive one; and India's sphere of influence for security reasons. The establishment of a new Far Eastern Naval Command of India in the Andamans in 1999 is also a case in point.[29] At the same time we cannot ignore the relevance of the existence of Balasore and Chandipur missile testing ranges and, therefore, the surrounding area is sensitive. Even though it is after four years that everything comes to light; however, this time gap of four years was so profitably used by the Indian army to sideline the Defence Minister George Fernandes. Even if it proved otherwise army's ploy was a successful one though the Myanmarese junta increased its doubts on Indian side's sincerity.

Beginning with the year 1999, new initiatives were again taken up to effectively control drug trafficking and curb insurgency. In July 1999, Kamal Pande, Home Secretary, Government of India and Thure Mying Maung, Deputy Minister for Home, Government of Myanmar met in New Delhi and agreed for "increased cooperation to tackle cross-border terrorism and drugs trafficking",[30] which was formalised by an agreement signed in Kohima. The two countries also agreed to coordinate in future military campaigns against ethnic separatists in border areas and take joint action against drug trafficking. This agreement was soon followed by exchanges of frequent visits of army personnel. General Ved Prakash Malik visited Myanmar twice in January and July 2000 followed by a visit of Admiral Sushilkumar to Myanmar in September 2001. Home Secretary Pande too went to Myanmar in August 2000 to confer with Myanmarese authorities in connection with security aspects. All these visits are symbols of closer ties and intensive discussion relating to insurgency, drug trafficking and control of arms trade through the porous Indo-Myanmar border. In return, General Maung Aye, Vice-Chairman of the SPDC visited Shillong in July 2000 followed by a high level Myanmar delegation led by Aye himself for a seven-day visit to India in November of the same year.

The visit that was led by General Maung Aye, Vice-Chairman of the SPDC, and Deputy Commander in Chief, Myanmar Defence Forces was probably the most important and significant one. His team consisted of Lt. General Tin Oo, the Secretary-2 of the SPDC, Lt. General Tin Hla, Deputy Prime Minister and Minister of Military Affairs, Maj. General Soe Win, member of the SPDC and the Commander of the North West Command, U Win Maung, Minister of Foreign Affairs, U Aung Thaung, Minister Industry-I, U Khin Maung Thein, Minister of Finance and Revenue, U Thaung, Minister of Science and Technology, Maj. General Tin Hlut, Minister of Electric Power, Brig. General Pyi Sone, Minister for Commerce and U Khin Maung Kyaw, Deputy Minister of Industry-II. A joint statement issued at the end of the week-long visit covered a wide range of areas for cooperation including economic cooperation, trade, cross border projects and activities, international terrorism, drug trafficking, cooperation in the field of culture, human resource development, science and technology, regional cooperation within the framework of Bangladesh, India, Myanmar, Sri Lanka, Thailand Economic Cooperation (BIMST-EC) the countries also under the aegis of the India-ASEAN dialogue partnership.[31]

The contents of the above joint statement made on 21 November, 2000 covered wide ranging areas for cooperation. What is relevant to us is that underdevelopment of the border area has been recognised by the two sides and agreed to develop transport and communication without which they find the task of containing insurgency in the area so difficult. International terrorism, drug trafficking have been identified clearly for areas of cooperation. Sanjay Hazarika informs us that Win Aung, Myanmarese Foreign Minister told a small group of journalists that as far as the North Eastern militants are concerned, Myanmar would cooperate with India to tackle this issue at the local military levels and on the border. Myanmar would not allow any group to "use our territory to make trouble" against India.[32] In short the aspects agreed upon for cooperation mainly cover the ones concerning the development of Indo-Myanmar border areas which would indirectly help containing insurgency.

Now, after 2000 nothing has been heard about KIO-India nexus. BBC Eastern India Correspondent Subir Bhaumik says that India has closed down bases of CNF and NUPA.[33] Exchange of visits and contacts of military commanders of India and Myanmar were frequent and are on the increase. On 13 February Jaswant Singh, Minister of External Affairs went to Myanmar to open a "gift road" connecting Kalewa and Kalemyo, a 160 km long India-built road along the Kabaw valley which is to be extended further up to Myitkyina through Mandalay.

While these developments were going on another incident tested the sincerity of both the sides. In November 2001 Myanmarese army captured 192 Manipuri militants during raids on seven camps of various Manipur outfits around Tamu in which top UNLF and PLA leaders were captured along with 40 kg of gold, currency worth of millions, currency printing machines, and 1600 weapons allegedly supplied by China.[34] India asked the Myanmarese government to extradite the militants. However, they said that they were Myanmarese. They released the militants when they were accused by India that Myanmarese government was giving asylum to two Taliban Pakistani nuclear scientists Bashiruddin Mohammad and Abdul Majid. Later the Myanmarese government released them under Chinese pressure.[35] However, the incident which invited charges and counter charges was overshadowed by the visit of Jaswant Singh, Minister of External Affairs, Government of India to Myanmar in April 2002.

Jaswant Singh's visit was timely. India, Myanmar and Thailand signed a Trilateral Agreement on 6 April, 2002. The agreement included: (i) construction of highway from Moreh in India to Mae Sot in Thailand through Bagan in Myanmar which is expected to be completed in two years; (ii) promotion of a highway from Kanchanaburi in Thailand to Dawei deep seaport in Myanmar and shipping links to seaports in India; (iii) the promotion of trade investment, tourism through facilitation of movement of goods and peoples across borders; (iv) cooperative efforts on human resource development and transfer of technology; and

(v) collective efforts to mobilize funds, resources and advisory services from various agencies for transport linkages.[36]

The aforesaid developments clearly show that the bilateral relationship between India and Myanmar has entered into a new era. Myanmar has improved its relations with both China and India in the line with its basic principles of foreign policy, i.e., (i) keeping balance and equidistance with both China and India; (ii) "maintenance of its security . . . by being friendly with all and allied with none".[37] India has taken the advantage at a time when Myanmar was internationally condemned and isolated; India also contributed partially in legitimising military rule in Myanmar. However, most important of all India hopes to contain insurgency in Northeast India more effectively than before. In the next ten/fifteen years it is quite expected that insurgent outfits will have a tough time for sanctuary, and training in the Kachin area as ceasefire agreement has been signed between Myanmar's military junta and the KIO/KIA though arms sell cannot be ruled out as arms have been allowed to be retained with KIO/KIA. There may be frictions between regional military commanders on the field in time of joint operations no doubt. However, mutual concern, understanding has been reached at the highest level. Therefore, it is expected that such ground realities will be amicably resolved. Deprivation of sanctuary, training, proper checking in small arms transfer, control of drug trafficking, development of border areas will put the insurgents into a disadvantageous position. In view of this there will be a lot of pressure on the insurgent groups of Northeast India along the Indo-Myanmar border. How long they are able to operate and survive there will largely depend much on their mutual trust and cooperation of India and Myanmar.

NOTES

1. Maj. Gen. (retd.) Dipankar Banerjee, *Myanmar and North East India* (Delhi Policy Group, New Delhi, 1997), p. 2.
2. B. Pakem, *India Burma Relations* (Omsons Publications, New Delhi, 1992), p. 219.
3. *Ibid.*
4. Dipankar Banerjee, n. 1, p. 4.

5. Pakem, n. 2. See also *Asian Recorder* (New Delhi), p. 19827.
6. Dipankar Banerjee, n. 1, p. 4.
7. Interview with Myanmarese student activists in November 2001.
8. John Bray, Burma, *The Politics of Constructive Engagement* (Royal Institute of International Affairs, London, 1995), p. 45.
9. *Eastern Courier* (New Delhi), 19 February, 1992.
10. There are a number of recent works dealing with Chinese influence and activities in Myanmar having security implications on India's North East and eastern borders. See for instance, Andrew Selth, "Burma and the Strategic Competition between China and India" in John Brandon, ed., *Burma/Myanmar in the Twenty-first Century: Dynamics of Continuity and Change* (Washington/Bangkok, 1997, pp. 146-68; Maj. Gen. (Retd.), Dipankar Banerjee, *Myanmar and North East India* (Delhi Policy Group, New Delhi, 1997); J. Mohan Malik,"Sino-Indian Rivalry in Myanmar: Implication for Regional Security", Contemporary *Southeast Asia* (Singapore), Vol. 16, No. 2, September 1994, pp. 137-56. Also Malik, "Myanmar's Role in Regional Security: Pawn or Pivot", *ibid.*, Vol. 19, No. 1, June 1997, pp. 52-73. The same also is discussed in Jaya Jaitley and Jaya Roy, eds., *Report on the International Convention for the Restoration of Democracy in Burma* (New Delhi, n.d.), pp. 132-59.
11. John Bray, n. 8.
12. Subir Bhaumik, "Burma Policy and Its Impact on Its (India's) North Eastern Region", paper presented at the National Seminar on Partnership of Development: "Holistic Approach to the North East" sponsored by the Indian Council of Social Science Research (ICSSR), New Delhi and organised by the North Eastern Regional Centre, ICSSR, Shillong from 8-9 May, 2002 at Gangtok, pp. 1-13. Further, the author is extremely thankful to Subir Bhaumik, BBC Eastern India Correspondent for granting a number of interactions in this connection during their stay for seminar at Gangtok.
13. See Appendix II.
14. Dipankar Banerjee, n. 1, p. 22.
15. The Government of India has declared 23 outfits as "Terrorist Organisations" by Prevention of Terrorism Act, 2002 out of which 10 of them operate in North East India. These proscribed outfits are (i) United Liberation Front of Assam (ULFA); (ii) National Democratic Front of Bodoland (NDFB); (iii) People's Liberation Army (PLA); (iv) United National Liberation Front (UNLF) (Manipur); (v) People's Revolutionary Party of Kangleipak (PREPAK); (vi) Kangleipak Communist Party (KCP); (vii) Kanglei Yawol Kanna Lup (KYKL); (viii) Manipur People's Liberation Front (MPLF); (ix) All Tripura Tiger Force (ATTF); and (x) National Liberation Front of Tripura (NLFT).
16. *Asian Recorder* (New Delhi), 1984, pp.18005-6.
17. See Appendix II.
18. Banerjee, n. 1, p. 23.

19. Subir Bhaumik, n. 12.
20. Ministry of External Affairs, Government of India, *Annual Report, 1992-93* (New Delhi), p. 18.
21. J.N. Dixit, *My South-Block Years: Memoirs of a Foreign Secretary* (New Delhi, 1997, reprint of 1996), p. 168.
22. *Ibid.*, p. 169.
23. Interview with Lt. General Ramesh Batra, GOC-in-C, Eastern Command on 6 May, 1995 to Subir Bhaumik. See Bhaumik, n. 12 End Notes 32.
24. Drug Control and Crime Prevention, United Nations, *World Drug Report 2000* (Oxford University Press, New York, 2000), p. 160.
25. Vijay Sakhuja, "Indian Ocean and the Safety of Sea Lines of Communication", *Strategic Analysis* (New Delhi), Vol. 25, No. 5 August, 2001, pp. 689-702. See also Rohan Gunaratna, "Illicit Transfer of Conventional Weapons: Role of State and Non-State Actors in South Asia", in Jayanath Dhanapala, *Small Arms Control: Old Weapons, New Issues* (Ashgate Publishing, Vermont, 1999), p. 266. See also Mohammad Shahidul Anam Khan, "Linkage between Arms Trafficking and the Drug Trade in South Asia", in Dhanapala, *ibid.*, p. 248. Among the Indian scholars Binalakshmi Nepram has highlighted the linkage between small arms, drugs and terrorism in the Indo-Myanmar border area in her book entitled: *South Asia's Fracture Frontier* (Mittal Publications, New Delhi, 2002). See also Binalakshmi, "Insurgency, Narcotics and Small Arms in India's North East, I and II", *Sangai Express* (Imphal), 29 and 30 September, 2000. See also Anindita Dasgupta, "Small Arms Prolification in India's North East Frontier", *Economic and Political Weekly* (Mumbai), 6 January, 2001. See also S.K. Ghosh, *India's North East Frontier Fifty Turbulent Years: Heavy Arms Traffick—A Menace to the Region's Stability* (Titagarh, 1997).
26. "Rebel Groups Silent: Army Grills Gun Runners in Port Blair", *Telegraph* (Calcutta), 13 February, 1998. See also *ibid.*, 12 February, 1998.
27. Subir Bhaumik, n. 12.
28. "Operation Leech: Rebels Await Trial, Andaman Nervous", *Hindustan Times, North East Special* (Hereinafter referred to as *HT*), 9 September, 2002; See also "Gun Running: CBI Says Army Suspect", *HT*, 8 September, 2002.
29. See Prakash Nanda, "Strategic Significance of the Andaman's", *Indian Defence Review* (New Delhi), July-September, 2002, pp. 12-14.
30. Subir Bhaumik, n. 12.
31. See text of *the Indo-Myanmar Joint Statement*, New Delhi, 21 November, 2000, in Appendix-I.
32. See Sanjay Hazarika, "Wisdom in Wooing Myanmar", *Statesman* (Kolkata) reproduced in *Imphal Free Press*, 12 December, 2000.
33. Subir Bhaumik, n. 12.
34. "Myanmar Junta Cracks on Indian Ultras", *HT*, 7 November, 2001.
35. "Myanmar Snubs India, Frees Ultras", *HT*, 17 March, 2002.

36. See Text of the Press Release on the Occasion of thc India-Myanmar-Thailand Ministerial Meeting on Transport Linkages, Yangon, 5-6 April, 2002 in Appendix-III.
37. R.G. Sawhney, "Burma" in U.S. Bajpai (ed.), *India and Its Neighbourhood* (Lancer International, New Delhi, 1986), p. 351. See also, Frederica M. Bunge (ed.), *Burma: A Country Study* (Washington D.C., 1983), p. 207.

APPENDIX-I

INDIA-MYANMAR JOINT STATEMENT
November 21, 2000, New Delhi

1. H.E. General Maung Aye, Vice Chairman, State Peace & Development Council (SPDC), Deputy Commander-in-Chief, Myanmar Defence Forces and Commander-in-Chief, Myanmar Army paid a seven-day visit to India from 14 to 21 November, 2000 at the invitation of H.E. Shri Krishan Kant, Vice President of India. General Maung Aye was accompanied by a high-level delegation consisting of H.E. Lt Gen. Tin Oo, Secretary-2, SPDC, H.E. Lt. Gen. Tin Hla, Deputy Prime Minister and Minister of Military Affairs, H.E. Maj. Gen. Soe Win, Member of the SPDC and Commander of the North West Command, H.E. U Win Aung, Minister for Foreign Affairs, H.E. U Aung Thuang, Minister for Industry-I, H.E. U Khin Maung Thein, Minister for Finance and Revenue, H.E. U Thaung, Minister for Science and Technology, H.E. Maj. Gen. Tin Htut, Minister for Electric Power, H.E. Brig. Gen. Pyi Sone, Minister for Commerce and H.E. U Khin Maung Kyaw, Dy. Minister of Industry-II, and other senior officials.

2. During this visit, the leaders of the two countries held discussions on bilateral, regional and international issues. They discussed measures to create favourable conditions for the rapid development of bilateral relations.

3. Relations between India and Myanmar are civilisational in nature and rooted in a common cultural and religious heritage and geographical contiguity. Leaders of both countries have always maintained a tradition of high level exchanges and personal rapport. With the visits by General Maung Aye this process has been enhanced.

4. In Delhi, H.E. General Maung Aye and Daw Mya San were accorded a warm ceremonial welcome by H.E. Shri Krishan Kant. H.E. General Maung Aye and Daw Ya Mya San called on H.E. Shri K.R. Narayanan, President of India and Shrimati Usha Narayan. He held discussions with H.E. the Vice President, H.E.

Shri Atal Bihari Vajpayee, Prime Minister, H.E. Shri Jaswant Singh, Minister of External Affairs, H.E. Shri L.K. Advani, Home Minister, Shri Omar Farooq Abdullah, Minister of State for Commerce & Industry, and Shrimati Sonia Gandhi, Leader of Opposition.

5. The discussions between the Prime Minister and the Vice-Chairman, State Peace & Development Council covered a wide range of areas, including economic cooperation, trade, cross border projects and activities, international terrorism, drug trafficking, cooperation in the field of culture, human resource development, science and technology, and regional cooperation within the framework of BIMST-EC, of which both countries are members, as also under the aegis of India-ASEAN dialogue partnership. The two sides expressed satisfaction at the all-round progress in relations in the past few years. At the same time, it was agreed that the present level of interaction, specially in the economic and commercial fields did not reflect the potential as such relations. Both sides reaffirmed their desire to promote bilateral relations to a qualitatively higher and dynamic stage. They also agreed that they could benefit from various regional cooperation programmes in which they are participants, such as BIMST-EC and India-ASEAN cooperation.

6. The two sides agreed to take steps to ensure peace and tranquillity along the India-Myanmar border, and to give content to cross border cooperation, which would directly benefit population living on both sides of the border. They recognised the need to establish the necessary infrastructure in terms of cross border transport and communication links, promote more frequent exchanges both at the government and people-to-people level, and actively encourage the business communities of both countries to take advantage of many economic complementarities between the two countries. The Tamu-Kelemyo highway which will link India's north east with the western part of the Myanmar and beyond would contribute significantly to this cross border cooperation. The highway is expected to be handed over soon to the Myanmar Government.

7. The two sides also discussed progress in other proposed cross border projects, viz. the Tamanthi Hydroelectric project and the Kalandan River Navigation, Road and Gas Pipeline Project, and agreed to take necessary steps to expedite ongoing investigations and feasibility studies.

8. An agreement to extend a US $ 15 million Indian credit to Myanmar was signed during the visit by the Finance Minister of the two countries. Both sides noted with satisfaction that an earlier Indian credit of US $10 million was utilised by the Myanmar side for setting up industrial plants and for supply of rolling stock. The new credit line will also be used for sourcing industrial and electrical equipment from India.

9. During his stay in India H.E. General Maung Aye and his delegation visited places of Buddhist pilgrimage. General Maung Aye also travelled to Bangalore where he visited a number of scientific and Industrial establishment and organisations working in the fields of Information Technology, industrial and agricultural machinery, electronics, agriculture, aeronautics and space research. In Delhi, the Confederation of India Industry hosted a luncheon in honour of General Maung Aye and his delegation to enable them to meet and interact with leading Indian businessmen and industrialists and discuss possibilities of cooperation General Maung Aye and his delegation also visited Agra and Udaipur.

10. H.E. General Maung Aye extended a cordial invitation to H.E. Krishan Kant, Vice President of India to pay an official visit to Myanmar. The invitation was accepted with pleasure. Mutually convenient dates for the visit will be decided through diplomatic channels.

11. On behalf of H.E. Senor General Than Shwe, Chairman State Peace and Development Council and Prime Minister of Myanmar, General Maung Aye extended cordial invitation to H.E. Shri K.R. Narayanan, President of India and Shri Atal Bihari Vajpayee, Prime Minister of India, respectively to pay visits to Myanmar. The invitations were accepted with pleasure and mutually convenient dates would be decided through diplomatic channels. The President and Prime Minister of India respectively

requested H.E. General Maung Aye to convey to H.E. Senior General Than Shwe an invitation to visit India at a mutually convenient date.

12. The Myanmar delegation thanked the Government and people of India for the warm and friendly reception and gracious hospitality extended to the delegation.

New Delhi
November 21, 2000.

APPENDIX-II

CEASEFIRE ETHNIC ARMIES

	Leader	*Ceasefire*	*Strength*
Arakan State			
1. Rakhine State All National Race Solidarity Party	Saw Tun U	06 April 97	100 men
Kachin State			
1. Kachin Independence Organisation/Army	Tu Jai	01 Oct. 93	5,000 men
2. New Democratic Army	Sakhone Ting Yin	15 Dec. 89	400 men
Karen (Kawthollei) State			
1. Democratic Karen Buddhist Army	Tha Htoo Kyaw	Dec. 94	1,000 men
2. National Karen Peace Army (former KNU)	Tha Mu Hel	Feb. 97	50 men
3. Phado Aung San Group (former KNU)	Phado Aung San	17 April 97	10 men
Kayah (Karenni) State			
1. Kayan National Guards	Gabriel Byan	27 Feb. 92	200 men
2. Karenni Nationalities People Liberation Front (PDF)	Htun Kyaw	09 May 94	300 men
Mon State			
1. New Mon State Party	Nai Shwe Kyin	29 Jun. 95	1,500 men
Shan State			
1. Kachin Defence Army	Mahtu Naw	11 Jan. 91	500 men
2. Myanmar National Democracy Alliance	Hpon Kyar Shin	31 Mar. 89	1,300 men
3. National Democracy Alliance Army	Sai Lin	30 Jun. 89	4,000 men

4. Pa-O National Organisation	Aung Kham Hti	18 Feb. 91	300 men
5. Palaung State Liberation Party	Ai Mone	21 Apr. 91	800 men
6. Shan State Army	Sai Nong/ Hso Hten	24 Sept. 89	1,500 men
7. Shan State (National) Army	Kang Yod		6,000 men
8. Shan State Nationalities People Liberation Organisation	Tha Kalei	09 Oct. 94	300 men
9. United Wa State Army	Pao Yuchang	May 89	15,000 men
10. Mong Tai Army	Khun Sa	02 Jan. 96	became SSNA, SSA*
Total	**20 groups**		**38,410 men**

* SSA and SSNA now come under Hso Hten in the Shan State Peace Committee. Compiled by the Euro-Burman Office.

Source: Burma Debate (Washington DC), Summer/Fall 2001, p. 38.

APPENDIX-III

PRESS RELEASE ISSUED ON THE OCCASION OF THE INDIA-MYANMAR-THAILAND MINISTERIAL MEETING ON TRANSPORT LINKAGES (Yangon, Myanmar, 5-6 April, 2002)

1. The India-Myanmar-Thailand Ministerial Meeting on Transport Linkages was held on 5 and 6 April, 2002 at the Sedona Hotel in Yangon, Myanmar.
2. The Ministerial Meeting was opened with a Keynote Address by His Excellency Lt. General Khin Nyunt, Secretary-I of the State Peace and Development Council of the Union of Myanmar.
3. In his address, His Excellency Secretary-I Lt. General Khin Nyunt recalled the historical, cultural and civilisation links that had existed among the three countries, and in particular, the common spiritual link provided by Buddhism. He spoke of the joint aspirations of the leaders and peoples of the three countries to restore and develop transport linkages in order to promote investment and the flow of trade, tourism and people to people contact.
4. His Excellency Secretary-I noted that the meeting was a landmark event and reaffirmed the commitment of Myanmar to successful cooperation among India, Myanmar and Thailand on transport linkages. His Excellency Secretary-I expressed the conviction that the meeting would result in a programme of action of transport linkages that would be of benefit to the three countries and to the two regions of Southeast and South Asia.
5. Present for the Opening of the Meeting were Ministers, Deputy Ministers, Heads of Diplomatic Missions and UN Agencies and invited guests.
6. The Meeting was attended by His Excellency Shri Jaswant Singh, Minister of External Affairs of the Republic of India, His Excellency U Win Aung, Minister of Foreign Affairs of the Union of Myanmar and His Excellency Dr. Surakiart

Sathirathai, Minister of Foreign Affairs of the Kingdom of Thailand. The Ministers were accompanied by their senior officials.

7. His Excellency U Win Aung chaired the Meeting. The Ministers discussed a wide range of issues pertaining to transport linkages among the three countries, including the possibility of constructing a new highway through Myanmar, which will link the three countries, and promote cooperation between Southeast Asia and South Asia.
8. The Ministers agreed that the objectives of the trilateral cooperation shall be to develop and promote cooperation in multi-model transport and other linkages, with a view to enhance trade and investment, tourism and people to people contact, so as to further contribute to the economic development of the three countries and two regions.
9. Cooperation between the three countries shall be supportive and complimentary to BIMST-EC, Mekong-Ganga Cooperation as well as ASEAN-India Dialogue Cooperation shall include the participation of both private and public sectors as well as funding by countries, regional organisations and international financial institutions.
10. The Meeting agreed on the following areas for cooperation:

    (a) construction of a highway from Moreh in India to Mae Sot in Thailand through Bagan in Myanmar to be completed within a timeframe of two years;
    (b) promotion of a highway from Kanchanaburi in Thailand to Dawei deep seaport in Myanmar and shipping links to seaports in India;
    (c) promotion of trade, investment and tourism through facilitation of movement of goods and peoples across borders;
    (d) cooperative efforts on human resource development and transfer of technology; and
    (e) collective efforts in acquiring funds and advisory services from countries, regional organisations and international financial institutions, for the transport linkages.

11. The Meeting agreed to establish the following cooperation mechanism with a view to effectively implement the objectives already agreed upon:

    (a) The Ministerial Meeting of the Foreign Ministers shall be held annually;
    (b) The Meeting shall propose, review and give policy guidelines to the Senior Officials Meeting (SOM) ;
    (c) The SOM shall be held annually back-to-back with the ASEAN-India Dialogue SOM and shall oversee the cooperation mechanism;
    (d) The Chairmanship shall be rotated in alphabetical order; and
    (e) The Ministries of Foreign Affairs shall be the focal point of the mechanism.

12. The Meeting agreed to set up two Task Forces—one on financing and the other on technical matters—to be chaired by Thailand and India respectively.
13. The respective host country shall provide secretariat services for the meetings held under the trilateral cooperation.
14. The Ministers agreed that the next Ministerial Meeting shall be held in Brunei Darussalam. It was further agreed that the next SOM meeting shall be held back-to-back with the ASEAN-India Dialogue SOM.
15. The Ministers expressed their satisfaction with the outcome of the Meeting, which was conducted in a friendly atmosphere and in the spirit of brotherly understanding and cooperation. The Ministers of India and Thailand expressed their deep appreciation to the Government of the Union of Myanmar for the warm welcome and generous hospitality accorded to them and their delegations during their stay in Yangon and for the excellent arrangements made for the meeting.

Ministry of Foreign Affairs
Yangon
Dated: 6 April, 2002.

INDEX